150 *of the* WORLD'S GREATEST
HYMN STORIES

THEN
SINGS
MY SOUL

THOMAS NELSON PUBLISHERS
Nashville

Published by Thomas Nelson, Inc., P.O. Box 141000, Nashville, Tennessee 37214.

Library of Congress Cataloging-in-Publication-Data is available.

Printed in Canada

7 8 9 10 — 07 06 05 04 03

TO
Ben and Victoria

Table of Contents

INDICES

The Cure for Shot Nerves

It was a small pond of brownish water near my motel, bound on one side by a freeway . . . an unlikely spot for a personal retreat. But I was in no shape to be choosy. I was exhausted, my nerves were shot, and I felt dangerously close to some sort of breakdown. The sun was warm, the birds were raising a carefree chorus, and, thankfully, no one else was around. As I began walking, the words of an old hymn I'd learned in college came to mind, and instinctively, almost unconsciously, I began singing it softly:

> *Praise the Savior, ye who know Him;*
> *Who can tell how much we owe Him?*
> *Gladly let us render to Him*
> *All we are and have.*

There followed a verse of:

> *The God of Abraham praise,*
> *Who reigns enthroned above;*
> *Ancient of everlasting days*
> *And God of love.*

Then Fanny Crosby's,

> *All the way My Savior leads me,*
> *What have I to ask beside?*
> *Can I doubt His tender mercy*
> *Who through life has been my guide?*

Ducks glided over the pond, and a couple of geese waddled past with a flourescent-yellow brood of goslings. I heard myself singing quietly the old Scottish rendition of the 23rd Psalm:

> *The Lord's My Shepherd, I'll not want.*
> *He makes me down to lie,*
> *In pastures green. He leadeth me*
> *The quiet waters by.*
>
> *My soul He doth restore again;*
> *And me to walk doth make,*

Within the paths of righteousness
Ev'n for His own Name's Sake.

That hour by the tiny lake was better for me than a month of therapy, and it did me more good than a dozen self-help books. Then and there I felt emerging twinges of a "restored soul."

What if I had not known those hymns?

This book is designed to reacquaint you with 150 of "those hymns." Yes, I know hymns are an endangered species in this day of praise choruses and video projectors. And, no, I'm not critical of the new praise and worship music. I sing it heartily at church, and I listen to contemporary Christian music on the radio.

But as we sing a new song to the Lord, let's not forget the old ones. It's the sturdy old hymns of the faith that strengthen and steady me when I'm weary and worn. They're the ones I sing while walking by the lake or when rising troubled in the night.

Hymns, especially those chock full of theology, such as Watts' and Wesley's, permeate our souls with the timeless veracities of Scripture.

Hymns help us praise God. They're shafts of brilliant sunlight through the clouds. They provide an almost mystical connection with the endless anthems of praise raising at this very moment before the Heavenly Throne. They unite the Lord's earth-bound church in heavenly harmony.

Hymns enable us to pray. Sometimes when we're too weary or worried for words, we can sing George Matheson's great, *O love that wilt not let me go, / I rest my weary soul in Thee . . . .* Or Hudson Taylor's favorite hymn, *Jesus, I am resting, resting / in the joy of what Thou art. / I am finding out the greatness / of Thy loving heart.*

Hymns give us a way of talking to ourselves, of encouraging ourselves in the Lord, as we do when we sing *Be still my soul, the Lord is on thy side.* They also give us a pulpit for preaching to others, exhorting others to come to Christ just as they are, without one plea.

And hymns connect us with generations now gone. Each week millions of Christians in local settings around the world, using hymns composed by believers from every era and branch of Christendom, join voices in united bursts of praise, speaking to one another in psalms and hymns and spiritual songs, singing and making melody in their hearts to the Lord.

In developing this volume, I'm fortunate to work again with a truly excellent editor—Teri Wilhelms. This is our sixth book together. I'm also thankful to Wayne Kinde and Phil Stoner of Thomas Nelson Publishers, editors, friends, choir members in their local churches, and lovers of the "songs of Zion."

My wife, Katrina, who proof-reads every word I write, straightens out many a mangled sentence and spots many an error. Thanks go out to Greg Johnson, my literary agent and friend, for his advice and assistance. My secretary, Sherry Anderson, goes beyond duty's call in offering and giving assistance. And my staff and church tolerate my literary pursuits and earn my everlasting gratitude. I'm especially indebted to Donelson's gifted worship leader, Jerry Carraway, who has labored at my side for almost twenty years and who loaned me some priceless volumes on hymnology as well as his own advice and expertise. He is responsible for the original music engravings that accompany all the hymn stories in this book.

And my thanks to you—for loving hymns. If a specific hymn has made an impact in your life or if you'd like to contact me, please do so at robertjmorgan.com.

Praise the Savior, ye who know Him
Who can tell how much we owe Him!
Gladly let us render to Him
All we are and have.

THEN
SINGS
MY SOUL

The Lord Bless You and Keep You

Numbers 6:24–26

Peter C. Lutkin

The Lord bless you and keep you; The

Lord lift His coun-te-nance up-on you, and give you peace,

and give you peace, and give you

The Lord make His face to shine up-

and give you peace; The Lord make His face to shine up-

peace; The Lord

on you, and be gra - - - cious un-to you, be gra-cious.

on you, and be gra-cious, and be gra-cious;

The Lord be gra-cious, gra-cious un - to you.

The Lord Bless You and Keep You

FOURTEENTH CENTURY B.C.

The LORD bless you and keep you; the LORD make His face shine upon you, and be gracious to you; the LORD lift up His countenance upon you, and give you peace.
Numbers 6:24–26

The Dead Sea Scrolls were, until recently, our oldest copies of biblical text. But in 1979, Villanova professor, Judith Hadley, was assisting archaeologist, Gabriel Barkay, in excavating a site in Jerusalem's Hinnom Valley. In a burial cave, she saw something resembling the metal cap of a pencil. It was a sensational find, a tiny silver scroll of great antiquity. Another was found nearby. These tiny amulets, dating to the Hebrew monarchy seven centuries before Christ, were so small and fragile they took several years to painstakingly clean and open.

When scientists finally unrolled them, they found the world's oldest extant copy of a biblical text, the words of Numbers 6:24–26: *The LORD bless you and keep you; The LORD make His face shine upon you, and be gracious to you; the LORD lift up His countenance upon you, and give you peace.*

While the amulets date from the seventh century B.C., the original words are far older, coming 1,400 years before Christ. As the Israelites wandered in the wilderness, the Lord commanded the priests to bless the people with this three-fold blessing.

These ancient lyrics have been set to music many times, but never more beautifully than by Peter Christian Lutkin in his classic tune BENEDICTION. During the Fanny Crosby/Ira Sankey era of gospel music, when so much was written for easy congregational singing, Lutkin wrote more elaborate melodies with a classical flare.

Lutkin was born in Wisconsin in 1888, and devoted his life to church music, studying the masters in Europe, excelling on the organ, and founding the School of Music at Northwestern Illinois. He helped start the American Guild of Organists. He died in 1931 and was buried in Rosehill Cemetery in Chicago.

In his *Notes from My Bible*, D. L. Moody said about the priestly blessing of Numbers 6: "Here is a benediction that can give all the time without being impoverished. Every heart may utter it, every letter may conclude with it, every day may begin with it, every night may be sanctified by it. Here is blessing—keeping—shining—the uplifting upon our poor life of all heaven's glad morning. It is the Lord Himself who (gives us) this bar of music from heaven's infinite anthem."

The LORD bless you and keep you;
The LORD make His face shine upon you, and be gracious to you;
The LORD lift up His countenance upon you, and give you peace.

3

Be Thou My Vision

Irish Hymn, c. 8th Century

Irish Folk Melody

1. Be thou my Vi - sion, O Lord of my heart;
2. Be thou my Wis-dom, and thou my true Word;
3. Rich - es I heed not, nor man's emp - ty praise;
4. High King of heav - en, my vic - to - ry won,

Naught be all else to me, save that thou art;
I ev - er with thee and thou with me, Lord;
Thou mine in - her - i - tance, now and al - ways;
May I reach heav-en's joys, O bright heaven's Sun!

Thou my best thought, by day or by night,
Thou my great Fa - ther, and I thy true son,
Thou and thou on - ly, first in my heart,
Heart of my own heart, what - ev - er be - fall,

Wak - ing or sleep - ing, thy pres-ence my light.
Thou in my dwell - ing, and I with thee one.
High King of heav - en, my trea - sure thou art.
Still be my Vi - sion, O Rul - er of all.

Be Thou My Vision

EIGHTH CENTURY

Go therefore and make disciples of all the nations, baptizing them in the name of the Father and of the Son and of the Holy Spirit. Matthew 28:19

O nly one missionary is honored with a global holiday, and only one is known by his own distinct color of green—St. Patrick, of course, missionary to Ireland.

Patrick was born in A.D. 373, along the banks of the River Clyde in what is now called Scotland. His father was a deacon, and his grandfather a priest. When Patrick was about 16, raiders descended on his little town and torched his home. When one of the pirates spotted him in the bushes, he was seized, hauled aboard ship, and taken to Ireland as a slave. There he gave his life to the Lord Jesus.

"The Lord opened my mind to an awareness of my unbelief," he later wrote, "in order that I might remember my transgressions and turn with all my heart to the Lord my God."

Patrick eventually escaped and returned home. His overjoyed family begged him to never leave again. But one night, in a dream reminiscent of Paul's vision of the Macedonian Man in Acts 16, Patrick saw an Irishman pleading with him to come evangelize Ireland.

It wasn't an easy decision, but Patrick, about 30, returned to his former captors with only one book, the Latin Bible, in his hand. As he evangelized the countryside, multitudes came to listen. The superstitious Druids opposed him and sought his death. But his preaching was powerful, and Patrick became one of the most fruitful evangelists of all time, planting about 200 churches and baptizing 100,000 converts.

His work endured, and several centuries later, the Irish church was still producing hymns, prayers, sermons, and songs of worship. In the eighth century, an unknown poet wrote a prayer asking God to be his Vision, his Wisdom, and his Best Thought by day or night.

In 1905, Mary Elizabeth Byrne, a scholar in Dublin, Ireland, translated this ancient Irish poem into English. Another scholar, Eleanor Hull of Manchester, England, took Byrne's translation and crafted it into verses with rhyme and meter. Shortly thereafter it was set to a traditional Irish folk song, "Slane," named for an area in Ireland where Patrick reportedly challenged local Druids with the gospel.

It is one of our oldest and most moving hymns:

> *Be Thou my vision, O Lord of my heart,*
> *Naught be all else to me save that Thou art.*
> *Thou my best thought by day or by night,*
> *Waking or sleeping, Thy presence my light.*

All Glory, Laud, and Honor

Theodulph of Orleans

Melchior Teschner

1. All glo - ry, laud, and hon - or To Thee, Re - deem - er, King.
2. The com - pa - ny of an - gels Are prais - ing Thee on high,
3. To Thee, be - fore Thy pas - sion, They sang their hymns of praise;

To whom the lips of chil - dren Made sweet ho - san - nas ring.
And mor - tal men and all things Cre - a - ted make re - ply.
To Thee, now high ex - alt - ed, Our mel - o - dy we raise.

Thou art the King of Is - ra - el, Thou Da - vid's roy - al Son,
The peo - ple of the He - brews With palms be - fore Thee went;
Thou didst ac - cept their prais - es; Ac - cept the praise we bring,

Who in the Lord's name com - est, The King and Bless - ed One.
Our praise and prayer and an - thems Be - fore Thee we pre - sent.
Who in all good de - light - est, Thou good and gra - cious King.

All Glory, Laud, and Honor

A.D. 820

Behold, your King is coming to you; He is just and having salvation, lowly and riding on a donkey, a colt, the foal of a donkey. Zechariah 9:9

*T*he mighty Charlemagne (742–814), King of the Franks, united most of western Europe under his crown. He was a visionary who advanced education and reformed the laws, economy, and culture of Europe.

When Charlemagne died, his son, Louis I, assumed the throne. At first, all went well. But in 817, he began dividing the empire among his nephew and his four sons, causing no end of problems. Twice he was deposed by his sons, and, though he regained his throne both times, he was never again able to rest securely.

Caught in the middle of this epic family conflict was Theodulph, Bishop of Orleans, a city south of Paris. Theodulph, born in Spain about 750, had gone to France as a church leader at Charlemagne's request. He was a brilliant man who worked hard to reform the clergy. He established schools and advanced education. He advocated high morals, built churches, and composed hymns of praise to God.

But during the political intrigues of Louis' reign, Theodulph was accused (falsely, it seems) of conspiring with King Bernard of Italy; and on Easter Sunday, 818, he was imprisoned in the monastery of Angers, a city southwest of Paris.

There, as he meditated on our Lord's triumphal entry into Jerusalem prior to His Crucifixion and Resurrection, Theodulph wrote the great Palm Sunday hymn, "All Glory, Laud, and Honor."

According to a tradition that can be neither confirmed nor denied, when King Louis later visited Angers, he momentarily halted by the monastery where Theodulph was held, and the bishop appeared at the window, singing "All Glory, Laud and Honor." The king was reportedly so moved that he ordered the bishop's release.

For whatever reason, we know Theodulph *was* released in 821, but he died on his way back to Orleans, or shortly after his return there.

Originally there were 78 verses (39 couplets) to this hymn! Theodulph had lots of time in his prison-monastery. The first several are the ones we commonly sing today. One stanza that has fallen by the wayside is this quaint verse:

> *Be Thou, O Lord, the Rider,*
> *And we the little ass,*
> *That to God's holy city*
> *Together we may pass.*

Jesus, the Very Thought of Thee

Att. to Bernard of Clairvaux

John B. Dykes

1. Je - sus, the ver - y thought of Thee
2. No voice can sing, no heart can frame,
3. O hope of ev - ery con - trite heart,
4. Je - sus, our on - ly joy be Thou,

With sweet - ness fills my breast;
Nor can the mem - 'ry find
O joy of all the meek,
As Thou our prize wilt be;

But sweet - er far Thy face to see
A sweet - er sound than Thy blest name,
To those who fall, how kind Thou art!
Je - sus, be Thou our glo - ry now

And in Thy pres - ence rest.
O Sav - ior of man - kind.
How good to those who seek.
And thro' e - ter - ni - ty.

Jesus, the Very Thought of Thee

TWELFTH CENTURY

These things I have spoken to you, that in Me you may have peace. In the world you will have tribulation; but be of good cheer, I have overcome the world. John 16:33

When Bernard (c. 1090–1153), a sickly youth in Dijon, France, was unable to fulfill military service, he became a monk. So successful was he that he eventually founded the famous monastery in nearby Clairvaux; in time almost 170 other monasteries sprang from Bernard's leadership. He became the most powerful preacher of his era, and is remembered as a pious man, a deeply contemplative mystic, the "honey-tongued doctor." Martin Luther called Bernard "the best monk that ever lived, whom I admire beyond all the rest put together."

He wasn't a perfect man, as seen in his support for the Second Crusade to liberate the Holy Land from Muslim control. But for 800 years, his words have been read and sung, and his good work has continued.

If you've never read Bernard, here are some excerpts from his writings and sermons:

- How do we know that Christ has really overcome death? Precisely in that he, who did not deserve it, underwent it . . . . But what kind of justice is this, you may say, that the innocent should die for the guilty? It is not justice, but mercy.
- I was made a sinner by deriving my being from Adam; I am made righteous be being washed in the blood of Christ.
- You will never have real mercy for the failings of another until you know and realize that you have the same failings in your soul.
- Thank you, Lord Jesus, for your kindness in uniting us to the church you so dearly love, not merely that we may be endowed with the gift of faith, but that, like brides, we may be one with you . . . , beholding with unveiled faces that glory which is yours in union with the Father and the Holy Spirit forever and ever. Amen.
- You wish me to tell you why and how God should be loved. My answer is that God Himself is the reason He is to be loved.

Several well-known hymns are attributed to St. Bernard: "Jesus, the Very Thought of Thee," "O Sacred Head Now Wounded," and a lesser-known hymn entitled "Open Wide are Thine Hands," the second verse of which says:

Lord, I am sad and poor, but boundless is Thy grace;
Give me the soul transforming joy for which I seek Thy face.

9

All Creatures of Our God and King

St. Francis of Assisi   *Geistliche Kirchengesänge* Cologne

1. All crea-tures of our God and King, Lift up your voice and with us sing, Al - le - lu - ia! Al - le - lu - ia! Thou ing sun with gold - en beam, Thou sil - ver moon with soft-er gleam, O praise Him! O praise Him! Al-le-lu - ia! Al - le - lu - ia! Al-le-lu - ia!

2. Let all things their Cre - a - tor bless, And wor-ship Him in hum-ble-ness. O praise Him! Al - le - lu - ia! Praise, the Fa - ther, praise the Son, And praise the spir - it, Three in One! O praise Him!

All Creatures of Our God and King

1225

I tell you that if these should keep silent, the stones would immediately cry out.
Luke 19:40

So many stories have arisen around St. Francis of Assisi that it's difficult to separate truth from fiction. We know he was born in 1182 in central Italy, son of a rich merchant. After a scanty education, Francis joined the army and was captured in war. He came to Christ shortly after his release, renounced his wealth, and began traveling about the countryside, preaching the gospel, living simply, seeking to make Christ real to everyone he met.

Francis loved nature, and many stories spotlight his interaction with animals. Once as he hiked through Italy's Spoleto Valley, he came upon a flock of birds. When they didn't fly away, he decided to preach them a little sermon: "My brother and sister birds," he reportedly said, "you should praise your Creator and always love Him. He gave you feathers for clothes, wings to fly, and all other things you need. It is God who made your home in thin, pure air. Without sowing or reaping, you receive God's guidance and protection."

The flock, it is said, then flew off rejoicing.

That perspective is reflected in a hymn Francis composed just before his death in 1225, called, "Cantico di fratre sole"—"Song of Brother Sun." It exhorts all creation to worship God. The sun and moon. All the birds. All the clouds. Wind and fire. All men of tender heart. All creatures of our God and King.

Though written in 1225, an English version didn't appear until 1919, when Rev. William H. Draper decided to use it for a children's worship festival in Leeds, England.

But is it sound theology to exhort birds and billowing clouds to lift their voices in praise? Yes! "All Creatures of our God and King" simply restates an older hymn— Psalm 148—which says:

Praise Him, sun and moon; | Praise Him, all you stars of light . . . . |
You great sea creatures and all the depths; | Fire and hail, snow and clouds; |
Stormy wind, fulfilling His word; | Mountains and all hills; |
Fruitful trees and all cedars; | Beasts and all cattle; |
Creeping things and flying fowl . . . | Let them praise the name of the LORD, |
For His name alone is exalted . . . | Praise the LORD!

The God of Abraham Praise

Thomas Olivers   Traditional Hebrew Melody

1. The God of A - br'ham praise, Who reigns en - throned a - bove,
2. He by Him - self hath sworn; We on His oath de - pend.
3. The God who reigns on high The great arch - an - gels sing,
4. The whole tri - um - phant host Give thanks to God on high;

The An - cient of e - ter - nal days And God of love.
We shall, on ea - gles' wings up - borne, To heav'n as - cend.
And "Ho - ly, ho - ly, ho - ly," cry, "Al - might - y King!"
"Hail, Fa - ther, Son and Ho - ly Ghost!" They ev - er cry.

Je - ho - vah, great I AM, By earth and heav'n con - fessed:
We shall be - hold His face; We shall His pow'r a - dore
Who was and is the same And ev - er - more shall be;
Hail, A - br'ham's God and mine! With heav'n our songs we raise:

We bow and bless the sa - cred name For - ev - er blest.
And sing the won - ders of His grace For - ev - er - more.
E - ter - nal Fa - ther, great I AM, We wor - ship Thee.
All might and maj - es - ty are Thine And end - less praise.

The God of Abraham Praise

1404/1770

I am the God of your father—the God of Abraham . . . Exodus 3:6

"*T*he God of Abraham Praise" is perhaps the most Jewish of all Christian hymns, and its writing covers many centuries. Its roots go back to the medieval Jewish scholar Moses Maimonides (1135–1204), who wrote a confession of faith containing thirteen creeds.

Centuries later, in 1404, another Jewish scholar, Daniel ben Judah, a judge and liturgical poet in Rome, deeply impressed with Maimonides' creed, composed the *Yigdal,* a doxology of thirteen stanzas widely sung in Jewish synagogues to this day.

Centuries later, in 1770, an opera vocalist named Meyer Lyon sang the *Yigdal* in London's Great Synagogue, Duke's Place. In the audience that night was Thomas Olivers.

Thomas (1725–1799) had been born in Tregynon, Wales, and orphaned about age four. He studied the craft of shoemaking, but he learned the art of sinning better, "the worst boy known in Tregynon for thirty years."

When he was eighteen, Thomas was thrown out of town, and he wandered down to Bristol, England, where evangelist George Whitefield happened to be preaching from Zechariah 3:2: "Is not this a brand plucked out of the fire?"

"When that sermon began," Thomas recalled, "I was one of the most abandoned and profligate young men living; before it ended I was a new creature. The world had changed for Tom Olivers." He became a traveling evangelist and passionate Christian worker.

On that Sabbath evening in 1770, when Thomas heard Meyer Lyon sing the *Yigdal,* he was so moved that he later approached Lyon, acquired the music, and adapted the Jewish Doxology into a Christian hymn of thirteen stanzas, beginning, "The God of Abraham Praise."

"Look at this," he told a friend, "I have rendered it from the Hebrew, giving it, as far as I could, a Christian character." Thomas annotated his hymn with footnotes, citing Scripture references for almost every line, the first being Exodus 3:6: "I am the God of thy Father, the God of Abraham." It appeared in 1785 in John Wesley's *Pocket Hymnbook.*

Modern congregations don't have the patience to sing all thirteen stanzas, so here is one of the lesser-known verses for you to ponder:

> *The God Who reigns on high the great archangels sing,*
> *And "Holy, holy, holy!" cry, "Almighty King!"*
> *Who was, and is, the same, and evermore shall be:*
> *Jehovah, Lord, the great I AM, we worship Thee!*

13

A Mighty Fortress Is Our God

Martin Luther   Martin Luther

1. A might-y for-tress is our God. A bul-wark nev-er fail - ing;
2. Did we in our own strength con-fide, Our striv-ing would be los - ing,
3. And though this world with dev-ils filled, Should threat-en to un-do us,
4. That word a-bove all earth-ly powers, No thanks to them, a-bid - eth;

Our helper He a-mid the flood Of mor-tal ills pre-vail - ing.
Were not the right man on our side, The man of God's own choos - ing.
We will not fear, for God hath willed, His truth to tri-umph through us.
The Spir-it and the gifts are ours Through Him who with us sid - eth.

For still our an-cient foe Doth seek to work us woe- His craft and power are
Dost ask who that may be? Christ Je-sus, it is He- Lord Sab-a-oth His
The prince of dark-ness grim, We trem-ble not for him- His rage we can en-
Let goods and kin-dred go, This mor-tal life al-so- The bo-dy they may

great, And, armed with cru-el hate, On earth is not His e - qual.
name, From age to age the same, And He must win the bat - tle.
dure, For lo, his doom is sure: One lit-tle word shall fell him.
kill; God's truth a-bid-eth still: His king-dom is for-ev - er.

A Mighty Fortress Is Our God

1529

God is our refuge and strength, a very present help in trouble. Psalm 46:1

We think of Martin Luther as a great reformer, Bible translator, political leader, fiery preacher, and theologian. But he was also a musician, having been born in an area of Germany known for its music. There in his little Thuringian village, young Martin grew up listening to his mother sing. He joined a boys' choir that sang at weddings and funerals. He became proficient with the flute (recorder), and his volcanic emotions often erupted in song.

When the Protestant Reformation began, Luther determined to restore worship to the German Church. He worked with skilled musicians to create new music for Christians, to be sung in the vernacular. He helped revive congregational singing and wrote a number of hymns.

Often he "borrowed" popular secular melodies for his hymns, though occasionally a tune brought criticism and he was "compelled to let the devil have it back again" because it was too closely associated with bars and taverns.

In the forward of a book, Luther once wrote: "Next to the Word of God, the noble art of music is the greatest treasure in the world. It controls our thoughts, minds, hearts, and spirits . . . . A person who . . . does not regard music as a marvelous creation of God . . . does not deserve to be called a human being; he should be permitted to hear nothing but the braying of asses and the grunting of hogs."

Luther's most famous hymn is "Ein' feste Burg ist unser Gott,"—"A Mighty Fortress Is Our God." Based on Psalm 46, it reflects Luther's awareness of our intense struggle with Satan. In difficulty and danger, Luther would often resort to this song, saying to his associate, "Come, Philipp, let us sing the 46th Psalm."

This is a difficult hymn to translate because the original German is so vivid. At least 80 English versions are available. The most popular in America was done by Frederic Henry Hodge. But an older version appeared in the Pennsylvania Lutheran Church Book of 1868:

> *A mighty fortress is our God, | A trusty Shield and Weapon; |*
> *He helps us free from every need, | That hath us now o'ertaken.*

The British version of "A Mighty Fortress" is Thomas Carlyle's translation:

> *A safe stronghold our God is still, | A trusty shield and weapon; |*
> *He'll help us clear from all the ill | That hath us now o'ertaken.*

15

Now Thank We All Our God

Martin Rinkart

Johann Crüger

1. Now thank we all our God, With heart and hands and voic - es,
2. O may this boun-teous God Through all our life be near us,
3. All praise and thanks to God The Fa - ther now be giv - en,

Who won-drous things hath done, In whom this world re - joic - es;
With ev - er joy - ful hearts And bless - ed peace to cheer us;
The Son, and Him who reigns With them in high-est heav - en,

Who, from our moth-ers' arms, Hath blessed us on our way
And keep us in His grace, And guide us when per - plexed,
The one e - ter - nal God, Whom earth and heav'n a - dore;

With count-less gifts of love, And still is ours to - day.
And free us from all ills In this world and the next.
For thus it was, is now, And shall be ev - er - more.

Now Thank We All Our God

1636

In everything give thanks; for this is the will of God in Christ Jesus for you.
1 Thessalonians 5:18

An old English preacher once said, "A grateful mind is a great mind," and the Bible agrees. There are 138 passages of Scripture on the subject of thanksgiving, and some of them are powerfully worded. Colossians 3:17 says: "And whatever you do in word or deed, do all in the name of the Lord Jesus, giving thanks to God the Father through Him." 1 Thessalonians 5:18 adds, "In everything give thanks; for this is the will of God in Christ Jesus for you."

Unfortunately, few hymns are devoted exclusively to thanking God. Among the small, rich handful we *do* have is "Now Thank We All Our God." The German Christians sing this hymn like American believers sing the "Doxology," yet it's loved on both sides of the Atlantic and around the world.

It was written by Martin Rinkart (1586–1649), a Lutheran pastor in the little village of Eilenberg, Saxony. He grew up as the son of a poor coppersmith, felt called to the ministry, and after his theological training began his pastoral work just as the Thirty Years' War was raging through Germany.

Floods of refugees streamed into the walled city of Eilenberg. It was the most desperate of times. The Swedish army encompassed the city gates, and inside the walls there was nothing but plague, famine, and fear. Eight hundred homes were destroyed, and people began dying in increasing numbers. There was a tremendous strain on the pastors, who expended all their strength in preaching the gospel, caring for the sick and dying, and burying the dead. One after another, the pastors themselves took ill and perished until at last only Martin Rinkart was left. Some days he conducted as many as fifty funerals.

Finally the Swedes demanded a huge ransom. It was Martin Rinkart who left the safety of the city walls to negotiate with the enemy, and he did it with such courage and faith that there was soon a conclusion of hostilities, and the period of suffering ended.

Rinkart, knowing there is no healing without thanksgiving, composed this hymn for the survivors of Eilenberg. It has been sung around the world ever since.

Now thank we all our God, with heart and hands and voices,
Who wondrous things has done, in Whom this world rejoices

The Lord's My Shepherd

Scottish Psalter, 1650

Jessie S. Irvine

1. The Lord's my shep - herd, I'll not want; He makes me down to lie In pas - - tures green; He lead - eth me The qui - et wa - ters by.

2. My soul He doth re - store a - gain, And me to walk doth make With - in the paths of right - eous - ness, E'en for His own name's sake.

3. Yea, though I walk in death's dark vale, Yet will I fear no ill, For Thou art with me, and Thy rod And staff me com - fort still.

4. My ta - ble Thou hast fur - nish - ed In pres - ence of my foes; My head Thou dost with oil a - noint, And my cup o - ver - flows.

The Lord's My Shepherd

1650

The LORD is my shepherd; I shall not want. Psalm 23:1

*O*ur oldest hymnal is the Book of Psalms, and Christians throughout history have wanted to obey the biblical injunction to praise the Lord using *"psalms,* hymns, and spiritual songs" (Ephesians 5:19; Colossians 3:16).

John Calvin, quoting Augustine, wrote, "We shall not find better songs nor more fitting for the purpose than the Psalms of David, which the Holy Spirit spoke . . . . And moreover, when we sing them, we are certain that God puts in our mouths these, as if He Himself were singing in us to exalt His glory."

But the Psalms were originally written in Hebrew, and, when translated, they don't typically have the rhyme or rhythm for easy singing.

In the early 1640s, Francis Rouse, an English Puritan, rendered all 150 Psalms from the Hebrew into metrical English. The General Assembly of the Church of Scotland, meeting in Edinburgh, took Rouse's translation and submitted it to revision committees. These committees spent six years comparing the metered Psalms with the original Hebrew, seeking to develop a singable translation that was accurate to the original Hebrew. They worked as painstakingly as if creating a new translation of the Bible.

Finally, in 1650, the *Scottish Psalter* was released and approved for congregations of the Church of Scotland. Its full title was: *The Psalms of David in Meeter: Newly translated, and diligently compared with the original Text, and former Translations: More plain, smooth, and agreeable to the Text, than any heretofore.*

Though the Scottish Psalter of 1650 is one of the great treasures of hymnody, the only portion widely sung beyond Scotland is its beautiful rendition of Psalm 23, set to the tune "Crimond," which begins:

> *The Lord's my Shepherd, I'll not want.*
> *He makes me down to lie*
> *In pastures green; He leadeth me*
> *The quiet waters by.*

The melody, CRIMOND, was composed about 1870 by a woman named Jessie Seymour Irvine. She was the daughter of the parish minister in the little Scottish town of Crimond, which is also famous for its unusual clock in the church tower. The clockmaker accidentally put six marks into one of the five minute sections on the clock face. As a result, each hour in Crimond is 61 minutes, making a day there 24 minutes longer than anywhere else on earth.

Well, it just gives a little extra time for singing "The Lord's My Shepherd."

19

Praise God, from Whom All Blessings Flow

Thomas Ken

att. to Louis Bourgeois

Praise God from whom all bless - ings flow.

Praise Him, all crea - tures here be - low.

Praise Him a - bove, ye heav'n - ly host.

Praise Fa - ther, Son and Ho - ly Ghost. A - men.

Praise God, from Whom All Blessings Flow

1674

Blessed be the God and Father of our Lord Jesus Christ, who has blessed us with every spiritual blessing in the heavenly places in Christ. Ephesians 1:3

Before Charles Wesley or Isaac Watts, there was Thomas Ken who has been called "England's first hymnist." He was born in 1637 in Little Berkhampstead on the fringes of greater London. When his parents died, he was raised by his half-sister and her husband who enrolled him in Winchester College, an historic boys' school. Thomas was later ordained to the ministry and returned to Winchester as a chaplain.

To encourage the devotional habits of the boys, Thomas wrote three hymns in 1674. This was revolutionary because English hymns had not yet appeared. Only the Psalms were sung in public worship. Ken suggested the boys use the hymns privately in their rooms.

One hymn was to be sung upon waking, another at bedtime, and a third at midnight if sleep didn't come. His morning hymn had thirteen stanzas, beginning with:

> *Awake, my soul, and with the sun thy daily stage of duty run;*
> *Shake off dull sloth and joyful rise, to pay thy morning sacrifice.*

His evening hymn, equally meaningful, included this verse:

> *All praise to Thee, my God, this night, for all the blessings of the light!*
> *Keep me, O keep me, King of kings, beneath Thine own almighty wings.*

All three hymns ended with a common stanza, which has since become the most widely-sung verse in the world.

> *Praise God, from Whom all blessings flow; / Praise Him, all creatures here below; /*
> *Praise Him above, ye heavenly host; / Praise Father, Son, and Holy Ghost.*

In 1680, Thomas was appointed chaplain to England's King Charles II. It was a thankless job, as Charles kept a variety of mistresses. Once the king asked to lodge a mistress in the chaplain's residence. Thomas rebuked him, saying, "Not for the King's Kingdom!" Afterward the king referred to him as "that little man who refused lodging to poor Nellie."

During the reign of the next king, James II, Thomas, by now a bishop, was sent to the Tower of London for his Protestant convictions. After his release, Thomas retired to the home of a wealthy friend where he died on March 11, 1711. He was buried at sunrise, and the Doxology was sung at his funeral.

Sing Praise to God Who Reigns Above

Johann J. Schütz

Bohemian Brethren's *Kirchengesänge*

1. Sing praise to God who reigns a-bove, The God of all cre-a - tion; The God of pow'r the God of love, The God of our sal - va - tion. With heal-ing balm my soul is filled, And ev - ery faith-less mur-mur stilled; To God, all praise and glo - ry!

2. What God's al-might - y power hath made, His gra-cious mer-cy keep - eth; By morn - ing glow or even - ing shade, His watch-ful eye ne'er sleep - eth. With - in the king-dom of His might, Lo, all is just and all is right; To God, all praise and glo - ry.

3. The Lord is nev - er far a - way, But, thru all grief dis-tress - ing, An ev - er-pre - sent help and stay, Our peace and joy and bless - ing. As with a mo-ther's ten - der hand, He leads His own, His cho-sen band, To God, all praise and glo - ry.

4. Thus all my toil - some way a - long, I sing a - loud His prais - es; That men may hear the grate - ful song. My voice un-wear - ied rais - es, Be joy - ful in the Lord my heart; Both soul and bod - y bear your part, To God all praise and glo - ry.

Sing Praise to God Who Reigns Above

1675

If My people ... will humble themselves, and pray and seek My face, and turn from their wicked ways, then I will ... forgive their sin .... 2 Chronicles 7:14

*E*vangelist Vance Havner once quipped, "When I was a boy, preachers used to talk about 'holding a revival.' What we really need is somebody who will turn a revival loose."

Well, that's what Philip Spener did in Germany, spurred on by his friend and attorney, Johann Jakob Schütz.

Years before, Martin Luther had been all aflame as he established the Protestant Reformation, and the early Lutherans were firebrands of holy zeal. But a generation later, Lutheranism had lost its steam. By the 1600s, church life tended to be formal and shallow. The doctrine was correct but cold. That's when Philip Spener accepted the call to pastor the Lutheran Church in Frankfort am Main. Rather than preaching from the prescribed texts, he began preaching through the entire Bible, calling for repentance and serious discipleship. In 1669, as he preached from the Sermon on the Mount, revival broke out in the church. People were converted, lives changed, families transformed.

No one was more excited than Johann Schütz, a lifelong resident of Frankfort and prominent city attorney. He suggested Spener take some of these converts and disciple them in small, home prayer and Bible study groups. Spener did so, and it became the talk of the town. These people were called "Pietists" in derision, but the revival spread throughout Germany and is known to history as the "Pietistic Movement."

Out of his joy for what was happening, Johann Schütz wrote a hymn in 1675:

> *Sing praise to God Who reigns above, the God of all creation,*
> *The God of power, the God of love, the God of our salvation.*
> *With healing balm my soul is filled and every faithless murmur stilled:*
> *To God all praise and glory.*

Schütz died in Frankfort at age 49, on May 22, 1690. But his hymn lives on. It was first published in the United States in 1879, where it appeared in *Hymnbook for the Use of Evangelical Lutheran Schools and Congregations*. It is sung to a traditional Bohemian melody named "Kirchengesänge."

The story of Spener and Schütz reminds us we should never give up on revival. If you don't see a revival starting around you, let it begin in your own heart, then let it overflow to others.

23

Fairest Lord Jesus

Anonymous German Hymn   *Schlesische Volkslieder* arr. by Richard S. Willis

1. Fair - est Lord Je - sus; Rul - er of all na - ture,
2. Fair are the mead - ows; Fair - er still the wood - lands,
3. Fair is the sun - shine; Fair - er still the moon - light
4. Beau - ti - ful Sav - ior! Lord of the na - tions!

O Thou of God and man the Son.
Robed in the bloom - ing garb of spring.
And all the twin - kling star - ry host.
Son of God and Son of man!

Thee will I cher - ish; Thee will I hon - or,
Je - sus is fair - er; Je - sus is pur - er;
Je - sus shines bright - er; Je - sus shines pur - er
Glo - ry and hon - or, Praise, ad - o - ra - tion,

Thou my soul's glo - ry, joy, and crown.
Who makes the woe - ful heart to sing.
Than all the an - gels heav'n can boast.
Now and for - ev - er - more be Thine!

Fairest Lord Jesus

1677

For unto us a Child is born, unto us a Son is given . . . And His name will be called Wonderful, Counselor, Mighty God, Everlasting Father, Prince of Peace.
Isaiah 9:6

*T*his hymn came from Roman Catholic Jesuits in Germany and originally had six verses. It first appeared in 1677 in a Jesuit hymnbook titled *Münster Gesangbuch*, but the text of the hymn was in existence at least fifteen years earlier, for it has been found in a manuscript dating back to 1662. Yet the origin of the words remains a mystery.

Who translated it into English? That, too, is largely a mystery. The first three stanzas are the work of an anonymous translator. The fourth stanza was by Joseph A. Seiss, and it first appeared in a Lutheran Sunday School book in 1873.

How appropriate that no human author draws attention from the great theme of this song. There's no source to distract from the subject, no story to detract from the Savior.

This hymn emphasizes the beauty and wonder of Christ, and it alludes to His dual nature, that He was both human and divine, God made flesh, the God-Man: *O Thou of God and man the Son . . . . Son of God and Son of Man . . . .*

It brings to mind one of the greatest observations ever made about Christ, uttered by the "Golden-mouthed" preacher of Antioch, John Chrysostom, in a fourth-century sermon: "I do not think of Christ as God alone, or man alone, but both together. For I know He was hungry, and I know that with five loaves He fed five thousand. I know He was thirsty, and I know that He turned the water into wine. I know He was carried in a ship, and I know that He walked on the sea. I know that He died, and I know that He raised the dead. I know that He was set before Pilate, and I know that He sits with the Father on His throne. I know that He was worshiped by angels, and I know that He was stoned by the Jews. And truly some of these I ascribe to the human, and others to the divine nature. For by reason of this He is said to have been both God and man."

Beautiful Savior! Lord of all the nations!
Son of God and Son of Man!
Glory and honor, praise, adoration,
Now and forever more be Thine.

Praise Ye the Lord, the Almighty

Joachim Neander

Straslund Gesangbuch

1. Praise to the Lord, the Al - might - y, The King of cre - a - tion!
2. Praise to the Lord, Who o'er all things So won-drous-ly reign - eth,
3. Praise to the Lord! O let all that is in me a - dore Him!
4. Praise to the Lord, Who doth pros - per Thy work and de - fend thee;

O my soul, praise Him, For He is thy health and sal - va - tion!
Shel - ters thee un - der His wings, Yes, so gent - ly sus - tain - eth!
All that hath life and breath, Come now with prais - es be - fore Him.
Sure - ly His good - ness and mer - cy Here dail - y at - tend thee.

All ye who hear, Now to His tem - ple draw near;
Hast Thou not seen How all thy long - ings have been
Let the a - men sound from His peo - ple a - gain:
Pon - der a - new what the Al - might - y can do,

Join me in glad ad - o - ra - tion!
Grant - ed in what He or - dain - eth?
Glad - ly for aye we a - dore Him.
If with His love He be - friend thee.

Praise Ye the Lord, the Almighty

1680

Where were you when I laid the foundations of the earth? Tell Me, if you have understanding. Job 38:4

T his hymn was written by Joachim Neander, born in 1650, whose father, grandfather, great-grandfather, and great-great-grandfather—all Joachim Neanders—had been preachers of the gospel. But as a student, Joachim was wild and rebellious. At 20, he joined a group of students who descended on St. Martin's Church in Bremen to ridicule and scoff the worshippers. But the sermon that day by Rev. Theodore Under-Eyck arrested him and led to his conversion. A few years later, he was the assistant preacher at that very church.

Joachim often took long walks near his home in Hochdal, Germany. They were worship walks, and he frequently composed hymns as he strolled, singing them to the Lord. He was the first hymnwriter from the Calvinist branch of Protestantism. When he was 30—the year he died—he wrote this while battling tuberculosis:

> *Praise Ye The Lord, The Almighty, the King of Creation.*
> *O my soul praise Him, for He is Thy health and Salvation.*

One of Joachim's favorite walking spots was a beautiful gorge a few miles from Dusseldorf. The Dussel River flowed through the valley, and Joachim Neander so loved this spot that it eventually was named for him—Neander Valley. The Old German word for "valley" was "tal" or "thal" with a silent "h."

Two hundred years later Herr von Beckersdorf owned the valley, which was a source for limestone, used to manufacture cement. In 1856, miners discovered caves which contained human bones. Beckersdorf took the bones to a local science teacher who speculated they belonged to one who died in the Flood.

But when William King, an Irish professor of anatomy, saw the bones, he claimed they were proof of evolution's famous "missing link." Other Neanderthal fossils were found, and for many years they were used to "prove" Darwin's theory of evolution. Today we know the Neanderthal was fully human, an extinct people group of great strength.

But, as one expert put it, "when Joachim Neander walked in his beautiful valley so many years ago, he could not know that hundreds of years later his name would become world famous, not for his hymns celebrating creation, but for a concept that he would have totally rejected: human evolution."*

---

*Marvin L. Lubenow, *Bones of Contention* (Grand Rapids: Baker Book House, 1992), p. 77. I am indebted to Lubenow for much of the information in this story, gleaned from chapter 6 of this excellent book, subtitled "A Creation's Assessment of Human Fossils."

Behold the Savior of Mankind

Samuel Wesley, Sr.

William Daman's *Booke of Musicke*

1. Be - hold the Sav - ior of man - kind Nailed to the shame - ful tree! How vast the love that Him in - clined To bleed and die for thee!

2. Hark, how He groans, while na - ture shakes, And earth's strong pil - lars bend! The tem - ple's veil in sun - der breaks; The sol - id mar - bles rend.

3. 'Tis done! the pre - cious ran - som's paid! "Re - ceive my soul!" He cries; See where He bows His sa - cred head! He bows His head and dies!

4. But soon He'll break death's en - vious chain, and in full glo - ry shine; O Lamb of God, was ev - er pain, Was ev - er love, like thine?

Behold the Savior of Mankind

1700

Christ has redeemed us from the curse of the law, having become a curse for us (for it is written, "Cursed is everyone who hangs on a tree"). Galatians 3:13

S amuel Wesley, Sr. was a penniless and unpopular Anglican pastor in tiny Epworth, England, and it riled him that his wife's kitchen Bible studies were more popular than his own sermons. Though they truly loved each other, Susanna once exclaimed, "It is a misfortune peculiar to our family that he and I seldom think alike."

Epworth's citizens, too, found Samuel dogmatic and often severe, and some expressed their disapproval in appalling ways. His crops were burned, his livestock maimed, and on February 9, 1709, his house was torched. Susanna was awakened by sparks falling onto the bed. Samuel cried, "Fire! Fire!" The thatched roof exploded, and the flames spread like a sheet of lightning. The parents, flying to rescue their children, were almost trapped. But everyone finally managed to escape through windows and the garden door. Or so they thought.

Peering back, they saw five-year-old John's terrified face pressed against an upstairs window. Instantly a human ladder formed; and just as the house caved in, John was snatched to safety. He never forgot the rescue: "I remember the circumstances as distinctly as though it were but yesterday. Seeing the room was very light, I put my head out and saw streaks of fire on top of the room. I . . . ran to the door, but could get no further, the floor beyond it being in a blaze. I climbed up a chest that stood near a window."

Among the things that perished that night was the manuscript of Samuel's compositions. He had often found relief in penning devotional poetry and hymns. He had hoped in this way to meet his family's financial needs—and to be remembered by posterity. That night, all was lost.

Well, almost all. Somehow one hymn was rescued. Appropriately, it was about another preacher with Whom Samuel identified, One Who was likewise disdained and attacked.

This is the only known surviving hymn from the father of the famous Wesley brothers, but it became the forerunner for the many wonderful hymns that later flowed from the pen of Samuel's famous hymn-writing son, Charles:

Behold the Savior of mankind
Nailed to the shameful tree!
How vast the love that Him inclined
To bleed and die for thee!

Behold the Glories of the Lamb

Isaac Watts   William Tans'ur

1. Be - hold the glo - - ries of the Lamb A - midst His Fa - ther's throne. Pre - pare new hon - ors for His Name, And songs be - fore un - known.

2. E - ter - nal Fa - - ther, who shall look In - to Thy se - cret will? Who but the Son should take that Book And o - - - pen ev - - ery seal?

3. Now to the Lamb that once was slain Be end - less bless - ings paid; Sal - va - tion, glo - ry, joy re - main For - ev - - - er on Thy head.

4. Thou hast re - deemed our souls with blood, Hast set the pris - oner free; Hast made us kings and priests to God, And we shall reign with Thee.

Behold the Glories
of the Lamb

1707

Worthy is the Lamb who was slain to receive power and riches and wisdom, and strength and honor and glory and blessing! Revelation 5:12

I saac Watts, Sr. was a clothier and a deacon in Above Bar Congregational Church in Southampton, England. He and his wife, Sarah were "Dissenters"—Non-Anglicans—a treasonous offense in those days. About the time Isaac, Jr. prematurely arrived, July 17, 1674, the elder Watts was arrested. Sarah reportedly nursed her newborn while seated on a stone outside the prison.

In time Watts was released, and the young couple soon discovered they had a precocious child. Young Isaac took to books almost from infancy. He learned Latin at age four, Greek at nine, and Hebrew at thirteen. He loved rhyme and verse. At age seven, he wrote this poem in childish script. Notice the acrostic—ISAAC:

> I am a vile polluted lump of earth
> So I've continued ever since my birth
> Although Jehovah grace does give me
> As sure this monster Satan will deceive me
> Come, therefore, Lord, from Satan's claws relieve me.

After Isaac graduated from grammar school in Southampton, a wealthy benefactor offered to send him to Oxford. But that would have required his becoming Anglican. Politely declining, Isaac enrolled in a college-level school for Dissenters in Stoke Newington, London, where he excelled.

After graduation from college, Isaac, about 19, returned to Southampton. He complained to his father about the dismal singing at church. Only versified arrangements of the Psalms were used. Martin Luther taught his followers to sing hymns, but John Calvin allowed only the singing of Scriptures. After a heated discussion, his father challenged Isaac to write a hymn.

Centering his thoughts on Revelation 5, he did so. This was the first of Isaac's 600-plus hymns, and has been called the first English hymn designed for congregational use. (It was published in 1707.) Above Bar Congregational Church liked Isaac's hymn so much, they requested a new one each week. Isaac, about 20, gladly complied. Those two years in Southampton became the richest hymn-writing period in Isaac Watts' life. Though barely out of school, he composed hymns that are still sung nearly three centuries later, earning him the title, "Father of English Hymnody."

Alas! and Did My Savior Bleed

Isaac Watts

Hugh Wilson

1. A - las! and did my Sav - ior bleed And did my Sov - ereign die? Would He de - vote that sa - cred head, For such a worm as I.
2. Was it for crimes that I have done, He suf - fered on the tree? A - maz - ing pi - ty, grace un - known, And love be - yond de - gree!
3. Well might the sun in dark - ness hide And shut His glo - ries in; When Christ the might - y Ma - ker died For man, the crea - ture's sin.
4. Thus might I hide my blush - ing face While His dear cross ap - pears; Dis - solve my heart in thank - ful - ness And melt mine eyes to tears.
5. But drops of grief can ne'er re - pay, The debt of love I owe; Here, Lord, I give my - self a - way, 'Tis all that I can do.

Alas! and Did My Savior Bleed

1707

But God forbid that I should boast except in the cross of our Lord Jesus Christ.
Galatians 6:14

After his graduation from college, Isaac Watts returned to Southampton, England, and spent two years writing hymns for Above Bar Congregational Church. He then moved to London to tutor children in a wealthy family of Dissenters. While there he joined Mark Lane Independent Chapel. Soon he was asked to be a teacher in the church, and in 1698, he was hired as associate pastor. There, on his twenty-fourth birthday, he preached his first sermon. In 1702, he became senior pastor of the church, a position he retained the rest of his life. He was a brilliant Bible student, and his sermons brought the church to life.

In 1707, his *Hymns and Spiritual Songs* was published. Isaac had written most of these hymns in Southampton while in late teens and early twenties. Included was a hymn now considered the finest hymn ever written in the English language. It was based on Galatians 6:14: "But God forbid that I should boast except in the cross of our Lord Jesus Christ." Originally the first stanza said: *When I survey the wondrous cross / Where the young Prince of Glory died . . .* In an enlarged 1709 edition, Watts rewrote the lines to say:

> *When I survey the wondrous cross*
> *On which the Prince of glory died,*
> *My richest gain I count but loss,*
> *And pour contempt on all my pride.*

Also included in the 1707 hymnbook was "Heavenly Joy on Earth," better known today as, "Come, We That Love the Lord," or "We're Marching to Zion."

Another hymn was, "Godly Sorrow Arising from the Sufferings of Christ," better known as: "Alas! and Did My Savior Bleed." This hymn later played a major role in the conversion of a great American hymnist. In 1851, Fanny Crosby, 31, attended a revival service at John Street Methodist Church in New York. "After a prayer was offered," she recalled, "they began to sing the grand old consecration hymn, 'Alas! and Did My Savior Bleed' and when they reached the third line of the fifth stanza, 'Here, Lord, I give myself away,' my very soul was flooded with celestial light."

How right that Watts should, long after his death, play a part in winning to Christ the author of a new generation of hymns and gospel songs!

I Sing the Mighty Power of God

Isaac Watts

from *Gesangbuch der Herzogl*, Württemberg

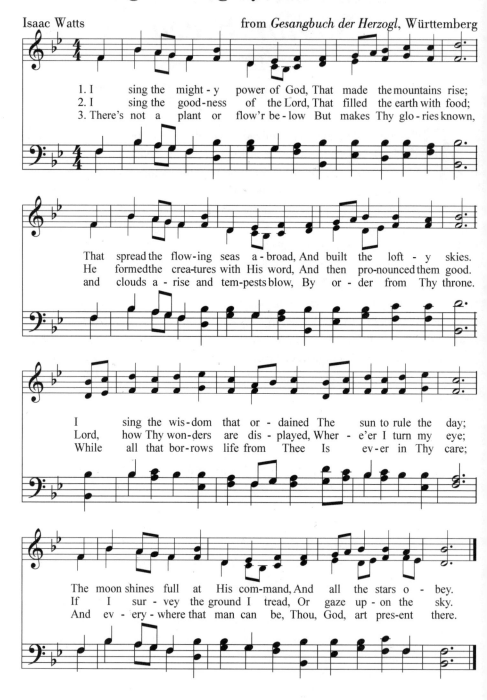

1. I sing the might-y power of God, That made the mountains rise;
2. I sing the good-ness of the Lord, That filled the earth with food;
3. There's not a plant or flow'r be-low But makes Thy glo-ries known,

That spread the flow-ing seas a-broad, And built the loft-y skies.
He formed the crea-tures with His word, And then pro-nounced them good.
and clouds a-rise and tem-pests blow, By or-der from Thy throne.

I sing the wis-dom that or-dained The sun to rule the day;
Lord, how Thy won-ders are dis-played, Wher-e'er I turn my eye;
While all that bor-rows life from Thee Is ev-er in Thy care;

The moon shines full at His com-mand, And all the stars o-bey.
If I sur-vey the ground I tread, Or gaze up-on the sky.
And ev-ery-where that man can be, Thou, God, art pres-ent there.

I Sing the Mighty Power of God

<u>1715</u>

He has made the earth by His power; He has established the world by His wisdom, and stretched out the heaven by His understanding. Jeremiah 51:15

A s Isaac Watts quietly pastored Mark Lane Chapel in London, the growing popularity of his hymns was causing a tempest. "Christian congregations have shut out divinely inspired Psalms," one man complained, "and taken in Watts' flights of fancy." The issue of singing hymns versus Psalms split churches, including the one in Bedford, England, once pastored by John Bunyan.

The controversy jumped the Atlantic. In May, 1789, Rev. Adam Rankin told the General Assembly of the Presbyterian Church, meeting in Philadelphia: "I have ridden horseback all the way from my home in Kentucky to ask this body to refuse the great and pernicious error of adopting the use of Isaac Watts' hymns in public worship in preference to the Psalms of David."

We don't know Isaac's reactions. Dr. Samuel Johnson later reported that "by his natural temper he was quick of resentment; but, by his established and habitual practice, he was gentle, modest, and inoffensive." But in 1712, Isaac suffered a breakdown from which he never fully recovered. He asked his church to discontinue his salary; but they raised it and hired a co-pastor who assumed the bulk of the pastoral duties. Watts remained as pastor the rest of his life, preaching whenever he could.

A wealthy couple in the church, Sir Thomas and Lady Abney, invited him to spend a week on their estate. Isaac accepted—and lived with them until his death 36 years later. He enjoyed the children in the home, and in 1715, he published *Divine and Moral Songs for Children*. It sold 80,000 copies in a year and has been selling ever since. In his preface, he said, "Children of high and low degree, of the Church of England or Dissenters, baptized in infancy or not, may all join together in these songs. And as I have endeavored to sink the language to the level of a child's understanding . . . to profit all, if possible, and offend none."

One hymn in this volume, intended for children, became popular with adults. Entitled, "Praise for Creation and Providence," it said:

> *I sing the mighty power of God, that made the mountains rise,*
> *That spread the flowing seas abroad, and built the lofty skies.*
> *I sing the wisdom that ordained the sun to rule the day;*
> *The moon shines full at God's command, and all the stars obey.*

Jesus Shall Reign

Isaac Watts   John Hatton

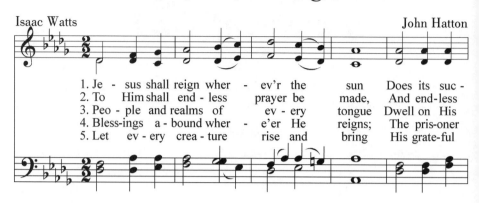

1. Je - sus shall reign wher - ev'r the sun Does its suc -
2. To Him shall end - less prayer be made, And end-less
3. Peo - ple and realms of ev - ery tongue Dwell on His
4. Bless-ings a - bound wher - e'er He reigns; The pris-oner
5. Let ev - ery crea - ture rise and bring His grate-ful

ces - sive jour - neys run; His king - dom spread from
prais - es crown His head. His name like sweet per -
love with sweet - est song; And in - fant voic - es
leaps to loose his chains; The wea - ry find e -
hon - ors to our King; An - gels de - scend with

shore to shore, 'Til moons shall wax and wane no more.
fume shall rise With ev - ery morn - ing sac - ri - fice.
shall pro - claim Their ear - ly bless - ings on His name.
ter - nal rest, And all the sons of want are blest.
songs a - gain, And earth re - peat the loud "A - men!"

Jesus Shall Reign

1719

His name shall endure forever; His name shall continue as long as the sun. And men shall be blessed in Him; All nations shall call Him blessed. Psalm 72:17

hile living on the Abney estate, Isaac devoted himself to a massive project, adapting the Book of Psalms for Christian worship. In 1719, *The Psalms of David Imitated in the Language of the New Testament* was published. In it, Watts worked his way through most of the 150 Psalms, paraphrasing them, injecting them with New Testament truth, and framing them in singing form.

He explained his approach with these words: "Where the Psalmist describes religion by the fear of God, I have often joined faith and love to it. Where he speaks of the pardon of sin through the mercies of God, I have added the merits of a Savior. Where he talks of sacrificing goats or bullocks, I rather choose to mention the sacrifice of Christ, the Lamb of God. Where He promises abundance of wealth, honor, and long life, I have changed some of these typical blessings for grace, glory, and life eternal, which are brought to light by the gospel, and promised in the New Testament."

Several of these have become favorites that have withstood the ages. His rendition of Psalm 72, for example, has been called the first missions hymn: "Jesus Shall Reign Where'er The Sun."

This hymn played a role in the life of Eric Liddell, Scottish Olympic hero of the 1924 games in Paris, who became a missionary to China with the London Missionary Society. His departure from Edinburgh was never-to-be-forgotten. His friends escorted him in a festooned carriage from Scottish Congregational Church to Waverley Station where multitudes had gathered. Before boarding the train, Eric spoke to the crowds, saying he was going abroad to endeavor to do his part in trying to unify the countries of the world under Christ. "Let our motto be 'Christ for the World, for the World Needs Christ,'" he shouted. He then led in two verses of "Jesus Shall Reign Where'er the Sun."*

If, on that memorable day, Eric had sang *all* the verses of "Jesus Shall Reign," he would have come to this one:

> *The saints shall flourish in His days,*
> *Dressed in the robes of joy and praise;*
> *Peace, like a river, from His throne*
> *Shall flow to nations yet unknown.*

---

*Eric Liddell served courageously in China until his death in 1945 in a Japanese internment camp.

O God, Our Help in Ages Past

Isaac Watts   William Croft

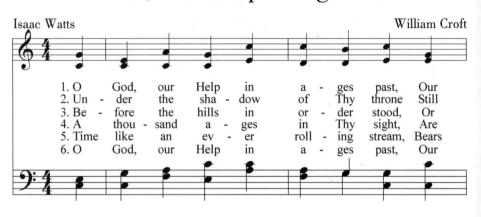

1. O God, our Help in a - ges past, Our
2. Un - der the sha - dow of Thy throne Still
3. Be - fore the hills in or - der stood, Or
4. A thou - sand a - ges in Thy sight, Are
5. Time like an ev - er roll - ing stream, Bears
6. O God, our Help in a - ges past, Our

Hope for years to come, Our Shel - ter from the
may we dwell se - cure; Suf - fi - cient is Thine
earth re - ceived her frame, From ev - er - last - ing
like an eve - ning gone; Short as the watch that
all its sons a - way; They fly, for - got - ten,
Hope for years to come, Be Thou my Guide while

storm - y blast, And our e - ter - nal Home!
arm a - lone, And our de - fense is sure.
Thou art God, To end - less years the same.
ends the night, Be - fore the ris - ing sun.
as a dream Dies at the open - ing day.
life shall last, And our e - ter - nal Home.

O God, Our Help in Ages Past

1719

Lord, You have been our dwelling place in all generations. Before the mountains were brought forth, or ever You had formed the earth and the world, even from everlasting to everlasting, You are God. Psalm 90:1–2

Another hymn in Isaac Watts' 1719 *Psalms of David Imitated* is based on Psalm 90, and is perhaps Watts' most bracing hymn. It was played on the radio by the BBC as soon as World War II was declared, and was later sung at the funeral service of Winston Churchill. Some of the original verses have fallen into disuse, but as you read them, think of the ailing hymnist, sitting at the desk in his room on the Abney estate, pouring over Psalm 90 and penning these words:

*Our God, our help in ages past, / Our hope for years to come, /
Our shelter from the stormy blast, / And our eternal home.*

*Under the shadow of Thy throne / Thy saints have dwelt secure; /
Sufficient is Thine arm alone, / And our defense is sure.*

*Before the hills in order stood, / Or earth received her frame, /
From everlasting Thou art God, / To endless years the same.*

*Thy Word commands our flesh to dust, / "Return, ye sons of men:" /
All nations rose from earth at first, / And turn to earth again.*

*A thousand ages in Thy sight / Are like an evening gone; /
hort as the watch that ends the night / Before the rising sun.*

*The busy tribes of flesh and blood, / With all their lives and cares, /
Are carried downwards by the flood, / And lost in following years.*

*Time, like an ever rolling stream, / Bears all its sons away; /
They fly, forgotten, as a dream / Dies at the opening day.*

*Like flowery fields the nations stand / Pleased with the morning light; /
The flowers beneath the mower's hand / Lie withering ere 'tis night.*

*Our God, our help in ages past, / Our hope for years to come, /
Be Thou our guard while troubles last, / And our eternal home.*

P.S.   We also have a great Christmas carol from this 1719 collection. As Watts studied Psalm 98, especially verses 4–9, he worded them this way: *Joy to the world, the Lord is come! Let earth receive her King!*

God Is the Refuge of His Saints

Isaac Watts

Lowell Mason

1. God is the ref - uge of His saints, When storms of sharp dis - tress in - vade; Ere we can of - fer our com - plaints, Be - hold Him pres - ent with His aid.

2. Let moun-tains from their seats be hurled Down to the deep, and bur - ied there; Con - vul - sions shake the sol - id world: Our faith shall nev - er yield to fear.

3. There is a stream, whose gen - tle flow Sup - plies the cit - y of our God, Life, love, and joy, still guid - ing through, And wat'r - ing our di - vine a - bode.

4. That sac - red stream, Thy ho - ly Word, That all our rag - ing fear con - trols; Sweet peace Thy prom - i - ses af - ford, And give new strength to faint - ing souls.

God Is the Refuge
of His Saints
<u>1719</u>

The LORD of hosts is with us; the God of Jacob is our refuge. Psalm 46:7

I n appearance, Isaac Watts was . . . well, odd. Standing five feet in his stockings, he had an outsized head and prominent nose, and his skin was tallowy. One woman, Elizabeth Singer, having never met him, fell in love with him through his hymns and poems, but when she saw him face-to-face, she was unsettled. He fell in love with her, but she couldn't bring herself to marry him, later saying, "I only wish I could admire the casket (jewelry box) as much as I admire the jewel."

In 1739, Watts suffered a stroke that left him able to speak but unable to write. A secretary was provided to transcribe his dictated poems and books, but over the next several years he became increasingly weak and bedridden. He died on November 25, 1748, and is buried in Bunhill Fields in London.

In addition to his 600 hymns, he wrote 52 other works, including a book of logic widely used in universities, and books on grammar, astronomy, philosophy, and geography. But it's his hymns—most of them written in his early twenties—for which we're most grateful.

Here's a lesser known Watts hymn. It is his rendition of Psalm 46, the same Scripture that had inspired Luther's "A Mighty Fortress." Watts takes a gentler approach:

> *God is the refuge of His saints, | When storms of sharp distress invade; |*
> *Ere we can offer our complaints, | Behold Him present with His aid.*
>
> *Loud may the troubled ocean roar; | In sacred peace our souls abide; |*
> *While every nation, every shore, | Trembles, and dreads the swelling tide.*
>
> *There is a stream, whose gentle flow | Supplies the city of our God, |*
> *Life, love, and joy, still guiding through, | And wat'ring our divine abode.*
>
> *That sacred stream—Thy holy Word— | That all our raging fear controls; |*
> *Sweet peace Thy promises afford, | And give new strength to fainting souls.*
>
> *Zion enjoys her Monarch's love, | Secure against a threatening hour; |*
> *Nor can her firm foundations move, | Built on His truth, and armed with power.*

Am I a Soldier of the Cross?

Isaac Watts

Thomas A. Arne

1. Am I a sol - dier of the cross,
2. Must I be car - ried to the skies
3. Are there no foes for me to face?
4. Sure I must fight, if I would reign;
5. Thy saints in all this glo - rious war
6. When that il - lus - trious day shall rise,

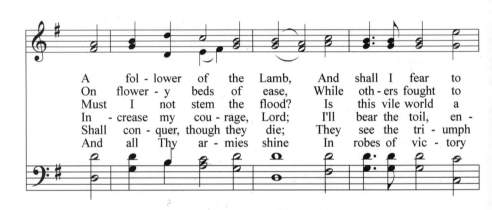

A fol - lower of the Lamb, And shall I fear to
On flower - y beds of ease, While oth - ers fought to
Must I not stem the flood? Is this vile world a
In - crease my cou - rage, Lord; I'll bear the toil, en -
Shall con - quer, though they die; They see the tri - umph
And all Thy ar - mies shine In robes of vic - tory

own His cause, Or blush to speak His name?
win the prize, And sailed through blood - y seas?
friend to grace, To help me on to God?
dure the pain, Sup - port - ed by Thy word.
from a - far, By faith they bring it nigh.
through the skies, The glo - ry shall be Thine.

Am I a Soldier of the Cross?

1724

Watch, stand fast in the faith, be brave, be strong. 1 Corinthians 16:13

his Isaac Watts hymn appeared after most of his others, not in a collection of hymns, but in a published volume of his sermons. It followed a sermon entitled "Holy Fortitude," based on 1 Corinthians 16:13: "Watch, stand fast in the faith, be brave, be strong."

Over a century later, this song played a role in American hymnology, bringing together the powerful gospel team of evangelist D. L. Moody and soloist Ira Sankey.

It happened this way. By the 1870s, D. L. Moody had become a world-famed evangelist, but he badly needed a musician to lead singing at his meetings. On a Saturday night in 1870, he preached at a convention in Indianapolis. At the last minute, a tax collector named Ira Sankey was asked to lead singing.

After the service, Moody assaulted Sankey with questions, "Where are you from? Are you married? What is your business?"

Sankey replied that he lived in Pennsylvania, was married, had two children, and worked for the government, whereupon Moody said abruptly, "You will have to give that up."

Sankey, dumbfounded, asked "What for?"

"To help me in my work. I have been looking for you for the last eight years."

The next day, Sankey received a card from Moody, suggesting they meet on a certain corner that evening at six. Sankey arrived first. When Moody showed up, he said nothing but entered a nearby store for a large box. He asked Sankey to stand on the box and sing.

Sankey dutifully hoisted himself up and sang Isaac Watts' *Am I a soldier of the cross, a follower of the Lamb, / and shall I fear to own His cause, or blush to speak His Name?*

Workers, going home from mills and factories, were arrested by Sankey's beautiful voice, and the crowd grew. Moody ascended the box and preached for twenty-five minutes before announcing that the meeting would continue in the Opera House. The Opera House was soon packed, and Moody preached the gospel with great power. Finally, he closed the meeting, saying, "Now we must close, as the brethren of the convention wish to come in to discuss the question, 'How to reach the masses!'"

That was the beginning of three remarkable decades. Moody and Sankey, soldiers of Christ, crisscrossed the world, singing and preaching and reaching the masses as few others, before or since.

And Can It Be That I Should Gain?

Charles Wesley

Thomas Campbell

1. And can it be that I should gain An in - t'rest in the Sa - vior's blood? Died He for me, who caused His pain? For me, who Him to death pur - sued? A - maz - ing love! How can it be That Thou, my God, shouldst die for me?

2. He left His Fa - ther's throne a - bove, So free, so in - fi - nite His grace; Emp - tied Him - self of all but love, And bled for A - dam's help - less race. 'Tis mer - cy all, im - mense and free! For, O my God it found out me!

3. No con - dem - na - tion now I dread; Je - sus, and all in Him, is mine! A - live in Him my liv - ing Head, And clothed in righ - teous - ness di - vine, Bold I ap - proach th'e - ter - nal throne, And claim the crown, through Christ my own.

4. Long my im - pris - oned spir - it lay Fast bound in sin and na - ture's night; Thine eye dif - fused a quick - 'ning ray, I woke, the dun - geon flamed with light; My chains fell off, my heart was free; I rose, went forth and fol - lowed Thee.

And Can It Be That I Should Gain?

1738

But He was wounded for our transgressions, He was bruised for our iniquities; The chastisement for our peace was upon Him, and by His stripes we are healed.
Isaiah 53:5

harles Wesley was born just before Christmas in 1707. He was premature and neither cried nor opened his eyes. His mother, Susanna, kept him tightly wrapped in wool until his actual due date, whereupon he opened his eyes and cried.

At age eight, he was taken to London to attend Westminster School. At thirteen, he became a King's Scholar at Westminster, and upon graduating, Charles enrolled at Oxford. He was nineteen and full of life. He later said, "My first year at college I lost in diversions."

During his second year at Oxford, he grew serious about spiritual things. Neither he nor his brother, John, had yet received Christ as Savior, but they began seeking to live the Christian life so methodically they were dubbed "Methodists" by fellow students.

Their studies completed, the brothers volunteered to go to Georgia, a new colony in America for those in Britain's debtors' prisons, founded by Colonel James Oglethorpe. But as a missionary, Charles was an utter failure. He was demanding and autocratic, and he insisted on baptizing infants, not by sprinkling, but by immersing them three times in succession. One angry woman fired a gun at him.

Charles left America ill and depressed. Some time later, John also returned in low spirits. Finding themselves in spiritual crisis, the brothers began attending meetings led by the Moravian Christian, Peter Boehler. Finally, on Sunday, May 21, 1738 Charles, 31, wrote, "I now found myself at peace with God, and rejoiced in hope of loving Christ. I saw that by faith I stood."

John came to Christ about the same time, saying, "I felt my heart strangely warmed."

On Tuesday, May 23, Charles wrote in his journal, "I began a hymn upon my conversion." We aren't certain which hymn he meant, but many historians think it was "And Can It Be," because of the vivid testimony of verse 4:

> *Long my imprisoned spirit lay,*
> *Fast bound in sin and nature's night;*
> *Thine eye diffused a quickening ray—*
> *I woke, the dungeon flamed with light;*
> *My chains fell off, my heart was free,*
> *I rose, went forth, and followed Thee.*

O for a Thousand Tongues to Sing

Charles Wesley

Carl G. Gläser; arr. by Lowell Mason

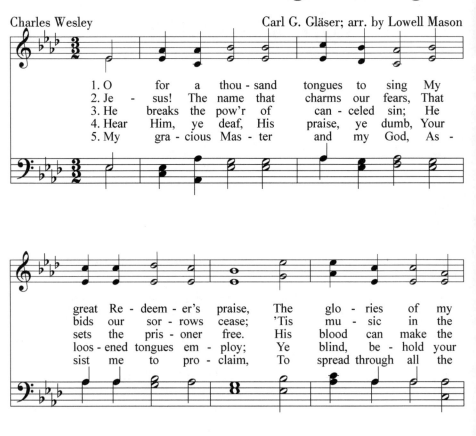

1. O for a thou - sand tongues to sing My
2. Je - sus! The name that charms our fears, That
3. He breaks the pow'r of can - celed sin; He
4. Hear Him, ye deaf, His praise, ye dumb, Your
5. My gra - cious Mas - ter and my God, As -

great Re - deem - er's praise, The glo - ries of my
bids our sor - rows cease; 'Tis mu - sic in the
sets the pris - oner free. His blood can make the
loos - ened tongues em - ploy; Ye blind, be - hold your
sist me to pro - claim, To spread through all the

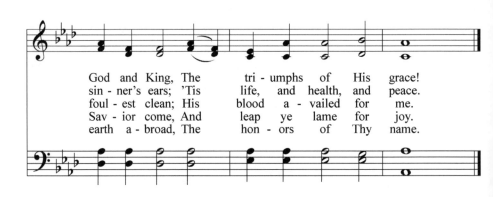

God and King, The tri - umphs of His grace!
sin - ner's ears; 'Tis life, and health, and peace.
foul - est clean; His blood a - vailed for me.
Sav - ior come, And leap ye lame for joy.
earth a - broad, The hon - ors of Thy name.

O for a Thousand Tongues to Sing

1739

. . . The whole multitude . . . began to rejoice and praise God with a loud voice for all the mighty works they had seen. Luke 19:37

*T*he Wesley brothers sent word of their conversion to their sainted mother, Susanna, who didn't know what to make of it. "I think you have fallen into an odd way of thinking," she replied. "You say that till within a few months you had no spiritual life and no justifying faith . . . . I heartily rejoice that you have attained to a strong and lively hope in God's mercy through Christ. Not that I can think that you were totally without saving faith before, but it is one thing to have faith, and another thing to be sensible we have it."

Well, Charles was now very sensible of having it. His life changed, and he gained victory over both his temper and his unfortunate drinking habit. "I was amazed to find my old enemy, intemperance, so suddenly subdued, that I almost forgot I was ever in bondage to him."

He also began to spread the news of what had happened to him. "In the coach to London," he wrote, "I preached faith in Christ. A lady was extremely offended . . . (and) threatened to beat me. I declared I deserved nothing but hell; so did she; and must confess it, before she could have a title to heaven. This was most intolerable to her."

New vitality came into Charles' public preaching. He discontinued the practice of reading his sermons, and began preaching extemporaneously.

He found a fruitful arena for ministry at the infamous Newgate Prison, and allowed himself to be locked up with condemned men on nights before their executions, that he might comfort and witness to them during their final hours.

As the first anniversary of his conversion approached, Charles wrote an eighteen-stanza hymn describing his praise to the Lord. It was titled, "For the Anniversary Day of One's Conversion," and the first stanza began: "Glory to God, and praise, and love . . . ." Verse seven began, "O for a thousand tongues to sing," inspired by a statement Charles had once heard: "Had I a thousand tongues, I would praise Him with them all."

Beginning with a 1767 hymnbook, the seventh stanza was made the first, and when John Wesley complied his *Collection of Hymns* in 1780, he chose this for the first hymn in the book. Congregations today usually sing verses seven, eight, nine, and ten of Wesley's original, which we know today as "O for a Thousand Tongues to Sing."

Hark! The Herald Angels Sing

Charles Wesley

Felix Mendelssohn

1. Hark! the her - ald an - gels sing, "Glo - ry to the new - born King;
2. Christ, by high - est heav'n a - dored, Christ, the ev - er - last - ing Lord;
3. Hail the heav'n born Prince of Peace! Hail the Sun of Righ-teous-ness!

Peace on earth and mer - cy mild, God and sin - ners rec - on - ciled."
Late in time be - hold Him come, Off - spring of a vir - gin's womb.
Light and life to all He brings, Ris'n with heal - ing in His wings.

Joy - ful, all ye na - tions, rise, Join the tri - umph of the skies;
Veiled in flesh the God - head see, Hail, th'in - car - nate De - i - ty!
Mild He lays His glo - ry by, Born that man no more may die;

With an - gel - ic hosts pro - claim, "Christ is born in Beth - le - hem."
Pleased as man with men to dwell, Je - sus our Em - man - u - el.
Born to raise the sons of earth, Born to give them sec - ond birth.

Hark! The Herald Angels Sing
1739

Then the angel said to them, "Do not be afraid, for behold, I bring you good tidings of great joy which will be to all people." Luke 2:10

U pon his conversion, Charles Wesley immediately began writing hymns, each one packed with doctrine, all of them exhibiting strength and sensitivity, both beauty and theological brawn. He wrote constantly, and even on horseback his mind was flooded with new songs. He often stopped at houses along the road and ran in asking for "pen and ink."

He wrote over 6,000 hymns during his life, and he didn't like people tinkering with the words. In one of his hymnals, he wrote: "I beg leave to mention a thought which has been long upon my mind, and which I should long ago have inserted in the public papers, had I not been unwilling to stir up a nest of hornets. Many gentlemen have done my brother and me (though without naming us) the honor to reprint many of our hymns. Now they are perfectly welcome to do so, provided they print them just as they are. But I desire they would not attempt to mend them, for they are really not able. None of them is able to mend either the sense or the verse. Therefore, I must beg of them these two favors: either to let them stand just as they are, to take things for better or worse, or to add the true reading in the margin, or at the bottom of the page, that we may no longer be accountable either for the nonsense or for the doggerel of other men."

But one man did the church a great favor by polishing up one of Charles' best-loved hymns. When Charles was 32, he wrote a Christmas hymn that began:

> *Hark, how all the welkin rings,*
> *"Glory to the King of kings;*
> *Peace on earth, and mercy mild,*
> *God and sinners reconciled!"*
> *Joyful, all ye nations, rise,*
> *Join the triumph of the skies;*
> *Universal nature say,*
> *"Christ the Lord is born to-day!"*

The word "welkin" was an old English term for "the vault of heaven." It was Charles' friend, evangelist George Whitefield, who, when he published this carol in his collection of hymns in 1753, changed the words to the now-beloved, "Hark! The Herald Angels Sing."

Christ the Lord Is Risen Today

Charles Wesley   from *Lyra Davidica*

1. Christ the Lord is risen to - day, Al - le - lu - ia!
2. Lives a - gain our glo - rious King, Al - le - lu - ia!
3. Love's re - deem - ing work is done, Al - le - lu - ia!
4. Soar we now where Christ has led, Al - le - lu - ia!

Sons of men and an - gels say: Al - le - lu - ia!
Where, O death, is now thy sting? Al - le - lu - ia!
Fought the fight, the bat - tle won, Al - le - lu - ia!
Fol - lowing our ex - alt - ed Head, Al - le - lu - ia!

Raise your joys and tri - umphs high, Al - le - lu - ia!
Dy - ing once He all doth save, Al - le - lu - ia!
Death in vain for - bids Him rise, Al - le - lu - ia!
Made like Him, like Him we rise, Al - le - lu - ia!

Sing, ye heavens, and earth, re - ply: Al - le - lu - ia!
Where thy vic - tor - y, O grave? Al - le - lu - ia!
Christ hath o - pened par - a - dise, Al - le - lu - ia!
Ours the cross, the grave, the skies, Al - le - lu - ia!

Christ the Lord
Is Risen Today

1739

And if Christ is not risen, then our preaching is empty and your faith is also empty.
1 Corinthians 15:14

John and Charles Wesley soon found themselves out of favor with many fellow Anglican ministers who spurned their fiery evangelistic preaching. Many pulpits were closed to them.

A friend from his Oxford days, George Whitefield, 22, who was having the same trouble, began preaching in the open air. In London, he asked Charles to stand with him as he preached to thousands in the open air at Blackheath, and Charles, too, got a vision for reaching the multitudes.

He made his first attempt in the outskirts of London. "Franklyn, a farmer, invited me to preach in his field," he wrote. "I did so to about 500. I returned to the house rejoicing." Soon he was preaching to thousands. "My load was gone, and all my doubts and scruples. God shone upon my path; and I knew this was his will concerning me."

A man named Joseph Williams heard Charles in Bristol: "I found him standing on a table-board, in an erect posture . . . surrounded by, I guess, more than a thousand people, some of them fashionable persons, but most of the lower rank of mankind. He prayed with uncommon fervency . . . He then preached about half an hour in such a manner as I have scarce ever heard any man preach . . . . I think I never heard any man labor so earnestly to convince his hearers they were all by nature in a sinful, lost, undone, damnable state; that notwithstanding, there was a possibility of their salvation, through faith in Christ . . . All this he backed up with many texts of Scripture, which he explained and illustrated, and then by a variety of the most forcible motives, arguments, and expostulation, did he invite, allure, quicken, and labor, if it were possible, to compel all, and every of his hearers, to believe in Christ for salvation."

Charles Wesley still preaches today in much the same way through his ageless hymns which are sung around the world each Sunday. Perhaps his most exuberant anthem is the one he simply called, "Hymn for Easter Day," published in 1739. It originally consisted of eleven stanzas. The "Alleluia's" were added later, but appropriately, for this is a hymn one never gets tired of singing:

> *Christ, the Lord, is risen today, Alleluia!*
> *Sons of men and angels say, Alleluia!*
> *Raise your joys and triumphs high, Alleluia!*
> *Sing, ye heavens, and earth, reply, Alleluia!*

Jesus, Lover of My Soul

Charles Wesley

Simeon B. Marsh

1. Je - sus, Lov - er of my soul, Let me to Thy bo - som fly,
2. Oth - er ref - uge have I none; Hangs my help-less soul on Thee.
3. Thou, O Christ, art all I want; More than all in Thee I find.
4. Plen-teous grace with Thee is found, Grace to cov - er all my sin.

While the near-er wa - ters roll, While the tem - pest still is high!
Leave, ah, leave me not a - lone; Still sup-port and com - fort me!
Raise the fall - en cheer the faint, Heal the sick and lead the blind.
Let the heal-ing streams a-bound; Make and keep me pure with - in.

Hide me O my Sav - ior hide, Till the storm of life is past.
All my trust on Thee is stayed; All my help from Thee I bring.
Just and ho - ly is Thy name; I am all un - righ-teous - ness.
Thou of life the Foun - tain art, Free - ly let me take of Thee.

Safe in - to the ha - ven guide. Oh, re-ceive my soul at last!
Cov - er my de - fense-less head, With the shad-ow of Thy wing.
False and full of sin I am; Thou art full of truth and grace.
Spring Thou up with - in my heart; Rise to all e - ter - ni - ty.

Jesus, Lover of My Soul
<u>1740</u>

For He Himself has said, "I will never leave you nor forsake you." So we may boldly say: "The Lord is my helper; I will not fear. What can man do to me?"
Hebrews 13:5b–6

Many stories have arisen around the writing of "Jesus, Lover of My Soul," but they all appear to be fictional. We don't know the exact occasion for his composition, but it was written shortly after Charles Wesley's conversion, and its words seem to anticipate the huge crowds, lawless mobs, midnight escapes, traveling dangers, and flea-infested beds he would encounter in coming years. Wesley's life, in brief, can be summed up as follows:

As the Methodist movement spread through England, Charles traveled horseback from place to place, an itinerant, homeless evangelist. His fiery preaching incited revival in some people and outrage in others.

In the midst of all this, his dear mother, Susanna, died on July 23, 1742. Her last words were, "Children, as soon as I am released, sing a psalm of praise to God." Later, preaching in Wales, Charles met Sally Gwynne, a beautiful girl half his age. A courtship followed, and Charles wanted to propose, but he was virtually penniless with no way of supporting a wife.

That's when he decided to publish his *Hymns and Sacred Poems*, as well as his journals and sermons, hoping the royalties would provide an income. Charles and Sally were married on April 8, 1749, Charles noting: "Not a cloud was to be seen from morning till night. I rose at four, spent three hours and a half in prayer or singing, with my brother . . . . At eight I led my Sally to church . . . . It was a most solemn season of love!"

They left immediately on a preaching tour, and Charles continued his itinerant ministry until 1756, when, at age 49, exhausted, he and Sally settled down. Charles busied himself preaching, visiting, counseling, fretting about his three unsaved children, trying to keep Methodism within the Church of England, and giving unsolicited advice to his brother, John. All the while, he worked tirelessly on his hymns and poems.

By early 1788, Charles was bedfast, not from sickness but from a lifetime of fatigue. By March, too weak to write, he dictated his last hymn to Sally:

In age and feebleness extreme, Who shall a sinful worm redeem?
Jesus, my only hope Thou art, strength of my failing flesh and heart;
Oh, could I catch a smile from Thee, and drop into eternity!

Hallelujah Chorus

from *The Messiah*

George Frideric Handel

George Frideric Handel

Hal - le - lu-jah! Hal - le - lu-jah! Hal-le - lu-jah! Hal-le-lu-jah! Hal-

le - lu-jah! Hal - le - lu-jah! Hal - le - lu-jah! Hal-le-

lu-jah! Hal-le - lu-jah! Hal - le - lu-jah! For the Lord

God om-nip - o - tent reign - eth. Hal - le - lu - jah!

Hallelujah Chorus
(from *The Messiah*)

1741

Let the heavens rejoice, and let the earth be glad; and let them say among the nations, the LORD *reigns.* 1 Chronicles 16:31

His father tried to discourage his musical interests, preferring that he enter the legal profession. But it was the organ, harpsichord, and violin that captured the heart of young George Frideric Handel. Once, accompanying his father to the court of Duke Johann Adolf, George wandered into the chapel, found the organ, and started improvising. The startled Duke exclaimed, "Who is this remarkable child?"

This "remarkable child" soon began composing operas, first in Italy then in London. By his 20s, he was the talk of England and the best paid composer on earth. He opened the Royal Academy of Music. Londoners fought for seats at his every performance, and his fame soared around the world.

But the glory passed. Audiences dwindled. His music became outdated, and he was thought of as an old fogey. Newer artists eclipsed the aging composer. One project after another failed, and Handel, now bankrupt, grew depressed. The stress brought on a case of palsy that crippled some of his fingers. "Handel's great days are over," wrote Frederick the Great, "his inspiration is exhausted."

Yet his troubles also matured him, softening his sharp tongue. His temper mellowed, and his music became more heartfelt. One morning Handel received by post a manuscript from Charles Jennens. It was a word-for-word collection of various biblical texts about Christ. The opening words from Isaiah 40 moved Handel: *Comfort ye, comfort ye my people. . . .*

On August 22, 1741, he shut the door of his London home and started composing music for the words. Twenty-three days later, the world had *Messiah.* "Whether I was in the body or out of the body when I wrote it, I know not," Handel later said, trying to describe the experience. *Messiah* opened in London to enormous crowds on March 23, 1743, with Handel leading from his harpsichord. King George II, who was present that night, surprised everyone by leaping to his feet during the *Hallelujah Chorus.* No one knows why. Some believe the king, being hard of hearing, thought it the national anthem.

No matter—from that day audiences everywhere have stood in reverence during the stirring words: *Hallelujah! For He shall reign forever and ever.*

Handel's fame was rekindled, and even after he lost his eyesight, he continued playing the organ for performances of his oratorios until his death in London, April 14, 1759.

O Come, All Ye Faithful

ascribed to John Francis Wade
translated by Frederick Oakeley

John Francis Wade

1. O come all ye faith - ful, Joy - ful and tri - um - phant, O
2. Sing choirs of an - gels, Sing in ex - ul - ta - tion, O
3. Yea, Lord, we greet Thee, Born this hap - py morn - ing;

come ye, O come ye to Beth - le - hem. Come and be -
sing all ye bright Hosts of heav'n a - bove. Glo - ry to
Je - sus to Thee be all glo - ry giv'n. Word of the

hold Him, Born the King of an - gels. O come let us a - dore Him, O
God, All glo - ry in the high - est.
Fa - ther Now in flesh ap - pear - ing.

come let us a - dore Him, O come let us a - dore Him, Christ the Lord.

Refrain

O Come, All Ye Faithful

1743

And when they had come into the house, they saw the young Child with Mary His mother, and fell down and worshiped Him. And when they had opened their treasures, they presented gifts to Him: gold, frankincense, and myrrh. Matthew 2:11

John Francis Wade, author of this hymn, was hounded out of England in 1745. He was a Roman Catholic layman in Lancashire; but because of persecution arising from the Jacobite rebellion, streams of Catholics fled to France and Portugal, where communities of English-speaking Catholics appeared.

But how could he, a refugee, support himself? In those days, the printing of musical scores was cumbersome, and copying them by hand was an art. In the famous Roman Catholic College and Ministry Center in Douay, France, Wade taught music and became renowned as a copyist of musical scores. His work was exquisite.

In 1743, Wade, 32, produced a copy of a Latin Christmas carol beginning with the phrase *Adeste Fidelis, Laeti triumphantes.* At one time historians believed he had simply discovered an ancient hymn by an unknown author, but most scholars now believe Wade himself composed the lyrics. Seven original hand-copied manuscripts of this Latin hymn have been found, all of them bearing Wade's signature.

John Wade passed away on August 16, 1786, at age 75. His obituary honored him for his "beautiful manuscripts" that adorned chapels and homes.

As time passed, English Catholics began returning to Britain, and they carried Wade's Christmas carol with them. More time passed, and one day an Anglican minister named Rev. Frederick Oakeley, who preached at Margaret Street Chapel in London, came across Wade's Latin Christmas carol. Being deeply moved, he translated it into English for Margaret Street Chapel. The first line of Oakeley's translation said: "Ye Faithful, Approach Ye."

Somehow, "Ye Faithful, Approach Ye," didn't catch on, and several years later Oakeley tried again. By this time, Oakeley, too, was a Roman Catholic priest, having converted to Catholicism in 1845. Perhaps his grasp of Latin had improved, because as he repeated over and over the Latin phrase *Adeste Fidelis, Laeti triumphantes* he finally came up with the simpler, more vigorous *O Come, All Ye Faithful, Joyful and Triumphant!*

So two brave Englishmen, Catholics, lovers of Christmas and lovers of hymns, living a hundred years apart, writing in two different nations, combined their talents to bid us come, joyful and triumphant, and adore Him born the King of angels.

O come, let us adore Him, Christ the Lord

When Morning Gilds the Skies

Katholisches Gesangbuch

Joseph Barnby

When Morning Gilds the Skies

1744

From the rising of the sun to its going down the LORD's name is to be praised.
Psalm 113:3

"rom the rising of the sun to its going down the LORD's name is to be praised," exclaims Psalm 113:3. That's the theme behind this anonymous Catholic hymn, "Beim frühen Morgenlicht," which first appeared in the German hymnbook *Katholisches Gesangbuch* in 1744.

It was translated into English a hundred years later by Edward Caswall, a Roman Catholic priest. Edward had grown up in an Anglican parsonage in Yately, England, where his father was a Church of England minister. Following in his father's footsteps, Edward became an Anglican curate in Stratford-sub-Castle, Wiltshire. But in 1847, he converted to Catholicism. He delighted in translating ancient hymns from Latin into English and is the translator who gave us St. Bernard's "Jesus, the Very Thought of Thee."

In translating "When Morning Gilds the Skies," he rendered the verses freely and even added some of his own. Those who love this hymn as much as I do will be pleased to learn the original English version had twenty-eight (fourteen double) stanzas. Here are some new ones for you to sing:

*When you begin the day, O never fail to say, / May Jesus Christ be praised! /
And at your work rejoice, to sing with heart and voice, / May Jesus Christ be praised!*

*Whene'er the sweet church bell peals over hill and dell, / May Jesus Christ be praised! /
O hark to what it sings, as joyously it rings, / May Jesus Christ be praised!*

*Be this at meals your grace, in every time and place; / May Jesus Christ be praised! /
Be this, when day is past, of all your thoughts the last / May Jesus Christ be praised!*

*When mirth for music longs, this is my song of songs: / May Jesus Christ be praised! /
When evening shadows fall, this rings my curfew call, / May Jesus Christ be praised!*

*When sleep her balm denies, my silent spirit sighs, / May Jesus Christ be praised! /
When evil thoughts molest, with this I shield my breast, / May Jesus Christ be praised!*

*Sing, sun and stars of space, sing, ye that see His face, / Sing, Jesus Christ be praised! /
God's whole creation o'er, for aye and evermore / Shall Jesus Christ be praised!*

Guide Me, O Thou Great Jehovah

William Williams

John Hughes

1. Guide me, O Thou great Je - ho - vah, Pil - grim through this
2. O - pen now the crys - tal foun - tain, Whence the heal - ing
3. When I tread the verge of Jor - dan, Bid my an - xious

bar - ren land; I am weak, but Thou art might - y,
stream doth flow; Let the fire and cloud - y pil - lar
fears sub - side; Death of death and Hell's de - struc - tion

Hold me with Thy pow'r - ful hand. Bread of heav - en, Bread of heav - en,
Lead me all my jour - ney through. Strong De - liv - 'rer, strong De - liv - 'rer,
Land me safe on Ca - naan's side. Songs of prais - es, songs of prais - es,

Feed me till I want no more; Feed me till I want no more.
Be Thou still my strength and shield; Be Thou still my strength and shield.
I will ev - er give to Thee; I will ev - er give to Thee.

Guide Me, O Thou Great Jehovah

1745

When you pass through the waters, I will be with you; and through the rivers, they shall not overflow you. When you walk through the fire, you shall not be burned, nor shall the flame scorch you. Isaiah 43:2

T he Great Awakening of the 1700s was a heaven-sent revival to many parts of the world. In America, the preaching of George Whitefield and Jonathan Edwards renewed Christian zeal and swept multitudes into the kingdom. In England, the open-air evangelism of Whitefield and the Wesley brothers did the same. In Wales, it was the electrifying preaching of Howell Harris and his convert, William Williams.

Williams, son of a wealthy farmer, graduated from the university as a physician, intending to become a medical doctor. But hearing a sermon that Harris preached while standing on a gravestone in Talgarth churchyard, he was converted. Soon thereafter, he changed professions to become a physician of the soul—a preacher.

During his 43 years of itinerant ministry, Williams traveled over 95,000 miles, drawing crowds of 10,000 or more. Once he spoke to an estimated 80,000, noting in his journal, "God strengthened me to speak so loud that most could hear."

Williams is best remembered, however, for his hymns. He has been called the "Sweet Singer of Wales," and the "Watts of Wales." In all, he composed over 800 hymns, his best known being this autobiographical prayer with its many Old Testament allusions, which first appeared in Williams' collection of Welsh hymns, *Alleluia* (1745), entitled "Strength to Pass Through the Wilderness."

Williams lived as a pilgrim, pressing through the snow of winter, the rains of springtime, and the heat of summer. He was both beaten by mobs (once nearly dying) and cheered by crowds, but in all his travels he sought only to do the will of God until his death at age 74.

Many years later, when President James Garfield was dying of an assassin's bullet, he seemed to temporarily rally and was allowed to sit by the window. His wife began singing this hymn, and the President, listening intently, began to cry. To his doctor, Willard Bliss, he said, "Glorious, Bliss, isn't it?"

This hymn was also sung at the funeral of England's Princess Diana.

Several stanzas of this hymn are today seldom sung. One of the best reads:

Musing on my habitation, musing on my heav'nly home;
Fills my soul with holy longings: Come, my Jesus, quickly come.
Vanity is all I see; Lord, I long to be with Thee.

O Happy Day, That Fixed My Choice

Philip Doddridge

Edward F. Rimbault

1. O hap-py day that fixed my choice On Thee, my Sav-ior and my God!
2. O hap-py bond that seals my vows To Him who mer-its all my love!
3. Tis done, the great trans-ac-tion's done; I am my Lord's and He is mine.

Well may this glow-ing heart re-joice, And tell its rap-tures all a-broad.
Let cheer-ful an-thems fill His house, While to that sa-cred shrine I move.
He drew me and I fol-lowed on, Charmed to con-fess the voice di-vine.

Hap-py day, hap-py day, When Je-sus washed my sins a-way!

He taught me how to watch and pray, And live re-joic-ing ev-ery day.

Hap-py day, hap-py day, When Je-sus washed my sins a-way!

O Happy Day, That Fixed My Choice

1755

Likewise, I say to you, there is joy in the presence of the angels of God over one sinner who repents. Luke 15:10

E ighteen of Monica Doddridge's nineteen children died in infancy. When number twenty arrived on June 26, 1702, he, too, appeared stillborn. But while being laid aside, he cried out. Monica determined then and there to raise Philip for the Lord. As a young child, he sat on her knees at the fireplace, which was lined with Delft tiles illustrating the history of the Bible. Using those tiles, Monica taught her son the lessons of Scripture.

When he was later orphaned, Philip wrote in his diary, "God is an immortal Father, my soul rejoices in Him; He hath hitherto helped me and provided for me; may it be my study to approve myself a more affectionate, grateful, and dutiful child."

But he was destitute, and though he longed to be a minister, there seemed no way to afford the necessary education. Friends advised him to prepare for another profession, but before making a final decision, Philip set apart a day for earnest prayer. While he was praying, the postman arrived with a letter from a wealthy benefactor offering to finance his training. It was such a timely answer that Philip resolved henceforth to live a life of prayer, and he trained himself to pray without ceasing, even while getting washed and dressed in the morning.

At age 27, Philip was asked to become the head of a seminary for Dissenting (non-Anglican) ministerial students in Northampton, England. His health was frail, and he didn't think he was well enough for the new responsibilities. But while passing a house, he overheard a child reading Deuteronomy 33:25: "As your days, so shall your strength be." He took it as from God and accepted the call.

The reputation of Northampton Academy radiated through England, and students flocked there, in part, because of Philip's chapel sermons and his powerful prayer life. For twenty-two years, Philip trained students, and his books became "must reading" for the Christians of his day—and ours.

By age 48, however, he was exhausted. Consumption struck his lungs, and he traveled to Lisbon for a therapeutic holiday. There he passed away on October 26, 1751.

Today Philip is best remembered for his book, *The Rise and Progress of Religion in the Soul,* and for his collection of nearly 400 hymns, published posthumously in 1755, and which included "O Happy Day."

Come, Thou Fount of Every Blessing

Robert Robinson   Traditional American Melody

1. Come, Thou fount of ev-ery bless-ing, Tune my heart to sing Thy grace.
2. Here I raise my Eb-e-ne-zer; Hith-er by Thy help I come.
3. Oh, to grace how great a debt-or Dai-ly I'm con-strained to be!

Streams of mer-cy, nev-er ceas-ing, Call for songs of loud-est praise.
And I hope, by Thy good plea-sure, Safe-ly to ar-rive at home.
Let thy grace, Lord, like a fet-ter, Bind my wan-d'ring heart to Thee:

Teach me some me-lo-dious son-net, Sung by flam-ing tongues a-bove.
Je-sus sought me when a stran-ger Wand'ring from the fold of God;
Prone to wan-der, Lord, I feel it, Prone to leave the God I love.

Praise the mount! I'm fixed up-on it, Mount of God's un-chang-ing love.
He, to res-cue me from dan-ger, In-ter-posed His pre-cious blood.
Here's my heart, Lord, take and seal it, Seal it for Thy courts a-bove.

Come, Thou Fount of Every Blessing

1758

The Lord is not slack concerning His promise, as some count slackness, but is longsuffering toward us, not willing that any should perish but that all should come to repentance. 2 Peter 3:9

Robert Robinson had a rough beginning. His father died when he was young, and his mother, unable to control him, sent him to London to learn barbering. What he learned instead was drinking and gang-life. When he was 17, he and his friends reportedly visited a fortune-teller. Relaxed by alcohol, they laughed as she tried to tell their futures. But something about the encounter bothered Robert, and that evening he suggested to his buddies they attend the evangelistic meeting being held by George Whitefield.

Whitefield was one of history's greatest preachers, with a voice that was part foghorn and part violin. That night he preached from Matthew 3:7: "But when he saw many of the Pharisees and Sadducees coming to his baptism, he said to them, "Brood of vipers! Who warned you to flee from the wrath to come?" Bursting into tears, Whitefield exclaimed, "Oh, my hearers! The wrath to come! The wrath to come!"

Robert immediately sobered up and sensed Whitefield was preaching directly to him. The preacher's words haunted him for nearly three years, until December 10, 1755, when he gave his heart to Christ.

Robert soon entered the ministry, and three years later at age 23, while serving Calvinist Methodist Chapel in Norfolk, England, he wrote a hymn for his sermon on Pentecost Sunday. It was a prayer that the Holy Spirit flood into our hearts with His streams of mercy, enabling us to sing God's praises and remain faithful to Him. "Come, Thou Fount of Every Blessing," has been a favorite of the church since that day.

Robinson continued working for the Lord until 1790, when he was invited to Birmingham, England, to preach for Dr. Joseph Priestly, a noted Unitarian. There, on the morning of June 8, he was found dead at age 54, having passed away quietly during the night.

Take a few moments to offer this hymn as a personal prayer, especially remembering those last insightful lines:

> *Let thy goodness, like a fetter, bind my wandering heart to thee.*
> *Prone to wander, Lord, I feel it, prone to leave the God I love;*
> *Here's my heart, O take and seal it, seal it for thy courts above.*

Father, Whate'er of Earthly Bliss

Anne Steele

Hans G. Nägeli

1. Fa - ther, what - e'er of earth - ly bliss Thy
2. Give me a calm and thank - ful heart, From
3. Let the sweet hope that Thou art mine My

sov - 'reign will de - nies,
ev - - - ery mur - mur free;
life and death at - tend,

Ac - cept - ed at Thy throne, let
The bless - ing of Thy grace im -
Thy pres - ence through my jour - ney

this My hum - ble prayer, a - rise:
part, And make me live to Thee.
shine, And crown my jour - ney's end.

Father, Whate'er of Earthly Bliss

<u>1760</u>

But may the God of all grace, who called us to His eternal glory by Christ Jesus, after you have suffered a while, perfect, establish, strengthen, and settle you. 1 Peter 5:10

*T*he Lord never wastes suffering in the lives of His children; He always blesses their sacrifices. That's the lesson of this once-widely-sung, now-seldom-heard hymn.

Anne Steele was born in Broughton, England, in 1716, the oldest daughter of a timber merchant. She faced her first tragedy at age three when her mother died. Her father, however, raised her for the Lord. Growing affluent in his business, he was able to pastor Broughton's Baptist church without salary, serving forty years. Anne joined the church at age 14, and became her dad's co-worker.

When she was 19, a severe hip injury left her an invalid. She nonetheless fell in love with one Robert Elscurot, who proposed to her. But he drowned the day before their wedding.

Out of her suffering, Anne began writing devotional material, and her ministry alongside her dad to the people of Broughton blossomed. In her mid-forties, Anne submitted her *Poems on Subjects Chiefly Devotional* for publication. Her father wrote in his diary, "This day Annie sent part of her composition to London to be printed. I entreat a gracious God, who enabled and stirred her up to such a work, to direct in it and bless it for the good of many . . . . I pray God to make it useful and keep her humble."

So many of these poems were converted to hymns that Anne is remembered as one of the foremost women hymnists of the eighteenth century. Her best-known hymn, "Desiring Resignation and Thankfulness," was written as a personal prayer:

> *Father, whate'er of earthly bliss | Thy sovereign will denies, |*
> *Accepted at Thy throne, let this | My humble prayer, arise:*
>
> *Give me a calm and thankful heart, | From every murmur free; |*
> *The blessing of Thy grace impart, | And make me live to Thee.*
>
> *Let the sweet hope that Thou art mine | My life and death attend, |*
> *Thy presence through my journey shine, | And crown my journey's end.*

The prayer of the final stanza was answered on November 11, 1778, the day of her death. As her weeping friends gathered around, she closed her eyes and whispered her last words: "I know that my Redeemer liveth."

There Is a Fountain

William Cowper

Traditional American Melody arranged by Lowell Mason

1. There is a foun-tain filled with blood Drawn from Im-man-uel's veins;
2. The dy-ing thief re-joiced to see That foun-tain in his day;
3. Dear dy-ing Lamb, Thy pre-cious blood Shall nev-er lose its pow'r
4. E'er since by faith I saw the stream Thy flow-ing wounds sup-ply,

And sin-ners, plunged be-neath that flood, Lose all their guilt-y stains:
And there may I, though vile as he, Wash all my sins a-way:
Till all the ran-somed Church of God Are saved, to sin no more:
Re-deem-ing love has been my theme, And shall be till I die:

Lose all their guilt-y stains, Lose all their guilt - y stains;
Wash all my sins a - way, Wash all my sins a - way;
Are saved, to sin no more, Are saved, to sin no more;
And shall be till I die, And shall be till I die,

And sin-ners, plunged be - neath that flood, Lose all their guilt-y stains.
And there may I, though vile as he, Wash all my sins a - way.
Till all the ran-somed Church of God Are saved, to sin no more.
Re - deem-ing love has been my theme, And shall be till I die.

There Is a Fountain

1772

Whom God set forth as a propitiation by His blood, through faith, to demonstrate His righteousness, because in His forbearance God had passed over the sins that were previously committed. Romans 3:25

illiam Cowper is one of God's gracious gifts to those suffering from depression. Like the Psalmist who cried, "Why are you cast down, O my soul?" (Psalm 42:5), Cowper shows us that our emotional struggles often give us heightened sensitivity to the heart of God and to the needs of others.

Cowper (pronounced Cooper), born in 1731, was the fourth child of a British clergyman and his wife. William's three siblings died, then his mother died while giving birth to the fifth child. William was six when he lost his mother, and it was a blow from which he never recovered. Years later, when someone sent him a picture of her, he wrote:

> *My mother! when I learn'd that thou wast dead,*
> *Say, wast thou conscious of the tears I shed?*
> *Hover'd thy spirit o'er thy sorrowing son,*
> *Wretch even then, life's journey just begun? . . .*
> *I heard the bell toll'd on thy burial day,*
> *I saw the hearse that bore thee slow away,*
> *And, turning from my nurs'ry window, drew*
> *A long, long sigh, and wept a last adieu!*

William, emotionally frail, was sent to a boarding school where for two years he was terrorized by a bully which further shattered his nerves. From ages 10 to 18, he had a better experience at Westminster School, developing a love for literature and poetry. His father wanted him to be an attorney, but, preparing for his bar exam, he experienced runaway anxiety. Concluding himself damned, he threw away his Bible and attempted suicide.

Friends recommended an asylum run by Dr Nathaniel Cotton, a lover of poetry and a committed Christian. Under Dr. Cotton's care, William slowly recovered. In the asylum in 1764, he found the Lord while reading Romans 3:25: ". . . whom God set forth as a propitiation by His blood, through faith . . . ." His life was still to hold many dark days of intense depression, but at least he now had a spiritual foundation. As he later put it:

> *There is a fountain filled with blood | Drawn from Immanuel's veins, |*
> *And sinners plunged beneath that flood, | Lose all their guilty stains.*

O for a Closer Walk with God

William Cowper

Johann G. Nägeli

1. O for a clos - er walk with God, A
2. Where is the bless - ed - ness I knew, When
3. What peace-ful hours I once en - joyed! How
4. Re - turn, O ho - ly Dove, re - turn, Sweet
5. The dear - est i - dol I have known, What -
6. So shall my walk be close with God, Calm

calm and heaven - ly frame, A light to shine up -
first I saw the Lord? Where is the soul - re -
sweet their mem - ory still! But they have left an
mes - sen - ger of rest! I hate the sins that
e'er that i - dol be, Help me to tear it
and se - rene my frame; So pur - er light shall

on the road That leads me to the Lamb!
fresh - ing view Of Je - sus and His Word?
ach - ing void The world can nev - er fill.
made Thee mourn, And drove Thee from my breast.
from Thy throne, And wor - ship on - ly Thee.
mark the road That leads me to the Lamb.

O for a Closer Walk with God

1772

As you therefore have received Christ Jesus the Lord, so walk in Him. Colossians 2:6

Soon after William Cowper was discharged from Cotton's mental asylum, he met Morley and Mary Unwin coming out of church. Morley, an evangelical clergyman, invited William to spend two weeks with them—and William ended up staying in the Unwin home for 22 years. He took up gardening as a hobby, which helped ward off his depressions.

When Morley was killed from falling off a horse, Mrs. Unwin, wanting to sit under the ministry of another evangelical preacher, decided to move to the village of Olney, population 2,000, where John Newton was vicar. Newton, ex-scoundrel and slave trader, had become a celebrated preacher in England. William moved with her, and he and Newton were soon fast friends. They frequently met in the lawn between their houses, and William begin assisting John in visiting the sick and dying, and in distributing benevolent funds.

In December, 1769, Mary Unwin fell ill and appeared to be dying. William's anxiety and depression returned with a vengeance. Mary, being quite a bit older than William, was a mother-figure to him. He prayed earnestly for her, and it was during this time that, examining his own spiritual condition, he wrote "O For a Closer Walk with God."

He said, "(Mary) is the chief of blessings I have met with in my journey since the Lord was pleased to call me . . . . Her illness has been a sharp trial to me. Oh, that it may have a sanctified effect . . . . I began to compose (these verses) yesterday morning before daybreak, but I fell asleep at the end of the first two lines. When I awaked, the third and fourth verses were whispered to my heart in a way I have often experienced."

The hymn begins, "O, for a closer walk with God, a calm and heavenly frame," then goes on to ask:

Where is the blessedness I knew, / When first I saw the Lord? /
Where is the soul refreshing view / Of Jesus and His Word?

Return, O holy Dove, return, / Sweet messenger of rest! /
I hate the sins that made Thee mourn / And drove Thee from my breast.

The dearest idol I have known, / Whate'er that idol be /
Help me to tear it from Thy throne, / And worship only Thee.

Fortunately, the danger passed, William's prayers were answered, and Mary recovered.

God Moves in a Mysterious Way

William Cowper

Scottish Psalter, 1615

1. God moves in a mys - te - rious way His
2. Deep in un - fath - om - a - ble mines Of
3. Ye fear - ful saints, fresh cour - age take; The
4. Judge not the Lord by fee - ble sense, But
5. Blind un - be - lief is sure to err, And

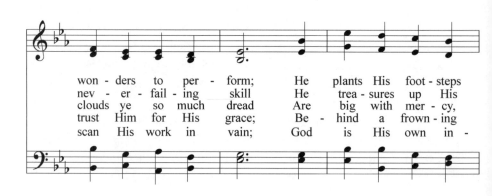

won - ders to per - form; He plants His foot - steps
nev - er - fail - ing skill He trea - sures up His
clouds ye so much dread Are big with mer - cy,
trust Him for His grace; Be - hind a frown - ing
scan His work in vain; God is His own in -

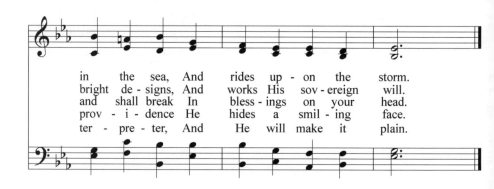

in the sea, And rides up - on the storm.
bright de - signs, And works His sov - ereign will.
and shall break In bless - ings on your head.
prov - i - dence He hides a smil - ing face.
ter - pre - ter, And He will make it plain.

God Moves in a Mysterious Way

1774

Jesus answered and said to him, "What I am doing you do not understand now, but you will know after this." John 13:7

William Cowper suffered another blow when his friend, John Newton, left Olney to become London's most celebrated pastor. Turning again to writing, William this time devoted his energy to secular poetry rather than spiritual hymns, earning him a prominent place in English literature. The publication of "The Task" made him famous throughout Britain. "Pity for Poor Africans," which appeared in 1788, contributed to John Newton and William Wilberforce's efforts to abolish slavery in the British Empire. William's translation of Homer, published in 1791, was widely lauded.

His depression was never far away, and it intensified as he aged. Shortly before his death he wrote *The Castaway*, in which he described himself as a sailor swept overboard into the Atlantic to perish. In this melancholia, William died on April 25, 1800.

There is a report, however, that on his deathbed his face suddenly lit up as he exclaimed, "I am not shut out of heaven after all!" And one of Cowper's lesser-known poems would make a fitting epitaph:

> *Sometimes a light surprises the Christian while he sings;*
> *It is the Lord, Who rises with healing in His wings . . . .*
>
> *In holy contemplation we sweetly then pursue*
> *The theme of God's salvation, and find it ever new.*
>
> *Set free from present sorrow, we cheerfully can say,*
> *Let the unknown tomorrow bring with it what it may.*
>
> *It can bring with it nothing but He will bear us through;*
> *Who gives the lilies clothing will clothe His people, too;*
>
> *Beneath the spreading heavens, no creature but is fed;*
> *And He Who feeds the ravens will give His children bread.*
>
> *Though vine nor fig tree neither their wonted fruit should bear,*
> *Though all the field should wither, nor flocks nor herds be there;*
>
> *Yet God the same abiding, His praise shall tune my voice,*
> *For while in Him confiding, I cannot but rejoice.*

Or as William put it elsewhere: "God moves in a mysterious way His wonders to perform."

Rock of Ages

Augustus M. Toplady

Thomas Hastings

1. Rock of A - ges, cleft for me, Let me hide my-self in Thee. Let the wa - ter and the blood, From Thy wound - ed side which flowed, Be of sin the dou - ble cure, Save from wrath and make me pure.

2. Could my tears for - ev - er flow? Could my zeal no lan - guor know? These for sin could not a - tone; Thou must save, and Thou a - lone. In my hand no price I bring; Sim - ply to thy cross I cling.

3. While I draw this fleet - ing breath, When my eyes shall close in death, When I rise to worlds un - known, And be - hold Thee on Thy throne, Rock of A - ges cleft for me, Let me hide my-self in Thee.

Rock of Ages
1776

My Father, who has given them to Me, is greater than all; and no one is able to snatch them out of My Father's hand. John 10:29

O n November 4, 1740, a baby in Farnham, England, was given the formidable name of Augustus Montague Toplady. His father died in a war, his mother spoiled him, his friends thought him "sick and neurotic," and his relatives disliked him.

But Augustus was interested in the Lord. "I am now arrived at the age of eleven years," he wrote on his birthday. "I praise God I can remember no dreadful crime; to the Lord be the glory." By age 12 he was preaching sermons to whoever would listen. At 14 he began writing hymns. At 16 he was soundly converted to Christ while attending a service in a barn. And at 22 he was ordained an Anglican priest.

As a staunch Calvinist, he despised John Wesley's Arminian theology and bitterly attacked the great Methodist leader. "I believe him to be the most rancorous hater of the gospel-system that ever appeared on this island," Augustus wrote.

"Wesley is guilty of satanic shamelessness," he said on another occasion, "of acting the ignoble part of a lurking, shy assassin."

In 1776 Augustus wrote an article about God's forgiveness, intending it as a slap at Wesley. He ended his article with an original poem:

> *Rock of Ages, cleft for me,*
> *Let me hide myself in Thee;*
> *Let the water and the blood,*
> *From Thy wounded side which flowed,*
> *Be of sin the double cure,*
> *Save from wrath and make me pure.*

Augustus Toplady died at age 38, but his poem outlived him and has been called "the best known, best loved, and most widely useful" hymn in the English language. Oddly, it is remarkably similar to something Wesley had written 30 years before in the preface of a book of hymns for the Lord's Supper: "O Rock of Salvation, Rock struck and cleft for me, let those two Streams of Blood and Water which gushed from thy side, bring down Pardon and Holiness into my soul."

Perhaps the two men were not as incompatible as they thought.*

---

*Taken from the author's book, *On This Day* (Nashville: Thomas Nelson Publishers, 1997), installment for November 4th.

All Hail the Power of Jesus' Name

Edward Perronet

Oliver Holden

1. All hail the power of Je-sus' name! Let an-gels pros-trate
2. Ye cho-sen seed of Is-rael's race, Ye ran-somed from the
3. Let ev-ery kin-dred, ev-ery tribe, On this ter-res-trial
4. O that with yon-der sa-cred throng, We at His feet may

fall; Bring forth the roy-al di - a - dem, And
fall, Hail Him who saves you by His grace, And
ball, To Him all maj-es - ty as - cribe, And
fall! We'll join the ev-er - last - ing song, And

crown Him Lord of all; Bring forth the roy - al
crown Him Lord of all; Hail Him who saves you
crown Him Lord of all; To Him all maj - es -
crown Him Lord of all; We'll join the ev - er -

di - a - dem, And crown Him Lord of all.
by His grace, And crown Him Lord of all.
ty as - cribe, And crown Him Lord of all.
last - ing song, And crown Him Lord of all.

All Hail the Power of Jesus' Name

1779

Who has gone into heaven and is at the right hand of God, angels and authorities and powers having been made subject to Him. 1 Peter 3:22

In the November, 1799, issue of *The Gospel Magazine,* edited by Augustus Toplady, there appeared an anonymous hymn entitled "On the Resurrection, the Lord is King":

> *All hail the power of Jesus' Name! Let angels prostrate fall;*
> *Bring forth the royal diadem, and crown Him Lord of all.*

The author, it was later revealed, was Rev. Edward Perronet.

Edward's Protestant grandparents had fled Catholic France, going first to Switzerland, then to England. Edward's father had become a vicar in the Anglican Church, and Edward followed in his footsteps.

For several years, he became closely allied with the Wesleys, traveling with them and sometimes caught up in their adventures. In John Wesley's journal, we find this entry: "Edward Perronet was thrown down and rolled in mud and mire. Stones were hurled and windows broken."

In time, however, Edward broke with the Wesleys over various Methodist policies, and John Wesley excluded his hymns from Methodist hymnals. Edward went off to pastor a small independent church in Canterbury, where he died on January 22, 1792. His last words were: *Glory to God in the height of His divinity! Glory to God in the depth of His humanity! Glory to God in His all-sufficiency! Into His hands I commend my spirit.*

Edward Perronet's hymn, "All Hail the Power," has earned him an indelible place in the history of church music. It also has a place in missionary history, being greatly used in evangelistic endeavors. Rev. E. P. Scott, for example, missionary to India, wrote of trying to reach a savage tribe in the Indian subcontinent. Ignoring the pleadings of his friends, he set off into the dangerous territory. Several days later, he met a large party of warriors who surrounded him, their spears pointed at his heart.

Expecting to die at any moment, Scott took out his violin, breathed a prayer, closed his eyes, and began singing, "All Hail the Power of Jesus' Name!" When he reached the words, "Let every kindred, every tribe," he opened his eyes. There stood the warriors, some in tears, every spear lowered. Scott spent the next two years evangelizing the tribe.

Amazing Grace

John Newton

Traditional American Melody

1. A - maz - ing grace! How sweet the
2. 'Twas grace that taught my heart to
3. Thro' man - y dan - gers, toils and
4. When we've been there ten thou - sand

sound! That saved a wretch like me!
fear, And grace my fears re - lieved.
snares I have al - read - y come.
years, Bright shin - ing as the sun,

I once was lost, but now am
How pre - cious did that grace ap -
'Tis grace that brought me safe thus
We've no less days to sing God's

found; Was blind, but now I see.
pear, The hour I first be - lieved.
far, And grace will lead me home.
praise, Than when we first be - gun.

Amazing Grace

1779

In Him we have redemption through His blood, the forgiveness of sins, according to the riches of His grace. Ephesians 1:7

I t's hard to shake off a mother's influence. John Newton's earliest memories were of his godly mother who, despite fragile health, devoted herself to nurturing his soul. At her knee he memorized Bible passages and hymns. Though she died when he was about seven, he later recalled her tearful prayers for him.

After her death, John alternated between boarding school and the high seas, wanting to live a good life but nonetheless falling deeper and deeper into sin. Pressed into service with the British Navy, he deserted, was captured, and after two days of suspense, was flogged. His subsequent thoughts vacillated between murder and suicide. "I was capable of anything," he recalled.

More voyages, dangers, toils, and snares followed. It was a life unrivaled in fiction. Then, on the night of March 9, 1748, John, 23, was jolted awake by a brutal storm that descended too suddenly for the crew to foresee. The next day, in great peril, he cried to the Lord. He later wrote, "That tenth of March is a day much remembered by me; and I have never suffered it to pass unnoticed since the year 1748—the Lord came from on high and delivered me out of deep waters."

The next several years saw slow, halting spiritual growth in John, but in the end he became one of the most powerful evangelical preachers in British history, a powerful foe of slavery, and the author of hundreds of hymns.

Here are some things you may not know about Newton's most famous hymn. His title for it wasn't originally "Amazing Grace" but "Faith's Review and Expectation." It is based in Newton's study of 1 Chronicles 17:16–17: "King David . . . said: 'Who am I, O Lord God? And what is my house, that You have brought me this far? And yet . . . You have also spoken of Your servant's house for a great while to come, and have regarded me according to the rank of a man of high degree . . . .'"

And here's a nearly forgotten verse that Newton added near the end of "Amazing Grace." Try singing it for yourself:

The earth shall soon dissolve like snow, the sun forbear to shine;
But God, Who called me here below, shall be forever mine.

Though Troubles Assail Us

John Newton

Traditional Welsh Melody

1. Though trou-bles as-sail us and dan-gers af-fright,
2. The birds, with-out gar-ner or store-house, are fed;
3. When Sa-tan as-sails us to stop up our path,
4. No strength of our own and no good-ness we claim;

Though friends should all fail us and foes all u-nite,
From them let us learn to trust God for our bread.
And cour-age all fails us, we tri-umph by faith.
Yet, since we have known of the Sav-ior's great name,

Yet one thing se-cures us, what-ev-er be-tide,
His saints what is fit-ting shall ne'er be de-nied
He can-not take from us, though oft He has tried,
In this our strong tow-er for safe-ty we hide:

The prom-ise as-sures us, "The Lord will pro-vide."
So long as 'tis writ-ten, "The Lord will pro-vide."
This heart-cheer-ing prom-ise, "The Lord will pro-vide."
The Lord is our pow-er, "The Lord will pro-vide."

Though Troubles Assail Us

1779

And Abraham called the name of the place, The-LORD-Will-Provide; as it is said to this day, "In the Mount of the LORD it shall be provided." Genesis 22:14

When he quit the seafaring life, John Newton worked in the docks of Liverpool as a surveyor of tides from 1755 to 1760. During these years he settled down spiritually and began to mature. He came into contact with the great evangelist, George Whitefield, and was energized by thoughts of preaching the evangelical faith. Encouraged by his godly wife, Mary, he began studying Hebrew and Greek and preparing for the ministry.

At age 39, he was ordained, and shortly thereafter appointed to the Anglican church in Olney, England. He labored there fifteen years, during which he and the great British poet, William Cowper, developed a lasting friendship. The two men met virtually every day in the garden between their homes, and together they produced a volume of hymns.

In 1779, Newton was appointed rector of St. Mary's Woolnoth, a quaint church in the heart of London's financial district. Here he preached for 28 years until his death at age 82.

Late in life, when his mind began failing, he told his friend William Jay, "My memory is nearly gone; but I remember two things, that I am a great sinner and that Christ is a Great Savior."

"Amazing Grace" is Newton's best-known hymn, but its popularity has obscured some of his other compositions. He wrote with incredible insight, yet his words are simple enough for children. Here is Newton's hymn based on Genesis 22:14:

Though troubles assail us and dangers affright,
Though friends should all fail us and foes all unite,
Yet one thing secures us, whatever betide,
The promise assures us, "The Lord will provide."

The birds, without garner or storehouse, are fed;
From them let us learn to trust God for our bread.
His saints what is fitting shall ne'er be denied.
So long as 'tis written, "The Lord will provide."

When Satan assails us to stop up our path,
And courage all fails us, we triumph by faith.
He cannot take from us, though oft he has tried,
This heart cheering promise, "The Lord will provide."

How Firm a Foundation

Rippon's *Selection of Hymns* Early American Melody

1. How firm a foun - da - tion, ye saints of the Lord,
2. Fear not; I am with thee. O be not dis - mayed,
3. When through fi - ery tri - als Thy path - way shall lie,
4. The soul that on Je - sus Hath leaned for re - pose,

Is laid for your faith In His ex - cel - lent Word!
For I am thy God, I will still give thee aid.
My grace, all suf - fi - cient, Shall be thy sup - ply.
I will not, I will not De - sert to its foes;

What more can He say Than to you He hath said,
I'll strength - en thee, help thee, And cause thee to stand,
The flames shall not hurt thee; I on - ly de - sign
That soul, though all hell Should en - deav - or to shake,

To you who for ref - uge To Je - sus have fled?
Up - held by My righ - teous, Om - nip - o - tent hand.
Thy dross to con - sume and thy gold to re - fine.
I'll nev - er, no nev - er, No nev - er for - sake.

How Firm a Foundation
1787

Fear not, for I am with you; be not dismayed, for I am your God. I will strengthen you, Yes, I will help you, I will uphold you with My righteous right hand. Isaiah 41:10

alk about long pastorates! John Rippon pastored Carter's Lane Baptist Church in London for 63 years, beginning in 1775. He had been born in 1751, so he was in his mid-twenties when he first mounted the Carter's Lane pulpit following his education at the Baptist College in Bristol, England.

During the years of Carter's Lane, John developed a vision for a church hymnal, which he edited, assisted by his Minister of Music, Robert Keene. The resulting volume, *A Selection of Hymns from the Best Authors, Intended to Be an Appendix to Dr. Watts' Psalms and Hymns,* was published in 1787. It was a runaway hit, especially among the Baptists, going through eleven British editions during Rippon's lifetime. An American edition appeared in 1820.

"How Firm a Foundation" first appeared here. No one knows its author, for the line reserved for the author's name simply bore the letter "K." Many scholars attribute the composition to Keene.

The unique power of this hymn is due to the fact that each of the seven original stanzas were based on various biblical promises. The first verse established the hymnist's theme—God's Word is a sufficient foundation for our faith. The author then selected precious promises from the Bible, and converted these into hymn stanzas, among them:

- Isaiah 41:10—*Fear not, for I am with you; be not dismayed, for I am your God. I will strengthen you, yes, I will help you, I will uphold you with My righteous right hand.*
- Isaiah 43:2—*When you pass through the waters, I will be with you; and through the rivers, they shall not overflow you. When you walk through the fire, you shall not be burned, nor shall the flame scorch you.*
- 2 Corinthians 12:9—*My grace is sufficient for you, for My strength is made perfect in weakness. Therefore most gladly I will rather boast in my infirmities, that the power of Christ may rest upon me.*
- Hebrews 13:5—*For He Himself has said, "I will never leave you nor forsake you."*

No wonder this hymn was first published under the title, "Exceedingly Great and Precious Promises."

There Is a Balm in Gilead

Traditional Spiritual

Traditional Spiritual

There is a balm in Gil-e-ad to make the wound-ed whole;

Fine

There is a balm in Gil-e-ad to heal the sin-sick soul.

1. Some - times I feel dis - cour - aged, And think my work's in vain,
2. If you can't preach like Pet - er, If you can't pray like Paul,

D.C. al Fine

But then the Ho - ly Spir - it Re - vives my soul a - gain.
Just tell the love of Je - sus, And say He died for all.

There Is a Balm in Gilead

About 1800

Who Himself bore our sins in His own body on the tree, that we, having died to sins, might live for righteousness—by whose stripes you were healed. 1 Peter 2:24

he first Africans on American shores arrived in chains. Their hellish voyage aboard slave ships was only the beginning of their sorrows. The breakup of their families, the oppression of bondage, the whips and shackles, their loss of dignity . . . it all combined to kill both body and spirit.

But the souls of the slaves found release through singing, and a unique form of music evolved called the "Negro Spiritual." Spirituals differed greatly from the hymns we've thus far studied. The classics of English hymnody were largely written by pastors like Isaac Watts and John Newton out of their studies of Scripture. African-American slaves, on the other hand, composed their songs in the fields and barns, the words dealing with daily pain and future hope.

Often the slaves were allowed to sing while working. If, for example, they were hauling a fallen tree, they would combine muscles and voices, using the musical rhythms for a "heave-ho" effect. Other times, risking the lash or branding iron, they'd slip into torch-lit groves to worship the Lord. With swaying bodies, they would stand, eyes half-closed, singing, "Go Down, Moses," "Roll, Jordan, Roll, "He's Got the Whole World in His Hands," and the classic "There Is a Balm in Gilead" based on Jeremiah 8:22.

"Hymns more genuine than these have never been sung since the psalmists of Israel relieved their burdened hearts," wrote Edith A. Talbot.

Fisk University, in Nashville, Tennessee, was established after the Civil War, and the famous Fisk Jubilee Singers popularized these Negro spirituals around the world. Composers began arranging spirituals in a way that appealed to the larger population and this gave rise to another type of Christian music, tagged by composer Thomas A. Dorsey as "gospel songs."

Few Negro spirituals can be precisely dated, nor are many specific authors known, but they have mightily influenced American Christian music. The roots of the children's Sunday school chorus, "Do Lord," for example, is in this old spiritual:

O do, Lord, remember me!
For Death is a simple thing,
And he go from door to door
And he knock down some, and he cripple up some,
And he leave some here to pray.
O do Lord, remember me!

Praise the Savior, Ye Who Know Him!

Thomas Kelly

Traditional German Melody

1. Praise the Sav - ior, ye who know Him! Who can
2. Je - sus is the name that charms us, He for
3. Trust in Him, ye saints, for - ev - er; He is
4. Keep us, Lord, O keep us cleav - ing to Thy

tell how much we owe Him? Glad - ly
con - flict fits and arms us; Noth - ing
faith - ful, chang - ing nev - er. Neith - er
self And still bel - iev - ing; 'Til the

let us ren - der to Him All we
moves and noth - ing harms us While we
force nor guile can sev - er Those He
hour of our re - ceiv - ing, Prom - ised

are and have.
trust in Him.
loves from Him.
joys with Thee.

Praise the Savior, Ye Who Know Him!

1806

Now therefore, our God, we thank You and praise Your glorious name. 1 Chronicles 29:13

Thomas Kelly of Kellyville, Ireland, was born July 13, 1769. His father, the Honorable Thomas Kelly, was an Irish judge. Planning to walk in his father's footsteps, Thomas enrolled at Trinity College, Dublin, and majored in law. But while in school, he was converted to Christ, and the Lord so convicted him about the ministry that, following graduation, he was ordained in the Irish Episcopal Church.

Thomas was aflame for Christ, and his robust messages about justification by faith troubled the Archbishop of Dublin who frowned on evangelical preaching. Eventually, Thomas was forbidden to preach in that diocese. He preached anyway, leaving the Irish church to become a Dissenter, a non-Anglican.

His keen biblical scholarship and splendid sermons flowed from a warm and winsome personality. Being a man of means, he devoted himself to helping those in need. He is forever remembered because of his acts of mercy during the Dublin famine of 1847.

Thomas also became the "Isaac Watts" of Ireland. He wrote 765 hymns, many of them published in 1802 in *A Collection of Psalms and Hymns*. Two years later, more were issued under the title, *Hymns on Various Passages of Scripture*. In 1815, another volume came out entitled, *Hymns of Thomas Kelly Not Before Published*.

Best known is his great Ascension hymn, "Look Ye Saints, the Sight is Glorious!" The easiest to sing and happiest to hear is his "Praise the Savior, Ye Who Know Him."

Praise the Savior, ye who know Him! Who can tell how much we owe Him?
Gladly let us render to Him all we are and have.

Jesus is the Name that charms us; He for conflict fits and arms us;
Nothing moves and nothing harms us while we trust in Him.

Trust in Him, ye saints, forever—He is faithful, changing never;
Neither force nor guile can sever those He loves from Him.

Keep us, Lord, O keep us cleaving to Thyself, and still believing;
Till the hour of our receiving, promised joys with Thee.

Then we shall be where we would be; then we shall be what we should be;
Things that are not now, nor could be, soon shall be our own.

The Star-Spangled Banner

Francis Scott Key

Attributed to John Stafford Smith

O say, can you see, by the dawn's ear - ly light,

What so proud - ly we hailed at the twi - light's last gleam-ing.

O say, does that star - span - gled ban - ner yet

wave O'er the land of the free and the home of the brave?

The Star-Spangled Banner

1814

For our citizenship is in heaven, from which we also eagerly wait for the Savior, the Lord Jesus Christ. Philippians 3:20

I t was a deadly September attack on America. Casualties on our own shores. The nation's capitol targeted. The White House in danger. Terror. Heroes.

One hero was Francis, a Georgetown attorney heavily involved in national politics. An evangelical Christian, Francis taught Bible classes and witnessed boldly, once telling a friend in Congress, "Christ alone can save you from the sentence of condemnation."

He also wrote hymns like this one:

> *Lord, with glowing heart I'd praise Thee, / For the bliss Thy love bestows, /*
> *For the pardoning grace that saves me, / And the peace that from it flows; /*
> *Help, O God, my weak endeavor; / This dull soul to rapture raise;*
> *Thou must light the flame, or never*
> *Can my love be warmed to praise.*

But nothing prepared Francis for the hostage-recovery mission he undertook at the request of the President of the United States. He was seeking the release of a prominent physician, Dr. Beanes, who had been taken captive. During that assignment he was detained by enemy troops and forced to watch a brutal assault on the eastern seaboard.

Toward the morning of September 14, 1814, when it became clear that American forces had withstood the 25-hour bombardment, Francis Scott Key penned another hymn, scribbling it on the back of an envelope. The first stanza we all know, but have you ever sung the last stanza of "The Star-Spangled Banner"?

> *Blest with victory and peace, may the heaven-rescued land*
> *Praise the Power that hath made and preserved us a nation!*
> *Then conquer we must when our cause it is just.*
> *And this be our motto: "In God is our trust."*
> *And the star-spangled banner in triumph shall wave*
> *O'er the land of the free and the home of the brave.*

After sunrise, the British released Francis, and back in Baltimore he wrote out this hymn in fuller form and showed it to his brother-in-law who promptly gave it to a printer who ran off handbills for distribution on the streets. One copy landed in the hands of an unknown musician who adapted it to the tune "To Anacreon in Heaven." So was born the patriotic hymn that was to become our national anthem.

Angels, from the Realms of Glory

James Montgomery

Henry T. Smart

1. An - gels from the realms of glo - ry, Wing your flight o'er
2. Shep - herds in the fields a - bi - ding, Watch-ing o'er your
3. Sag - es, leave your con - tem-pla-tions, Bright - er vi - sions
4. Saints, be - fore the al - tar bend-ing, Watch-ing long in
5. All cre - a - tion, join in prais-ing, God, the Fath - er,

all the earth; Ye who sang cre - a - tion's sto - ry,
flocks by night; God with man is now re - sid - ing,
beam a - far; Seek the great De - sire of na - tions,
hope and fear; Sud - den - ly the Lord, de-scend-ing,
Spir - it, Son; Ev - er - more your voic - es rais-ing,

Now pro - claim Mes - si - ah's birth.
Yon - der shines the in - fant Light.
Ye have seen His na - tal star.
In His tem - ple shall ap - pear.
To th'et - er - nal Three in One.

Come and wor-ship, come and wor-ship; Wor-ship Christ, the new-born King!

Angels, from the Realms of Glory

1816

Praise Him, all His angels; Praise Him, all His hosts! Psalm 148:2

Like all Moravians, John Montgomery had a burden for world evangelism. He was the only Moravian pastor in Scotland, but he and his wife felt God's call to be missionaries to the island of Barbados. Tearfully placing their six-year-old son, James, in a Moravian settlement in Bracehill near Bally-mena, County Antrim, Ireland, they sailed away. James never saw them again, for they perished in Barbados.

Left with nothing, James was enrolled in a school in England. When he didn't do well, he was apprenticed by school authorities to a baker. Baking wasn't for James. He ran away and spent his teenage years drifting from pillar to post, writing poetry and trying his hand at one thing then another. He eventually settled down in Sheffield, England.

In his early twenties, James began working for the local newspaper, the *Sheffield Register*, and there he found his niche. He loved writing. It was a politically active newspaper, and when its owner had to suddenly flee the country to avoid persecution and imprisonment, James purchased the paper and renamed it the *Sheffield Iris*. His editorials, too, proved unpopular with local officials. On two separate occasions he was thrown into jail. But he emerged from prison a celebrity, and he used his newly acquired fame to promote his favorite issues.

Chief among them was the gospel. Despite the loss of his parents, James Montgomery remained devoted to Christ and to the Scriptures, and he championed the cause of foreign missions and of the British Bible Society.

As the years passed, he became the most respected leader in Sheffield, and his writings were eagerly read by its citizens. Early on Christmas Eve, 1816, James, 45, opened his Bible to Luke 2, and was deeply impressed by verse 13. Pondering the story of the heralding angels, he took his pen and started writing. By the end of the day, his new Christmas poem was being read in the pages of his newspaper. It was later set to music and was first sung on Christmas Day, 1821, in a Moravian Church in England: "Angels, from the Realms of Glory."

His parents would have been proud.

Silent Night

Joseph Mohr

Franz Gruber

1. Si - lent night, ho - ly night, All is calm, all is bright. Round yon vir - gin moth - er and child; Ho - ly in - fant, so ten - der and mild, Sleep in heav - en - ly peace; Sleep in heav - en - ly peace.

2. Si - lent night, ho - ly night, Shep - herds quake at the sight. Glo - ries stream from heav - en a - far, Heaven-ly hosts sing "Al - le - lu - ia. Christ the Sa - vior is born; Christ the Sav - ior is born."

3. Si - lent night, ho - ly night, Won - drous star, lend thy light. With the an - gels, let us sing, Al - le - lu - ia to our King. Christ the Sa - vior is born; Christ the Sa - vior is born.

4. Si - lent night, ho - ly night, Son of God, love's pure light. Ra - diant beams from Thy ho - ly face, With the dawn of re - deem - ing grace. Je - sus, Lord, at Thy birth; Je - sus, Lord, at Thy birth.

Silent Night
1818

Therefore the Lord Himself will give you a sign: Behold, the virgin shall conceive and bear a Son, and shall call His name Immanuel. Isaiah 7:14

I t was Christmas Eve in the Austrian Alps. At the newly constructed Church of St. Nicholas in Oberndorf, a Tyrol village near Salzburg, Father Joseph Mohr prepared for the midnight service. He was distraught because the church organ was broken, ruining prospects for that evening's carefully planned music. But Father Joseph was about to learn that our problems are God's opportunities, that the Lord causes all things to work together for good to those who love Him. It came into Father Joseph's mind to write a new song, one that could be sung organless. Hastily, he wrote the words, "Silent night, holy night, all is calm, all is bright . . . ." Taking the text to his organist, Franz Gruber, he explained the situation and asked Franz to compose a simple tune.

That night, December 24, 1818, "Silent Night" was sung for the first time as a duet accompanied by a guitar at the aptly named Church of St. Nicholas in Oberndorf.

Shortly afterward, as Karl Mauracher came to repair the organ, he heard about the near-disaster on Christmas Eve. Acquiring a copy of the text and tune, he spread it throughout the Alpine region of Austria, referring to it as "Tiroler Volkslied."

The song came to the attention of the Strasser Family, makers of fine chamois-skin gloves. To drum up business at various fairs and festivals, the four Strasser children would sing in front of their parent's booth. Like the Von Trapp children a century later, they became popular folk singers throughout the Alps.

When the children—Caroline, Joseph, Andreas, and Amalie—began singing "Tri-oler Volkslied" at their performances, audiences were charmed. It seemed perfect for the snow-clad region, and perfect for the Christian heart. "Silent Night" even came to the attention of the king and queen, and the Strasser children were asked to give a royal performance, assuring the carol's fame.

"Silent Night" was first published for congregational singing in 1838 in the German hymnbook, *Katholisches Gesang—und Gebetbuch für den öffentlichen und häuslichen Gottesdienst zunächst zum Gebrauche der katholischen Gereinden im Königreiche Sachsen.* It was used in America by German-speaking congregations, then appeared in its current English form in a book of Sunday school songs in 1863.

Were it not for a broken organ, there would never have been a "Silent Night."

Jesus, I My Cross Have Taken

Henry F. Lyte

attributed to Wolfgang A. Mozart

1. Je-sus, I my cross have tak - en, All to leave and fol - low Thee;
2. Let the world de - spise and leave me; They have left my Sav - ior, too.
3. Hast-en on from grace to glo - ry, Armed by faith and winged by prayer;

Des - ti - tute, de - spised, for - sa - ken, Thou from hence my all shalt be.
Hu - man hearts and looks de-ceive me; Thou art not, like man, un - true.
Heav'n's e - ter - nal days be - fore me, God's own hand shall guide me there.

Per - ish ev - ery fond am - bi - tion, All I've sought, and hoped and known;
And while Thou shalt smile up - on me, God of wis - dom, love and might,
Soon shall close my earth - ly mis - sion, Swift shall pass my pil - grim days;

Yet how rich is my con - di - tion. God and heav'n are still my own!
Foes may hate and friends may shun me. Show Thy face and all is bright.
Hope shall change to glad fru - i - tion; Faith to sight, and prayer to praise.

Jesus, I My Cross Have Taken

1824

Then Jesus said to His disciples, "If anyone desires to come after Me, let him deny himself, and take up his cross, and follow Me." Matthew 16:24

J ust as the most beautiful skies combine billowing clouds with shimmering sunlight, Henry Francis Lyte's colorful, bittersweet life contributed to the pensive depth of his beautiful hymns. Henry was born in Scotland in 1793. His father, Captain Thomas Lyte, moved the family to Ireland, then abandoned them, and young Henry was raised by his mother who taught him the Bible and instructed him about prayer. After he entered Portora Royal School in Northern Ireland, his mother died, leaving Henry a nine-year-old orphan with no means of support.

Portora Royal School was superintended by wise and kindly Rev. Robert Burrows, who saw something special in Henry. He invited him into his home, accepted him as part of his family, and paid for his education. Henry excelled. At age 16, he was awarded financial assistance to Trinity College in Dublin, and he traveled there intending to enter the medical school. But something was pulling him toward the ministry, and he wound up instead in the Divinity School.

By this time, Henry had grown into a handsome teenager, six feet tall with dark curly hair and a winning personality. He proved a hard worker, a brilliant student, and a gifted poet who repeatedly won awards for his compositions.

After college, Henry, 21, was ordained and began preaching at St. Munn's Church in Taghmon, Ireland, an inland city south of Dublin. There he made friends with another pastor, Rev. Abraham Swanne. When Swanne became critically ill, Henry cared for him and for his family, spending long hours talking to the dying man. The two clergymen realized they were both blind guides, lost, without adequate personal relationships with Christ. As they searched the Scriptures together, both Henry and his dying friend came to a deeper faith. He later wrote, "I began to study my Bible and preach in another manner than I had done previously." It was this incident that inspired his wonderful hymn, written in 1824 (revised in 1833):

> *Jesus, I my cross have taken, | All to leave and follow Thee. |*
> *Destitute, despised, forsaken, | Thou from hence my all shall be. |*
>
> *Man may trouble and distress me, | 'Twill but drive me to Thy breast, |*
> *Life with trials hard may press me, | Heaven will bring me sweeter rest.*

In the Cross of Christ I Glory

John Bowring   Ithamar Conkey

1. In the cross of Christ I glo - ry,
2. When the woes of life o'er - take me,
3. When the sun of bliss is beam - ing,
4. Bane and bless - ing, pain and plea - sure,

Tow'r - ing o'er the wrecks of time;
Hopes de - ceive and fears an - noy;
Light and love up - on my way;
By the cross are sanc - ti - fied;

All the light of sa - cred sto - ry
Nev - er shall the cross for - sake me,
From the cross the ra - diance stream - ing
Peace is there that knows no mea - sure,

Gath - ers round its head sub - lime.
Lo! it glows with peace and joy.
Adds more lus - ter to the day.
Joys that thro' all time a - bide.

In the Cross of Christ I Glory

1825

So Moses made a bronze serpent, and put it on a pole; and so it was, if a serpent had bitten anyone, when he looked at the bronze serpent, he lived. Numbers 21:9

When the World Trade Center collapsed following the terrorist attacks of September 11, 2001, workers excavating the site found a cross-shaped beam that, standing upright amid the ruin and debris, became a make-shift center of worship. The picture of that cross was published around the world and served as a symbol of hope.

A similar story is associated with this hymn. On the island of Macao in the region of Hong Kong, a magnificent cathedral was destroyed. Only the front wall remained. Atop it was a great metal cross, blackened with age, silhouetted against the sky. It is said that hymnist John Bowring was so inspired by the story of this cathedral that he wrote the hymn, "In the cross of Christ I glory, tow'ring o'er the wrecks of time."

The validity of that story is questionable, but we do have a verified story about RATHBUN, the tune to which this hymn is set. It was composed by Ithamar Conkey, organist at Central Baptist Church in Norwich, Connecticut.

In 1849, Central's pastor had planned a series of sermons on the seven last words of Christ on the Cross. According to the *Norwich Bulletin:* "One Sunday during the series it was a very rainy day. Mr. Conkey was sorely disappointed that the members of the choir did not appear, as only one soprano came. Mr. Conkey was so discouraged and disheartened that after the prelude he closed the organ and locked it and went to his home on Washington Street. The pastor and choir gallery were at opposite ends of the church, and he could leave without attracting the attention of the congregation. That afternoon, as he sat down at the piano for practice, his mind was distracted with the thoughts of the sermons Dr. Hiscox had prepared and the words of the hymn, 'In the Cross of Christ I Glory.' He then and there composed the music that is now so universally familiar in churches of every denomination, known as RATHBUN. He admitted afterward the inspiration was a vivid contradiction of his feelings at the morning service."

But why did he name his tune RATHBUN?

The one choir member who showed up on that rainy Sunday in 1849 . . . that one faithful soprano . . . was named Mrs. Beriah S. Rathbun.

Holy, Holy, Holy! Lord God Almighty

Reginald Heber   John B. Dykes

1. Ho-ly, ho-ly, ho - ly, Lord God Al - might - y!
2. Ho-ly, ho-ly, ho - ly! All the saints a - dore Thee,
3. Ho-ly, ho-ly, ho - ly! Though the dark - ness hide Thee,
4. Ho-ly, ho-ly, ho - ly! Lord God Al - might - y!

Ear - ly in the morn - ing our song shall rise to Thee.
Cast - ing down their gold - en crowns A - round the glass - y sea;
Though the eye of sin - ful man Thy glo - ry may not see.
All Thy works shall praise Thy name In earth, and sky, and sea.

Ho - ly, ho - ly, ho - ly! Mer - ci - ful and might - y!
Cher - u - bim and ser - a - phim Fall - ing down be - fore Thee,
On - ly Thou art ho - ly; There is none be - side, Thee
Ho - ly, ho - ly, ho - ly! Mer - ci - ful and might - y!

God in three Per - sons, Bless - ed Trin - i - ty!
Which wert, and art, And ev - er - more shall be.
Per - fect in power, In love, and pur - i - ty.
God in three Per - sons, Bless - ed Trin - i - ty.

Holy, Holy, Holy!
Lord God Almighty

1826

And they do not rest day or night, saying: "Holy, holy, holy, Lord God Almighty, Who was and is and is to come!" Revelation 4:8

R eginald Heber was born April 21, 1783, to a minister and his wife in an English village. After a happy childhood and a good education in the village school, he enrolled at Oxford where he excelled in poetry and became fast friends with Sir Walter Scott. Following graduation, he succeeded his father as vicar in his family's parish, and for sixteen years he faithfully served his flock.

His bent toward poetry naturally gave him a keen and growing interest in hymnody. He sought to lift the literary quality of hymns, and he also dreamed of publishing a collection of high-caliber hymns corresponding to the church year for use by liturgical churches. But the Bishop of London wouldn't go along with it, and Heber's plans were disappointed.

He continued writing hymns for his own church, however, and it was during the sixteen years in the obscure parish of Hodnet that Heber wrote all 57 of his hymns, including the great missionary hymn, "From Greenland's Icy Mountains," which exhorted missionaries to take the gospel to faraway places like "Greenland's icy mountains," and "India's coral strand."

> *From Greenland's icy mountains, | From India's coral strand, |*
> *Where Afric's sunny fountains | Roll down their golden sand; |*
> *From many an ancient river, | From many a palmy plain, |*
> *They call us to deliver | Their land from error's chain.*

This hymn represented an earnest desire for Reginald, for he felt God was calling him as a missionary to "India's coral strand." His desire was fulfilled in 1822, when, at age 40, he was appointed to oversee the Church of England's ministries in India.

Arriving in Calcutta, he set out on a 16-month tour of his diocese, visiting mission stations across India. In February of 1826, he left for another tour. While in the village of Trichinopoly on April 3, 1826, he preached to a large crowd in the hot sun, and afterward plunged into a pool of cool water. He suffered a stroke and drowned.

It was after his death that his widow, finding his 57 hymns in a trunk, succeeded in publishing his *Hymns Written and Adapted to the Weekly Service of the Church Year.* In this volume was the great Trinitarian hymn based on Revelation 4:8–11, "Holy, Holy, Holy, Lord God Almighty."

My Faith Looks Up to Thee

Ray Palmer

Lowell Mason

1. My faith looks up to Thee, Thou Lamb of Cal-va-ry, Sa-vior di-vine! Now hear me while I pray; Take all my guilt a-way. Oh let me from this day Be whol-ly Thine!

2. May Thy rich grace im-part Strength to my faint-ing heart, My zeal in-spire. As Thou hast died for me, Oh may my love to Thee Pure, warm and change-less be, A liv-ing fire.

3. While life's dark maze I tread, And griefs a-round me spread Be Thou my Guide. Bid dark-ness turn to day; Wipe sor-row's tears a-way; Nor let me ev-er stray From Thee a-side!

4. When ends life's tran-sient dream, When death's cold sul-len stream Shall o'er me roll, Blest Sa-vior, then in love, Fear and dis-trust re-move. Oh bear me safe a-bove, A ran-somed soul.

My Faith Looks Up to Thee
1830

But rejoice to the extent that you partake of Christ's sufferings, that when His glory is revealed, you may also be glad with exceeding joy. 1 Peter 4:13

In the early 1830s, Lowell Mason moved to Boston from Savannah, where for sixteen years he had worked in a bank while directing church choirs on the side. In relocating to Boston, he wanted to focus exclusively on his musical interests. Soon he was directing three choirs, publishing hymns, compiling a songbook, and trying to get music education in the Boston public schools.

One day in 1832, he bumped into Ray Palmer. Palmer, 24, was exhausted. For years, he had burned the candle on both ends, working as a clerk in a dry goods store, attending classes at Yale, teaching at a girl's school in New York City, and preparing for the ministry.

Now, Mason wanted Palmer to write for him, to compose some hymns for his projected hymnbook.

Palmer, too tired to produce anything new, hesitatingly opened his little leather journal and showed Mason a poem he had written two years before. It was a personal prayer for renewed zeal and courage, composed in his rented room one night in 1830 when he had felt sick, tired, and lonely.

He later explained that he had wept that winter's evening upon finishing this poem: "The words for these stanzas were born out of my own soul with very little effort," he said. "I recall that I wrote the verses with tender emotion. There was not the slightest thought of writing for another eye, least of all writing a hymn for Christian worship."

After reading the words, Mason ducked into a nearby store for a piece of paper and hurriedly copied them down. That evening in his studio, he poured over this poem, hammering out the perfect tune for it. Shortly after, the two men met again and Mason told the young man, "Mr. Palmer, you may live many years and do many good things, but I think you will be best known to posterity as the author of 'My Faith Looks Up to Thee.'"

Lowell Mason was right. Ray Palmer did go on to do many good things and to write many fine hymns. But he is remembered by posterity for his first hymn, one written before he had even entered the ministry.

O For a Faith that Will Not Shrink

William H. Bathurst

J. C. Lowry

1. O for a faith that will not shrink, Tho' pressed by ev-'ry foe, That will not trem-ble on the brink Of an-y earth-ly woe!
2. That will not mur-mur nor com-plain, Be-neath the chas-tening rod But in the hour of grief or pain, Will lean up-on its God.
3. A faith that shines more bright and clear When tem-pests rage with-out; That when in dan-ger knows no fear, In dark-ness feels no doubt.
4. Lord give us such a faith as this; And then what-e'er may come, We'll taste e'en here the hal-lowed bliss, Of an e-ter-nal home.

O For a Faith that Will Not Shrink

1831

And the apostles said to the Lord, "Increase our faith." So the Lord said, "If you have faith as a mustard seed, you can say to this mulberry tree, 'Be pulled up by the roots and be planted in the sea,' and it would obey you. Luke 17:5–6

T his hymn strikes a chord in most Christians, for we often find ourselves *worrying* when we should be *worshipping* and *waiting*. The German Christian, George Müeller, was a man who learned to replace fear with faith. When asked about his ability to trust God in crises, he replied, "My faith is the same faith which is found in every believer. It has been increased little by little for the last 26 years. Many times when I could have gone insane from worry, I was at peace because my soul believed the truth of God's promises. God's Word, together with the whole character of God, as He has revealed Himself, settles all questions. His unchangeable love and His infinite wisdom calmed me . . . . It is written, 'He who did not spare His own Son, but delivered Him up for us all, how shall He not with Him also freely give us all things.'"

If your faith needs bolstering, make this hymn your own personal prayer. It was written by William Bathurst, who was born near Bristol, England, on August 28, 1796. He grew up in privileged surroundings. His father, Charles Bragge, a member of Parliament, changed his name to Bathurst when he inherited the family estate at Lydney Park, Gloucestershire.

After graduating from Oxford, William became an Anglican minister in a village near Leeds, England, for 32 years (1820–1852). But he grew uncomfortable with the Anglican Church, especially regarding the baptism and burial practices demanded by the Book of Common Prayer. He eventually resigned his pulpit and assumed the family estate at Lydney Park. He died at the estate on November 25, 1877, and was buried in the nearby churchyard.

"O For a Faith that Will Not Shrink" is the best-known of William's 200 hymns. Originally entitled, "The Power of Faith," it was written as William studied Luke 17:5–6, where the disciples asked Jesus, "Lord, increase our faith."

*O for a faith that will not shrink | Though pressed by ev'ry foe, |
That will not tremble on the brink | Of any earthly woe.*

*A faith that shines more bright and clear | When tempests rage without; |
That when in danger knows no fear, | In darkness feels no doubt.*

My Country, 'Tis of Thee

Samuel F. Smith

Thesaurus Musicus

1. My coun - try, 'tis of Thee, Sweet land of lib - er - ty, Of Thee I sing: Land where my fa - thers died, Land of the pil - grims' pride, From ev - ery moun - tain side Let free - dom ring!

2. My na - tive coun - try, thee, Land of the no - ble, free, Thy name I love: I love Thy rocks and rills, Thy woods and tem - pled hills; My heart with rap - ture thrills Like that a - bove.

3. Let mu - sic swell the breeze, And ring from all the trees Sweet free - dom's song: Let mor - tal tongues a - wake; Let all that breathe par - take; Let rocks their si - lence break, The sound pro - long.

4. Our fa - thers' God, to Thee, Au - thor of lib - er - ty, To Thee we sing: Long may our land be bright With free - dom's ho - ly light; Pro - tect us by Thy might, Great God, our King!

My Country, 'Tis of Thee

1831

Blessed is the nation whose God is the LORD . . . Psalm 33:12

*T*his patriotic hymn was written by Samuel Francis Smith, a native Bostonian, born on October 21, 1808. After attending Boston Latin School, he enrolled in Harvard, then attended Andover Seminary. While there, Samuel became fascinated by the work of Adoniram Judson, America's first missionary, and he developed a lifelong passion for world evangelism.

It was also during Samuel's first year at Andover that hymn publisher, Lowell Mason, sought his help. Mason had a stack of German songs and materials needing translation. Learning that Samuel was proficient in German, he recruited the young student to translate them.

On a cold February afternoon, about a half hour before sunset, Samuel sat in his sparsely furnished room, pouring over the materials. He was struck by the words of "Gott segne Sachsenland" ("God Bless our Saxon Land"), set to the tune we know as "America" (used in Great Britain for "God Save the Queen").

"I instantly felt the impulse to write a patriotic hymn of my own adapted to this tune," Samuel later said. "Picking up a scrap of paper which lay near me, I wrote at once, probably within half an hour, the hymn, 'America' as it is now known."

A friend, William Jenks, took a copy to the pastor of Boston's Park Street Congregational Church. There "America" was first sung by the Juvenile Choir at a Sunday School Rally, on July 4, 1831.

In the years that followed, Samuel Francis Smith grew into a powerful Baptist preacher, pastor, college professor, hymnist, linguist, writer, and missionary advocate. He traveled the world in support of evangelism, and he rejoiced when his son became a missionary to Rangoon. Samuel lived to ripe old age and remained active till the end. He died suddenly in his late-eighties at the Boston train station en route to a preaching appointment.

But he has always been most revered for the patriotic hymn he wrote as a 23-year-old student. As his friend and Harvard classmate, Oliver Wendell Holmes, put it at a class reunion:

> *And there's a nice youngster of excellent pith,—*
> *Fate tried to conceal him by naming him Smith;*
> *But he shouted a song for the brave and the free,—*
> *Just read on his medal, "My country, of thee!"*

Lead, Kindly Light

John Henry Newman

John B. Dykes

1. Lead, kind-ly Light, a - mid th'en - cir - cling gloom, lead Thou me on!
2. I was not ev - er thus, nor prayed that Thou shouldst lead me on;
3. So long Thy power hath blest me, sure it still will lead me on.

The night is dark, and I am far from home; lead Thou me on!
I loved to choose and see my path; but now lead Thou me on!
O'er moor and fen, o'er crag and tor - rent, till the night is gone,

Keep Thou my feet; I do not ask to see
I loved the gar - ish day, and, spite of fears,
And with the morn those an - gel fac - es smile,

The dis - tant scene; one step e - nough for me.
Pride ruled my will. Re - mem - ber not past years!
which I have loved long since, and lost a - while!

Lead, Kindly Light

1833

The steps of a good man are ordered by the LORD.—Psalm 37:23

*I*n the 1800s, more than 250 Church of England pastors converted to Roman Catholicism, largely through the influence of John Henry Newman.

Newman, born in London on February 21, 1801, was raised to love and read the Bible. He was a sensitive youth, and concluded early in life that God intended him to stay single. After graduating from Trinity College, Oxford, at age 19, he was ordained and became Vicar of St. Mary's, the university church at Oxford. His preaching attracted large crowds.

By 1833, his hard work and sensitive nature left him exhausted, and he embarked on a therapeutic voyage to the coasts of North Africa, Italy, Greece, and Sicily. While in Rome he found himself attracted to Catholicism. Proceeding on to Sicily, he contracted a fever and nearly died. Emotionally spent, homesick, weak, and worried, he sailed for home, but the winds died, stranding the vessel motionless on the Mediterranean for weeks.

The dispirited young man nearly broke under the strain. On June 16, 1833, alone in his cabin, he wrestled with God until he gained victory in his heart. From this experience, he penned one of the most famous hymns in the English language:

Lead, kindly Light! Amid th' encircling gloom, | Lead Thou me on; |
The night is dark, and I am far from home, | Lead Thou me on; |
Keep thou my feet; | I do not ask to see the distant scene; | One step enough for me.

"Lead, Kindly Light" was published the next year in a British magazine under the title, "Faith—Heavenly Leanings." It later appeared under the titles, "Light in the Darkness," and "The Pillar of Cloud."

By 1841 Newman was clearly turning away from the Anglican Church. On October 9, 1845, he shocked England by converting to Roman Catholicism. Two years later, he was ordained a priest and, eventually, a cardinal.

Try praying this hymn the next time you need guidance. The Lord leads us step by step. He provides for us day by day. And He cares for us moment by moment.

⌐⌐⌐

God never gives guidance for two steps at a time. I must take one step, and then I get light for the next. This keeps the heart in abiding dependence upon God.—C. H. Mackintosh

O Worship the King

Robert Grant

Johann Michael Haydn

1. O wor-ship the King, All glo-rious a-bove, And
2. O tell of His might, And sing of His grace, Whose
3. Thy boun-ti-ful care, What tongue can re-cite? It
4. Frail child-ren of dust, And fee-ble as frail, In

grate-ful-ly sing His power and His love: Our
robe is the light, Whose can-o-py space. His
breathes in the air; It shines in the light. It
Thee do we trust, Nor find Thee to fail. Thy

Shield and De-fend-er, The An-cient of Days, Pa-
char-iots of wrath, The deep thun-der-clouds form, And
streams from the hills; It de-scends to the plain, And
mer-cies how ten-der! How firm to the end! Our

vil-ioned in splen-dor, And gird - ed with praise.
dark is His path On the wings of the storm.
sweet-ly dis-tills In the dew and the rain.
Mak-er, De-fend-er, Re-deem - er, and Friend!

O Worship the King

1833

I will sing to the LORD as long as I live; I will sing praise to my God while I have my being. Psalm 104:33

harles Grant, director of the East India Company, was respected throughout India as one of Britain's finest statesmen. He was also a deeply committed Christian, an evangelical in the Anglican Church, who used his position in India to encourage missionary expansion there.

In 1778, just as England was reeling from the American Revolution, Charles returned to the British Isles to become a Member of Parliament from Inverness, Scotland.

His son, Robert, six years old at the time, grew up in a world of power, politics, and privilege. But he also grew up as a devout and dedicated follower of Christ. As a young man, Robert attended Magdalene College, Cambridge, then entered the legal profession. His intelligence and integrity were obvious. He became King's Sargent in the Court of the Duchy of Lancaster, and, in 1818, he entered Parliament. Among his legislative initiatives was a bill to remove civil restrictions against the Jews.

One day in the early 1830s, as Robert studied Psalm 104, he compared the greatness of the King of kings with the majesty of British royalty. Psalm 104:1 says of God: "O Lord my God, You are very great: You are clothed with honor and majesty." Verses 2–3 add that God covers Himself "with light as with a garment" and "makes the clouds His chariot." Verse 5 reminds us that God "laid the foundations of the earth." All of creation reflects God's greatness, verse 24 proclaiming, "O Lord, how manifold are Your works!" Verse 31 says, "May the glory of the Lord endure forever."

Robert filled his heart with these verses, and from his pen came one of the most magnificent hymns in Christendom:

> *O worship the King, all glorious above,*
> *And gratefully sing His power and His love;*
> *Our Shield and Defender, the Ancient of Days,*
> *Pavilioned in splendor and girded with praise.*

In 1832, Robert was appointed Judge Advocate General, this hymn was published in 1833, and he was knighted in 1834. Soon thereafter, at age 50, Sir Robert returned to India, land of his early childhood, to be Governor of Bombay. He died there on July 9, 1838. A nearby medical college was built in his honor and named for him. But his most lasting memorial is this majestic hymn of praise, calling us to worship the King of kings.

The Solid Rock

Edward Mote

William B. Bradbury

1. My hope is built on noth-ing less Than Je - sus' blood and
2. When dark-ness seems to hide His face, I rest on His un -
3. His oath, His cov - e - nant, His blood, Sup - port me in the
4. When He shall come with trum-pet sound, O may I then in

righ - teous-ness. I dare not trust the sweet - est frame, But whol - ly
chang - ing grace. In ev - ery high and storm - y gale, My an - chor
whelm-ing flood. When all a - round my soul gives way, He then is
Him be found! Dressed in His righ-teous - ness a - lone, Fault-less to

lean on Je - sus' name.
holds with - in the veil.
all my Hope and Stay.
stand be - fore the throne!

On Christ the sol - id Rock I stand, All

oth-er ground is sink-ing sand. All oth-er ground is sink-ing sand.

The Solid Rock

1834

For no other foundation can anyone lay than that which is laid, which is Jesus Christ. 1 Corinthians 3:11

 dward Mote was born into poverty on January 21, 1797, in London. His parents, innkeepers, wouldn't allow a Bible in their house, but somehow Edward heard the gospel as a teenager and came to Christ. He eventually became a skilled carpenter and the owner of his own cabinet shop.

"One morning," he recalled, "it came into my mind as I went to labor to write a hymn on the 'Gracious Experience of a Christian.' As I went up to Holborn I had the chorus: *On Christ the solid Rock I stand / All other ground is sinking sand.* In the day I had four verses complete, and wrote them off.

"On the Sabbath following, I met brother King . . . who informed me that his wife was very ill, and asked me to call and see her. I had an early tea and called afterwards. He said that it was his usual custom to sing a hymn, read a portion, and engage in prayer before he went to meeting. He looked for his hymnbook but could find it nowhere. I said, 'I have some verses in my pocket; if he liked, we would sing them.' We did, and his wife enjoyed them so much that after service he asked me, as a favor, to leave a copy of them for his wife.

"I went home, and by the fireside composed the last two verses, wrote the whole off, and took them to sister King . . . As these verses so met the dying woman's case, my attention to them was the more arrested, and I had a thousand printed for distribution."

In 1852, Edward, 55, gave up his carpentry to pastor the Baptist Church in Horsham, Sussex, where he ministered 21 years. He resigned in 1873, in failing health, saying, "I think I am going to heaven; yes, I am nearing port. The truths I have been preaching, I am now living upon and they'll do very well to die upon. Ah! The precious blood." He passed away at age 77.

Here's an interesting verse from Mote's original that is omitted from most hymnals today:

> *I trust His righteous character,*
> *His council, promise, and His power;*
> *His honor and His Name's at stake*
> *To save me from the burning lake;*
> *On Christ, the solid Rock, I stand,*
> *All other ground is sinking sand.*

Just As I Am

Charlotte Elliott

William B. Bradbury

1. Just as I am, with - out one plea, But that Thy blood was shed for me, And that Thou bidst me come to Thee, O Lamb of God, I come, I come!
2. Just as I am, and wait - ing not To rid my soul of one dark blot; To Thee whose blood can cleanse each spot, O Lamb of God, I come, I come!
3. Just as I am, though tossed a - bout With many a con - flict, many a doubt, Fight - ings and fears with-in, with - out, O Lamb of God, I come, I come!
4. Just as I am, poor, wretch - ed, blind; Sight, rich - es, heal - ing of the mind. Yea, all I need, in Thee to find, O Lamb of God, I come, I come!
5. Just as I am, Thou wilt re - ceive, Wilt wel - come, par - don, cleanse, re - lieve. Be - cause Thy prom - ise I be - lieve, O Lamb of God, I come, I come!

Just As I Am

1836

All that the Father gives Me will come to Me, and the one who comes to Me I will by no means cast out. John 6:37

S he was an embittered woman, Charlotte Elliott of Brighton, England. Her health was broken, and her disability had hardened her. "If God loved me," she muttered, "He would not have treated me this way."

Hoping to help her, a Swiss minister, Dr. Cesar Malan, visited the Elliotts on May 9, 1822. Over dinner, Charlotte lost her temper and railed against God and family in a violent outburst. Her embarrassed family left the room, and Dr. Malan was left alone with her.

"You are tired of yourself, aren't you?" he asked. "You are holding to your hate and anger because you have nothing else in the world to cling to. Consequently, you have become sour, bitter, and resentful."

"What is your cure?" asked Charlotte.

"The faith you are trying to despise."

As they talked, Charlotte softened. "If I wanted to become a Christian and to share the peace and joy you possess," she finally asked, "what would I do?"

"You would give yourself to God just as you are now, with your fightings and fears, hates and loves, pride and shame."

"I would come to God just as I am? Is that right?"

Charlotte did come just as she was, and her heart was changed that day. As time passed she found and claimed John 6:37 as a special verse for her: ". . . he who comes to Me I will by no means cast out."

Years later, her brother, Rev. Henry Elliott, was raising funds for a school for the children of poor clergymen. Charlotte wrote a poem, and it was printed and sold across England. The leaflet said: *Sold for the Benefit of St. Margaret's Hall, Brighton: Him That Cometh to Me I Will in No Wise Cast Out.* Underneath was Charlotte's poem— which has since become the most famous invitational hymn in history.

Charlotte lived to be 82 and wrote about 150 hymns, though she never enjoyed good health. As her loved ones sifted through her papers after her death, they found over a thousand letters she had kept in which people expressed their gratitude for the way this hymn had touched their lives.

Nearer, My God, to Thee

Sarah F. Adams

Lowell Mason

1. Near - er, my God, to Thee, Near - er to Thee,
2. Though like the wan - der - er, The sun gone down,
3. There let the way ap - pear, Steps un - to heav'n;
4. Then, with my wak - ing tho'ts Bright with Thy praise,
5. Or if, on joy - ful wing Cleav - ing the sky,

E'en though it be a cross That rais - eth me!
Dark - ness be o - ver me, My rest a stone;
All that Thou send - est me, In mer - cy giv'n;
Out of my ston - y griefs Beth - el I'll raise,
Sun, moon, and stars for - got, Up - ward I fly,

Still all my song shall be, Near - er, my God, to Thee;
Yet in my dreams I'd be, Near - er, my God, to Thee;
An - gels to beck - on me, Near - er, my God, to Thee;
So by my woes to be, Near - er, my God, to Thee;
Still all my song shall be, Near - er, my God, to Thee;

Near - er, my God, to Thee, Near - er to Thee!
Near - er, my God, to Thee, Near - er to Thee!
Near - er, my God, to Thee, Near - er to Thee!
Near - er, my God, to Thee, Near - er to Thee!
Near - er, my God, to Thee, Near - er to Thee!

Nearer, My God, to Thee

1840

Then he dreamed, and behold, a ladder was set up on the earth, and its top reached to heaven. Genesis 28:12

I t was reported that the band aboard the *Titanic* gallantly played "Nearer, My God, to Thee" as the great liner sank to its watery grave on April 14, 1912. A Canadian survivor told of being comforted by its strains. Historians, however, have never been able to nail down the validity of the story.

Never mind. It's a great hymn anyway, written by a woman named Sarah Flower Adams. She was born in Harlow, England, in the winter of 1805. Her father was a newspaper editor and a man of prominence.

Sarah herself grew up enjoying the spotlight. She showed great interest in the stage and dreamed of being an actress. In 1834, she married William Bridges Adams, a civil engineer. The couple lived in London where Sarah could be near the great theaters. In 1837, she played "Lady MacBeth" in the Richmond Theater in London to rave reviews.

Her frail health hampered her career, however, and she found herself focusing more on her literary gifts. It's said that she wrote quickly, as if under compulsion; and seldom did editors find anything to change in her work. Among her compositions were hymns of praise to the Lord. Sarah's sister, Eliza, a gifted musician, often wrote the music for her hymns. The two were very close.

One day in 1841, their pastor, Rev. William Johnson Fox of London's South Place Unitarian Church, paid a visit. He was compiling a church hymnbook and he wanted to include some of their hymns. He further mentioned that he was frustrated at his inability to find a hymn to go along with the upcoming Sunday's message, which was from the story of Jacob at Bethel in Genesis 28:20–22.

Sarah offered to write a hymn based on those verses. For the rest of the week she poured over the passage, visualizing Jacob's sleeping with a stone for his pillow as he dreamed of a ladder reaching to heaven. The following Sunday, South Place Unitarian Church sang Sarah's "Nearer, My God, to Thee."

Eliza, who was suffering from tuberculosis, died in 1846. Sarah had faithfully cared for her sister during the illness, but by the time Eliza died, Sarah, too, was showing signs of consumption.

She passed away on August 14, 1848, at age 43.

I Heard the Voice of Jesus Say

Horatius Bonar   John B. Dykes

1. I heard the voice of Je-sus say, "Come un-to Me and rest;
2. I heard the voice of Je-sus say, "Be-hold, I free-ly give
3. I heard the voice of Je-sus say, "I am this dark world's Light;

Lay down, thou wea-ry one, lay down Thy head up-on My breast."
The liv-ing wa-ter; thirst-y one, stoop down, and drink, and live."
Look un-to Me, thy morn shall rise, and all thy day be bright."

I came to Je-sus as I was, wea-ry and worn and sad;
I came to Je-sus, and I drank of that life-giv-ing stream;
I looked to Je-sus, and I found in Him my Star, my Sun;

I found in Him a rest-ing place, and He has made me glad.
My thirst was quenched, my soul re-vived, and now I live in Him.
And in that light of life I'll walk, till travel-ing days are done.

I Heard the Voice
of Jesus Say
1846

Come to Me, all you who labor and are heavy laden, and I will give you rest.
Matthew 11:28

A nyone can work with adults, but it takes a special person to communicate with children. Among the early hymnists, none connected with youngsters better than Horatius Bonar, "the prince of Scottish hymnists."

Horatius was born just before Christmas in 1808, one of eleven children. Two of his siblings—John and Andrew—also became outstanding preachers. After studying for the ministry at the University of Edinburgh and serving an internship at Leith, Horatius was ordained and began pastoring in Kelso. Later he moved to Edinburgh where he became one of Scotland's most famous pulpiteers.

He began writing hymns while at Kelso, and many of them were especially for children. Later, in his church in Edinburgh where only the Scottish version of the Psalms were sung, only the children were allowed to sing his hymns. On one occasion in the adult services, two of his church leaders stormed out in protest when a hymn was announced. But the children never protested. They loved his visits to Sunday School when he would lead them in exuberant singing.

Horatius wrote "I Heard the Voice of Jesus Say" for his Sunday School children in 1846. On the page containing the words, he doodled four faces and the head of a man wearing a hat. He based his three verses on three wonderful promises of Jesus in Matthew 11:28, John 4:14, and John 8:12. The first half of each stanza echoes our Lord's promise, and the last half of each stanza frames our response.

Where did his love for children come from? He and his wife had lost five of their children in rapid succession. But God gave him hundreds of children in his Sunday Schools. And that's not all . . .

Many years later, a surviving Bonar daughter was widowed and returned home to live with her parents. She had five young children. Writing to a friend, Horatius said, "God took five children from life some years ago, and He has given me another five to bring up for Him in my old age."

Horatius was nearly 80 when he preached in his church for the last time. Among his last requests was that no biography of him be written. He wanted all the glory to be Christ's alone.

Abide with Me

Henry F. Lyte

W. H. Monk

1. A - bide with me! Fast falls the e - ven - tide.
2. Swift to its close ebbs out life's lit - tle day.
3. I need Thy pres - ence Ev - ery pass - ing hour.
4. I fear no foe, With Thee at hand to bless;

The dark - ness deep - ens; Lord, with me a - bide!
Earth's joys grow dim; Its glo - ries pass a - way.
What but Thy grace Can foil the temp - ter's power?
Ills have no weight, And tears no bit - ter - ness.

When oth - er help - ers fail And com - forts flee,
Change and de - cay In all a - round I see;
Who, like Thy - self, My guide and stay can be?
Where is death's sting? Where, grave, thy vic - to - ry?

Help of the help - less, O a - bide with me!
O Thou, who chang - est not, a - bide with me!
Through cloud and sun - shine, Lord, a - bide with me.
I tri - umph still, If Thou a - bide with me.

Abide with Me

1847

If you abide in Me, and My words abide in you, you will ask what you desire, and it shall be done for you. John 15:7

Henry Francis Lyte, vicar in the fishing village of Lower Brixham, Devonshire, England, ministered faithfully for twenty-three years to his seafaring people.

Though a humble couple, he and his wife, Anne, lived in an elegant estate, Berry Head. It had reportedly been provided by King William IV, who had been impressed with Henry's ministry. At water's edge, its coastal views were among the most beautiful on the British Isles. Henry laid out walking trails through the estate's forty-one acres and enjoyed the tranquility of the house and grounds. There he wrote most of his sermons, poems, and hymns.

But Henry's lung condition hung over the home like a blackening cloud. Lower Brixham suffered damp winters, and while in his early fifties Henry realized his lung disorder had deteriorated into tuberculosis. On September 4, 1847, age 54, he entered his pulpit with difficulty and preached what was to be his last sermon. He had planned a therapeutic holiday in Italy. "I must put everything in order before I leave," he said, "because I have no idea how long I will be away."

That afternoon he walked along the coast in pensive prayer then retired to his room, emerging an hour later with a written copy of "Abide With Me." Some accounts indicate he wrote the poem during that hour; others say that he discovered it in the bottom of his desk as he packed for his trip to Italy, and that it had been written a quarter century earlier. Probably both stories are true. It is likely that, finding sketches of a poem he had previously started, he prayerfully revised and completed it that evening.

Shortly afterward, Henry embraced his family a final time and departed for Italy. Stopping in Avignon, France, he again revised "Abide With Me"—it was evidently much on his mind—and posted it to his wife. Arriving on the French Riviera, he checked into the Hotel de Angleterre in Nice, and there on November 20, 1847, his phthisic lungs finally gave out. Another English clergyman, a Rev. Manning of Chichester, who happened to be staying in the same hotel, attended him during his final hours. Henry's last words were, "Peace! Joy!"

When news of his death reached Brixham, the fishermen of the village asked Henry's son-in-law, also a minister, to hold a memorial service. It was on this occasion that "Abide With Me" was first sung.

It Came upon the Midnight Clear

Edmund H. Sears

Richard Storrs Willis

It Came upon the Midnight Clear

1849

And suddenly there was with the angel a multitude of the heavenly host praising God and saying: "Glory to God in the highest, and on earth peace, goodwill toward men!" Luke 2:13–14

E dmund Hamilton Sears is the author of two Christmas carols that are mirror images of each other, written fifteen years apart.

He was born in Sandisfield, Massachusetts, on April 6, 1819, and attended Union College in Schenectady, then Harvard Divinity School. He was ordained in the Unitarian ministry and chose to devote himself to small towns in Massachusetts, where he had time to study, think, and write.

At 24, he wrote "Calm on the Listening Ear," a Christmas carol based on the song of the angels in Luke 2. It proved very similar to the more-famous carol he would later write. Having the same meter and theme, and it can be sung to the same tune:

Calm on the listening ear of night | Come heaven's melodious strains, |
Where wild Judea stretches far | Her silver-mantled plains. |
Celestial choirs, from courts above, | Shed sacred glories there, |
And angels, with their sparkling lyres, | Make music on the air.

Fifteen years later, he wrote its more famous twin. "It Came upon the Midnight Clear" is an unusual carol in that there is no mention of Christ, of the newborn Babe, or of the Savior's Mission. Sears, after all, was Unitarian. The author's only focus is the angelic request for peace on earth.

Notice again the date of the hymn. It was written as the clouds of civil strife were darkening the United States, setting the stage for the War Between the States. We can grasp the concern that drove Edmund to write this hymn by reading a stanza now usually omitted from most hymnals:

Yet with the woes of sin and strife/ The world hath suffered long; |
Beneath the angel-strain have rolled | Two thousand years of wrong; |
And man, at war with man, hears not | The love song which they bring: |
O hush the noise, ye men of strife, | And hear the angels sing!

Edmund Sears became well-known because of his hymns and books. He was awarded a Doctor of Divinity degree in 1871, and took a preaching tour of England where he was met by large congregations. He died in Weston, Massachusetts, on January 16, 1876.

In Heavenly Love Abiding

Anna L. Waring

Felix Mendelssohn

1. In heav'n-ly love a - bid - ing, No change my heart shall fear;
2. Wher - ev - er He may guide me, No want shall turn me back;
3. Green pas-tures are be - fore me, Which yet I have not seen;

And safe is such con - fid - ing, For noth-ing chang - es here.
My Shep-herd is be - side me, And noth-ing can I lack.
Bright skies will soon be o'er me, Where dark-est clouds have been.

The storm may roar with - out me, My heart may low be laid,
His wis - dom ev - er wak - eth; His sight is nev - er dim.
My hope I can - not mea - sure; My path to life is free;

But God is round a - bout me, And can I be dis - mayed?
He knows the way He tak - eth, And I will walk with Him.
My Sav - ior has my trea-sure, And He will walk with me.

In Heavenly Love Abiding
<u>1850</u>

Have I not commanded you? Be strong and of good courage; do not be afraid, nor be dismayed, for the LORD your God is with you wherever you go. Joshua 1:9

One of our most reassuring hymns is Anna L. Waring's, "In Heavenly Love Abiding." Anna was born into a Quaker family in Wales in 1823. As a teen, she joined the Church of England and was baptized in 1842. She was a lifelong student of the Hebrew language and daily read from the Book of Psalms in the original text. Anna's special burden was for those behind bars, and she devoted herself to prison ministry and to causes like the Discharged Prisoners' Aid Society.

In 1850, she published a little volume of nineteen hymns, among them this one—"In Heavenly Love Abiding"—which Anna called, "Safety in God."

Here's another, lesser-known Anna Waring hymn, based on Psalm 31:15: "My times are in Your hand."

Father, I know that all my life / Is portioned out for me, /
And the changes that are sure to come, / I do not fear to see; /
But I ask Thee for a present mind / Intent on pleasing Thee.

I ask Thee for a thoughtful love, / Through constant watching wise, /
To meet the glad with joyful smiles, / And to wipe the weeping eyes; /
And a heart at leisure from itself, / To soothe and sympathize.

I would not have the restless will / That hurries to and fro, /
Seeking for some great thing to do, / Or secret thing to know; /
I would be treated as a child, / And guided where I go.

Wherever in the world I am, / In whatsoe'er estate, /
I have a fellowship with hearts / To keep and cultivate; /
And a work of lowly love to do / For the Lord on whom I wait.

So I ask Thee for the daily strength, / To none that ask denied, /
And a mind to blend with outward life / While keeping at Thy side; /
Content to fill a little space, / If Thou be glorified.

Crown Him with Many Crowns

Matthew Bridges/Godfrey Thring

George J. Elvey

1. Crown Him with man - y crowns, The Lamb up - on His throne. Hark!
2. Crown Him the Lord of love: Be - hold His hands and side, Rich
3. Crown Him the Lord of life, Who tri - umphed o'er the grave. Who
4. Crown Him the Lord of heaven: One with the Fath - er known, One

how the heaven - ly an - them drowns All mu - sic but its own! A -
wounds, yet vi - si - ble a - bove, In beau - ty glo - ri - fied; No
rose vic - tor - ious to the strife, For those He came to save. His
with the Spir - it Through Him given From yon - der glor - ious throne. All

wake, my soul and sing Of Him who died for Thee; And
an - gel in the sky Can ful - ly bear that sight, But
glo - ries now we sing, Who died and rose on high. Who
hail, Re - deem - er, hail! For Thou hast died for me; Thy

hail Him as thy match - less King Through all e - ter - ni - ty.
down - ward bends His won - dering eye At mys - ter - ies so bright.
died e - ter - nal life to bring, And lives that death may die.
praise and glo - ry shall not fail Through-out e - ter - ni - ty.

Crown Him with Many Crowns

1851

. . . and on His head were many crowns . . . Revelation 19:12

T he original form of this hymn was written by Matthew Bridges and consisted of six eight-line stanzas. He thought of his hymn as a sermon in song, based on Revelation 19:12. ". . . and on His head were many crowns." He called his hymn, "The Song of the Seraphs." Matthew, who once wrote a book condemning Roman Catholics, ended up converting to Catholicism in 1848. He followed John Henry Newman out of the Church of England.

In 1874, Godfrey Thring, a staunch Anglican clergyman feared that some of Bridges' verses smacked too much of Catholic doctrine. Verse two, for example, said:

> *Crown Him the virgin's Son, the God incarnate born,*
> *Whose arm those crimson trophies won which now His brow adorn;*
> *Fruit of the mystic rose, as of that rose the stem;*
> *The root whence mercy ever flows, the Babe of Bethlehem.*

It seems odd to us now that such a verse would cause controversy, but in the end Godfrey wrote six new verses for the same song. "Crown Him with Many Crowns," therefore became a six-verse hymn that was written twice!

Over the years, these twelve stanzas have become intermingled in the hymnbooks, with editors mixing and matching the verses. Here are the first lines of all twelve verses, the first six by Bridges, the last six by Thring:

- Stanza 1: *Crown Him with many crowns, the Lamb upon His throne . . .*
- Stanza 2: *Crown Him the virgin's Son, the God incarnate born . . .*
- Stanza 3: *Crown Him the Lord of love, behold His hands and side . . .*
- Stanza 4: *Crown Him the Lord of peace, Whose power a scepter sways . . .*
- Stanza 5: *Crown Him the Lord of years, the Potentate of time,*
- Stanza 6: *Crown Him the Lord of Heaven, one with the Father known . . .*
- Stanza 7: *Crown Him with crowns of gold . . . .*
- Stanza 8: *Crown Him the Son of God, before the worlds began . . .*
- Stanza 9: *Crown Him the Lord of light . . . .*
- Stanza 10: *Crown Him the Lord of life, who triumphed over the grave . . .*
- Stanza 11: *Crown Him the Lord of lords, who over all doth reign . . . .*
- Stanza 12: *Crown Him the Lord of heaven, enthroned in worlds above . . .*

Good King Wenceslas

John M. Neale

Swedish Carol

Good King Wenceslas

1854

But when you give a feast, invite the poor, the maimed, the lame, the blind. And you will be blessed, because they cannot repay you; for you shall be repaid at the resurrection of the just." Luke 14:13–14

This story is about two men—a Bohemian Duke and an Anglican minister—who lived nearly a thousand years apart.

Wenceslas was born in Bohemia, in modern Czechoslovakia, in the early 900s. His father, the Czech ruler, Duke Ratislav, gave him a good education supervised by his godly grandmother. When his father died, Wenceslas, seeing his mother mishandle affairs of state, stepped in at age 18, seizing the reins of government. From the beginning, he proved a different sort of king. He sought good relations with surrounding nations, particularly with Germany. He took steps to reform the judicial system, reducing the number of death sentences and the arbitrary power of judges. He encouraged the building of churches and showed heartfelt concern for the poor. He reportedly cut firewood for orphans and widows, often carrying the provisions on his own shoulders through the snow.

Wenceslas' brief reign ended suddenly. His pagan and rebellious brother, Boleslav, murdered him on September 28, 929, as he left for church. His people venerated him as a martyr, and today Wenceslas is the patron saint of Czechoslovakia.

He would be hardly remembered, however, but for John Mason Neale, an Anglican minister with a passion for returning church architecture and music to their ancient grandeur. Neale helped establish a committee to investigate and restore dilapidated church buildings in Great Britain. He was particularly upset at the ugly stoves installed to heat churches in Victorian times.

Disliking the hymns of Isaac Watts, he also sought to return church music to its medieval roots. Neale worked hard to translate ancient Greek, Latin, and Syrian hymns into English. In so doing, he gave us the Christmas carols, "Good Christian Men Rejoice," (a fourteenth century text set to a fourteenth-century tune), and "O Come, O Come Emmanuel," (a ninth-century text set to a fifteenth-century tune). He also translated the Palm Sunday hymn "All Glory, Laud, and Honor."

Good King Wenceslas is not a translation, but an original poem written by Neal to honor a godly monarch's concern for the poor. Neale himself worked with the needy, serving as warden of a charitable residence for indigent old men.

John Neale's antiquated opinions were widely scorned in his own day, but we're still singing his songs.

Still, Still with Thee

Harriet B. Stowe

Felix Mendelssohn

1. Still, still with Thee, when pur-ple morn-ing break-eth,
2. A-lone with Thee, a-mid the my-stic sha-dows,
3. Still, still with Thee, as to each new-born morn-ing,
4. So shall it be at last, in that bright morn-ing,

When the bird wak - eth, and the shad-ows flee;
The sol-emn hush of na-ture new-ly born;
A fresh and sol - emn splen-dor still is given,
When the soul wak - eth and life's sha-dows flee;

Fair - er than morn - ing, love-li-er than day - light,
A - lone with Thee in breath-less ad - o - ra - tion,
So does this bless - èd con-scious-ness, a - wak - ing,
O in that hour, fair - er than day - light dawn - ing,

Dawns the sweet con - scious - ness, I am with Thee.
In the calm dew and fresh-ness of the morn.
Breathe each day near - ness un - to thee and heaven.
Shall rise the glo - rious thought, I am with Thee.

Still, Still with Thee

1855

How precious also are Your thoughts to me, O God! How great is the sum of them!
If I should count them, they would be more in number than the sand; when I
awake, I am still with You. Psalm 139:17–18

arriet Beecher Stowe, daughter of the famous Congregational pastor Lyman Beecher, is best known for her novel, *Uncle Tom's Cabin*, which sold 10,000 copies its first week of publication and contributed to the outbreak of the Civil War by arousing public sentiment against slavery.

Harriet was a remarkable woman. She raised seven children and managed a household while maintaining a career—which was unusual in those days—and taught in a college. She was also a social crusader. She wrote thirty books and countless articles and poems. After *Uncle Tom's Cabin* was published, she became an international celebrity in America and England. But her life was crowded with tragedy as well, including the drowning of her son while he was a freshman in college, the alcoholism and disappearance of another son, and the morphine addiction of a daughter who was given the medication as a pain-killer following childbirth.

How did she manage it all?

First, she had dedicated herself wholly to Christ at age 14, after listening to a sermon by her father. "As soon as my father came home and was seated in his study," she recalled, "I went up to him and fell in his arms, saying, 'Father, I have given myself to Jesus, and He has taken me.' I never shall forget the expression of his face as he looked down into my earnest childish eyes . . . 'Is that so?' he said, holding me silent to his heart as I felt the hot tears fall on my head."

Second, Harriet rose each morning at 4:30 to meet with the Lord before the day began. She enjoyed watching the sunrise, listening to the birds, and sensing the all-encompassing presence of God. It is this habit Harriet described in her best-known hymn, written while meditating on Psalm 139:17–18: "How precious also are Your thoughts to me, O God! How great is the sum of them. If I should count them, they would be more in number than the sand; When I awake, I am still with You."

> *Still, still with Thee, when purple morning breaketh,*
> *When the bird waketh, and the shadows flee;*
> *Fairer than morning, lovelier than daylight,*
> *Dawns the sweet consciousness, I am with Thee.*

> *Alone with Thee, amid the mystic shadows,*
> *The solemn hush of nature newly born;*
> *Alone with Thee in breathless adoration,*
> *In the calm dew and freshness of the morn.*

What a Friend We Have in Jesus

Joseph M. Scriven

Charles C. Converse

1. What a Friend we have in Je-sus, All our sins and griefs to bear!
2. Have we tri-als and temp-ta-tions? Is there trou-ble an-y-where?
3. Are we weak and heav-y-lad-en, Cum-bered with a load of care?

What a priv-i-lege to car-ry, Ev-ery-thing to God in prayer!
We should nev-er be dis-cour-aged; Take it to the Lord in prayer.
Pre-cious Sav-ior, still our ref-uge! Take it to the Lord in prayer.

Oh, what peace we of-ten for-feit, Oh, what need-less pain we bear.
Can we find a friend so faith-ful, Who will all our sor-rows share?
Do Thy friends de-spise, for-sake Thee? Take it to the Lord in prayer.

All be-cause we do not car-ry Ev-ery-thing to God in prayer!
Je-sus knows our ev-ery weak-ness; Take it to the Lord in prayer.
In His arms He'll take and shield Thee; Thou wilt find a so-lace there.

What a Friend We Have in Jesus

1855

. . . the peace of God, which surpasses all understanding, will guard your hearts and minds through Christ Jesus. Philippians 4:6–7

Joseph Scriven watched in shock as the body of his fiancée was pulled from the lake. Their wedding had been planned for the next day. Reeling from the tragedy, he made up his mind to immigrate to America. Packing up his belongings in Dublin, Ireland, he sailed for Canada, leaving his mother behind. He was about 25 years old.

Ten years later, in 1855, he received word that his mother was facing a crisis. Joseph wrote this poem and sent it to her. Mrs. Scriven evidently gave a copy to a friend who had it published anonymously, and it quickly became a popular hymn, though no one knew who had written it.

Meanwhile, Joseph fell in love again. But tragedy struck a second time when his bride, Eliza Catherine Roche, contracted tuberculosis and died in 1860 before their wedding could take place.

To escape his sorrow, Joseph poured himself into ministry, doing charity work for the Plymouth Brethren and preaching among the Baptists. He lived a simple, obscure life in Port Hope, Canada, cutting firewood for widows, giving away his clothes and money to those in need. He was described as "a man of short stature, with iron-gray hair, close-cropped beard, and light blue eyes that sparkled when he talked." Ira Sankey later wrote:

> Until a short time before his death it was not known that he had a poetic gift. A neighbor, sitting up with him in his illness, happened upon a manuscript copy of "What a Friend We Have in Jesus." Reading it with great delight and questioning Mr. Scriven about it, he said that he had composed it for his mother, to comfort her in a time of special sorrow, not intending that anyone else should see it. Some time later, when another Port Hope neighbor asked him if it was true he composed the hymn, his reply was, "The Lord and I did it between us."

On October 10, 1896, Joseph became critically ill. In his delirium, he rose from his bed and staggered outdoors where he fell into a small creek and drowned at age 66. His grave was arranged so that his feet were opposite those of his lost love, Eliza Catherine Roche, that at the resurrection they might arise facing one another.

More Love to Thee, O Christ

Elizabeth P. Prentiss

William H. Doane

1. More love to Thee, O Christ, More love to Thee!
2. Once earth-ly joy I craved, Sought peace and rest.
3. Then shall my lat-est breath Whis-per Thy praise.

Hear Thou the prayer, I make on bend-ed knee.
Now Thee a-lone I seek; Give what is best.
This be the part-ing cry My heart shall raise;

This is my ear-nest plea: More love, O Christ to Thee;
This all my prayer shall be: More love, O Christ to Thee;
This still my prayer shall be: More love, O Christ to Thee;

More love to Thee, More love to Thee!
More love to Thee, More love to Thee!
More love to Thee, More love to Thee!

More Love to Thee, O Christ

1856

It is good for me that I have been afflicted, that I may learn Your statutes. Psalm 119:71

There's a little-known verse about sickness in the Bible, found in Isaiah 38:17. King Hezekiah, after the terrible illness that nearly cost his life, said, "Indeed it was for my own peace that I had great bitterness." Other translations put it:

- *It was for my own good that I had such hard times*—CEV
- *Surely it was for my benefit that I suffered such anguish*—NIV
- *It was for my welfare that I had great bitterness*—NRSV

Elizabeth Payson was born in Portland, Maine, on October 26, 1818. Her father, Edward Payson, was a famous Congregational minister, so revered that a thousand children were reportedly named for him. His writings and sermons are popular to this day.

In 1845, Elizabeth, a school teacher at the time, married a Presbyterian minister, George Lewis Prentiss, and the couple moved to New York where George began teaching at Union Theological Seminary. Elizabeth enjoyed writing, and her books, *Stepping Heavenward* and *The Flower of the Family,* became best-sellers.

Her health, however, was frail, and she suffered chronic insomnia. One day in 1856, following the deaths of two of her children, her health faltered and anxiety overwhelmed her. Inspired by the hymn "Nearer My God, To Thee," Elizabeth worked on a poem-prayer to the Lord. The words came easily at first, but by the end her creative energy evaporated, and she left the poem unfinished.

Thirteen years later, while rummaging through a stack of old papers, Elizabeth found this unfinished poem. As she re-read it, it didn't impress her as being very good. But when George insisted she finish it, she dutifully scribbled an ending in pencil. He printed a few copies, one of which landed on the desk of musician William Howard Doane in Cincinnati, who set the verses to music and published it in his *Songs of Devotion.*

"To love Christ more," Elizabeth once said, "is the deepest need, the constant cry of my soul . . . . Out in the woods and on my bed and out driving, when I am happy and busy, and when I am sad and idle, the whisper keeps going up for more love, more love, more love!"

Stand Up, Stand Up for Jesus

George Duffield, Jr.

George J. Webb

1. Stand up, stand up for Je - sus, Ye sol - diers of the cross;
2. Stand up, stand up for Je - sus, The trum - pet call o - bey;
3. Stand up, stand up for Je - sus, Stand in His strength a - lone;
4. Stand up, stand up for Je - sus, The strife will not be long,

Lift high His roy - al ban - ner, It must not suf - fer loss;
Forth to the might - y con - flict In this His glo - rious day.
The arm of flesh will fail you, Ye dare not trust your own.
This day, the noise of bat - tle, The next, the vic - tor's song.

From vic - t'ry un - to vic - t'ry His ar - my shall He lead,
Ye that are men, now serve Him A - gainst un - num - bered foes;
Put on the Gos - pel a - rmor, Each piece put on with prayer;
To Him that o - ver - com - eth, A crown of life shall be;

Till ev - 'ry foe is van - quished And Christ is Lord in - deed.
Let cou - rage rise with dan - ger, And strength to strength op - pose.
Where du - ty calls, or dan - ger, Be nev - er want - ing there.
He with the King of Glo - ry Shall reign e - ter - nal - ly.

Stand Up, Stand Up for Jesus

<u>1858</u>

Stand therefore, having girded your waist with truth, having put on the breastplate of righteousness. Ephesians 6:14

Dudley Tyng served as his father's assistant at Philadelphia's Church of the Epiphany and was elected its pastor when his father retired in 1854. He was only 29 when he succeeded his father at this large Episcopal church, and at first it seemed a great fit. But the honeymoon ended when Dudley began vigorously preaching against slavery. Loud complaints rose from the more conservative members, resulting in Dudley's resignation in 1856.

He and his followers organized the Church of the Covenant elsewhere in the city, and his reputation grew. He began noontime Bible studies at the YMCA, and his ministry reached far beyond his own church walls. Dudley had a burden for leading husbands and fathers to Christ, and he helped organize a great rally to reach men.

On Tuesday, March 30, 1858, five thousand men gathered. As Dudley looked over the sea of faces he felt overwhelmed. "I would rather this right arm were amputated at the trunk than that I should come short of my duty to you in delivering God's message," he told the crowd.

Over a thousand men were converted that day.

Two weeks later Dudley was visiting in the countryside, watching a corn-thrasher in the barn. His hand moved too close to the machine and his sleeve was snared. His arm was ripped from its socket, the main artery severed. Four days later his right arm was amputated close to the shoulder. When it appeared he was dying, Dudley told his aged father: "Stand up for Jesus, father, and tell my brethren of the ministry to stand up for Jesus."

Rev. George Duffield of Philadelphia's Temple Presbyterian Church was deeply stirred by Dudley's funeral, and the following Sunday he preached from Ephesians 6:14 about standing firm for Christ. He read a poem he had written, inspired by Dudley's words:

> *Stand up, stand up for Jesus, | Ye soldiers of the cross; |*
> *Lift high His royal banner, | It must not suffer loss.*

The editor of a hymnal heard the poem, found appropriate music, and published it. "Stand Up, Stand Up for Jesus" soon became one of America's favorite hymns, extending Dudley's dying words to millions.

Eternal Father, Strong to Save

William Whiting

John B. Dykes

1. E - ter - nal Fa - ther, strong to save, Whose
2. O Christ! Whose voice the wa - ters heard And
3. Most Ho - ly Spir - it! Who didst brood Up -
4. O Trin - i - ty of love and power! Our

arm hath bound the rest - less wave, Who bid'st the might - y
hushed their rag - ing at Thy Word, Who walk - edst on the
on the cha - os dark and rude, And bid its an - gry
fam - 'ly shield in dan - ger's hour; From rock and tem - pest,

o - cean deep Its own ap - point - ed lim - its keep; Oh,
foam - ing deep, And calm a - midst its rage didst sleep; Oh,
tu - mult cease, And give, for wild con - fu - sion, peace; Oh,
fire and foe, Pro - tect us where - so - ev'r we go; Thus

hear us when we cry to Thee, For those in per - il on the sea!
hear us when we cry to Thee, For those in per - il on the sea!
hear us when we cry to Thee, For those in per - il on the sea!
ev - er - more shall rise to Thee Glad hymns of praise from land and sea.

Eternal Father, Strong to Save
1860

Behold, He who keeps Israel shall neither slumber nor sleep. Psalm 121:4

salm 121 has been called the "Traveler's Psalm" because it requests God's watch-care over the comings and goings of His people: "The LORD shall preserve your going out and your coming in from this time forth, and even forevermore."

Nineteenth century hymnbooks usually had an entire collection of hymns echoing prayers for God's protection of travelers, especially for sailors. *Hymns for Christian Melody*, for example, published in 1832 by Rev. David Marks contains 24 hymns under the section: "Mariners." An 1857 hymnal published by the Freewill Baptist Printing Establishment in Dover, New Hampshire, devotes pages 928 to 943 to hymns for sailors.

The most famous mariners' hymn, "Eternal Father, Strong to Save," was written in 1869. It is called the "Navy Hymn" because of its association with the Naval Academy in Annapolis. It was Franklin Roosevelt's favorite hymn and was sung at his funeral. In November of 1963, its solemn strains accompanied the casket of John F. Kennedy as it was carried up the steps of the U.S. Capitol to lie in state.

The deeply moving melody was written by the famous composer, John B. Dykes, who named it MELITA after the island where Paul was shipwrecked in Acts 27.

Little is known about the author of the words, William Whiting of London. He was Master of an Anglican school for musicians, and he wrote several hymns; but only "Eternal Father, Strong to Save," is widely sung today. William reportedly wrote this hymn as a prayer for a friend who was preparing to sail to America:

> *Eternal Father, strong to save, | Whose arm hath bound the restless wave, |*
> *Who biddest the mighty ocean deep | Its own appointed limits keep; |*
> *Oh, hear us when we cry to Thee, | For those in peril on the sea!*

There follows a verse addressed to the Son, and one to the Holy Spirit. Then a closing verse requests traveling mercies from the Trinity. In more recent years, other verses have been added by various writers:

- *Lord, guard and guide the men who fly | Though the great spaces in the sky . . .*
- *Eternal Father, Lord of hosts, | Watch over the men who guard our coasts . . . .*
- *God, Who dost still the restless foam, | Protect the ones we love at home . . . .*
- *O Father, King of earth and sea, | We dedicate this ship to Thee . . . .*

Jesus Loves Me

Anna B. Warner

William B. Bradbury

1. Je-sus loves me! this I know, For the Bi-ble tells me so;
2. Je-sus loves me! He who died, Heav-en's gate to o-pen wide;
3. Je-sus take this heart of mine, Make it pure and whol-ly Thine;
4. Je-sus loves me! He will stay, Close be-side me all the way;

Lit - tle ones to Him be-long, They are weak, but He is strong.
He will wash a - way my sin, Let His lit - tle child come in.
Thou has bled and died for me, I will hence-forth live for Thee.
He's pre-pared a home for me, And some-day His face I'll see.

Yes, Je - sus loves me, Yes, Je - sus loves me,

Yes, Je - sus loves me, The Bi - ble tells me so.

Jesus Loves Me

1860

That Christ may dwell in your hearts through faith; that you, being rooted and grounded in love, may be able to comprehend with all the saints what is the width and length and depth and height—to know the love of Christ which passes knowledge; that you may be filled with all the fullness of God. Ephesians 3:17–19

Anna and Susan Warner lived in a lovely townhouse in New York City where their father, Henry Whiting Warner, was a successful lawyer. But the "Panic of 1837" wrecked the family's finances, forcing them to move into a ramshackle Revolutionary War-era home on Constitution Island on the Hudson, right across from the Military Academy at West Point.

Needing to contribute to the family income, Anna and Susan began writing poems and stories for publication. Anna wrote "Robinson Crusoe's Farmyard," and Susan wrote, "The Wide, Wide World." The girls thus launched parallel literary careers which resulted in 106 publications, eighteen of them co-authored.

One of their most successful joint projects was a novel titled *Say and Seal* in which a little boy named Johnny Fox is dying. His Sunday School teacher, John Linden, comforts him by taking him in his arms, rocking him, and making up a little song: "Jesus loves me, this I know, for the Bible tells me so . . . ."

The novel became a best-seller, second only to *Uncle Tom's Cabin;* and when hymnwriter William Bradbury read the words of John Linden's little song (written by Anna), he composed a childlike musical score to go along with them. "Jesus Loves Me," soon became the best-known children's hymn on earth.

Despite their success, the Warner sisters never seemed able to recover from the staggering financial reverses of 1836. Years later a friend wrote, "One day when sitting with Miss Anna in the old living room she took from one of the cases a shell so delicate that it looked like lace work and holding it in her hand, with eyes dimmed with tears, she said, 'There was a time when I was very perplexed, bills were unpaid, necessities must be had, and someone sent me this exquisite thing. As I held it I realized that if God could make this beautiful home for a little creature. He would take care of me.'"

For forty years, Susan and Anna conducted Bible classes for cadets at West Point, and both were buried with full military honors. They are the only civilians buried in the military cemetery at West Point. To this day, their home on Constitution Island is maintained by West Point as a museum to their memory.

I Gave My Life for Thee

Frances R. Havergal

Phillip P. Bliss

1. I gave My life for thee, My pre-cious blood I shed,
2. My Fa-ther's house of light, My glo-ry-cir-cled throne,
3. I suf-fered much for thee, More than thy tongue can tell,
4. And I have brought to thee, Down from My home a-bove,

That thou might'st ran-somed be, And quick-ened from the dead;
I left, for earth-ly night, For wan-d'rings sad and lone;
Of bit-t'rest ag-o-ny, To res-cue thee from hell;
Sal-va-tion full and free, My par-don and My love;

I gave, I gave My life for thee, What hast thou giv'n for Me?
I left, I left it all for thee, Hast thou left aught for Me?
I've borne, I've borne It all for thee, What hast thou borne for Me?
I bring, I bring Rich gifts to thee, What hast thou brought to Me?

I gave, I gave My life for thee, What hast thou giv'n for Me?
I left, I left it all for thee, Hast thou left aught for Me?
I've borne, I've borne It all for thee, What hast thou borne for Me?
I bring, I bring Rich gifts to thee, What hast thou brought to Me?

I Gave My Life for Thee

1860

For even the Son of Man did not come to be served, but to serve, and to give His life a ransom for many. Mark 10:45

W
ho said there's no place for the arts in Christianity?

In the early 1700s, there lived in Germany a young nobleman named Nikolaus Ludwig von Zinzendorf. His father had died when he was six weeks old, and Nikolaus was raised on a huge estate by three women—his mother, his grandmother, and his aunt, all of them devout Christians.

After graduating from the university at Wittenberg, the young count embarked on a grand tour of Europe. It was in the art museum at Düsseldorf that he had a life-altering experience with Christ. Housed in the museum was a painting by Domenico Feti entitled *Ecce Homo* ("Behold the Man"). It was a portrait of the thorn-crowned Christ gazing at the viewer. Beneath the painting were the words, "I have done this for you; what have you done for me?" Zinzendorf said to himself, "I have loved Him for a long time, but I have never actually done anything for Him. From now on I will do whatever He leads me to do."

As a result of that decision, Zinzendorf became one of the most influential leaders in Christian history, initiating the great Moravian missions movement which gave rise to global Protestant missions. He also wrote the great hymn, "Jesus, Thy Blood and Righteousness."

Many years later, on January 10, 1858, another young Christian visited the Düsseldorf art museum. Frances Havergal, about 17, was tired and sat down opposite the same painting. As she studied the picture and read the accompanying inscription, a few words of a hymn came to mind. Frances jotted them down. Later, back in England, she worked on her poem some more, but grew discouraged with it and threw it in the fire. Somehow it fell out of the grate. Several months later, Frances showed it to her father who was so moved that he wrote a tune for the words (although the tune most frequently used in American churches is by Philip Bliss). In 1860, it was published:

> *I gave my life for thee,*
> *My precious blood I shed,*
> *That thou might'st ransomed be,*
> *And quickened from the dead;*
> *I gave, I gave my life for thee,*
> *What hast thou given for me?*

141

Battle Hymn of the Republic

Julia Ward Howe   American Melody

1. Mine eyes have seen the glo - ry Of the com - ing of the Lord;
2. I have seen Him in the watch-fires Of a hun-dred cir - cling camps;
3. He has sound - ed forth the trum - pet That shall nev - er sound re - treat;
4. In the beau - ty of the lil - ies, Christ was born a - cross the sea,

He is tramp-ling out the vin - tage Where the grapes of wrath are stored;
They have build - ed Him an al - tar In the eve - ning dews and damps;
He is sift - ing out the hearts of men Be - fore His judg - ment seat;
With a glo - ry in His bos - om That trans - fig - ures you and me;

He hath loosed the fate - ful light - ning Of His ter - ri - ble swift sword;
I can read His righ - teous sen - tence By the dim and flar - ing lamps;
O be swift, my soul, to an - swer Him! Be ju - bi - lant, my feet!
As He died to make men ho - ly, Let us live to make men free,

His   truth   is   march - ing   on.
His   day   is   march - ing   on.
Our   God   is   march - ing   on.
While   God   is   march - ing   on.

Battle Hymn of the Republic

1861

Who is this King of glory? The LORD strong and mighty, the Lord mighty in battle.
Psalm 24:8

After the September 11, 2001 attacks on the Pentagon and the World Trade Center, a national service of prayer and remembrance was conducted at Washington's National Cathedral. America's most powerful leaders prayed together, listened to brief sermons by evangelist Billy Graham and others, then joined voices to sing the defiant anthem, "Battle Hymn of the Republic." Its words seemed to perfectly signal America's intention to battle the forces of terror in the world.

"Battle Hymn of the Republic" was written by Julia Ward Howe, a leader in women's rights and an ardent foe of slavery. Julia, who came from a wealthy New York family, was married to prominent Boston philanthropist and humanitarian, Dr. S. G. Howe. They were both crusaders for progressive political and moral issues of the day.

In 1861, during the darkest days of the Civil War, the Howes visited Washington, and Julia toured a nearby Union Army Camp on the Potomac in Virginia. There she heard soldiers singing a tribute to John Brown, who had been hanged in 1859 for attempting to lead an insurrection of slaves at Harper's Ferry: "John Brown's Body Lies a-mold'ring in the Grave." The music was rousing, but the words needed improvement. Julia's pastor, who accompanied her, asked her to consider writing new and better verses. That night, after the Howes retired to their room at the Willard Hotel, the words came.

> I went to bed and slept as usual, but awoke the next morning in the gray of the early dawn, and to my astonishment found that the wished-for lines were arranging themselves in my brain. I lay quite still until the last verse had completed itself in my thoughts, then hastily arose, saying to myself, I shall lose this if I don't write it down immediately. I searched for an old sheet of paper and an old stub of a pen which I had had the night before, and began to scrawl the lines almost without looking, as I learned to do by often scratching down verses in the darkened room when my little children were sleeping. Having completed this, I lay down again and fell asleep, but not before feeling that something of importance had happened to me.

Julia gave her song to a friend who worked at *The Atlantic Monthly*. The magazine published it in February, 1862, sending her a check for five dollars.

143

He Leadeth Me

Joseph H. Gilmore

William B. Bradbury

1. He lead-eth me, O bless-ed thought! O words with heaven-ly com-fort fraught!
2. Some-times 'mid scenes of deep-est gloom, Some-times where E - den's bow-ers bloom,
3. Lord, I would clasp Thy hand in mine, Nor ev - er mur-mur nor re - pine;
4. And when my task on earth is done, When by Thy grace. the vic-t'ry's won,

What -e'er I do, where-e'er I be, Still 'tis God's hand that lead-eth me.
By wa - ters still, o'er trou-bled sea, Still 'tis His hand that lead-eth me!
Con -tent what - ev - er lot I see, Since 'tis my God that lead-eth me.
E'en death's cold wave I will not flee, Since God through Jor - dan lead-eth me.

He lead-eth me, He lead-eth me, By His own hand He lead-eth me;

His faith-ful fol-lower I would be, For by His hand He lead-eth me.

He Leadeth Me

1862

. . . He leads me in the paths of righteousness for His name's sake. Psalm 23:3b

*O*n autumn nights as we sleep peacefully in our beds, millions of songbirds travel under cover of darkness, heading south. Somehow, they know their way. God has given them a state-of-the-art internal guidance system.

We're more valuable than many sparrows. If God guides His creation, will He not also guide His children? The Psalmist thought so, saying, "He leadeth me . . . He leadeth me . . ." (Psalm 23:2–3).

Dr. Joseph H. Gilmore, son of a Governor of New Hampshire, gave this account of writing his famous hymn on this theme:

As a young man recently graduated . . . , I was supplying for a couple of Sundays the pulpit of the First Baptist Church in Philadelphia. At the mid-week service, on the 26th of March, 1862, I set out to give the people an exposition of the Twenty-third Psalm, which I had given before on three or four occasions, but this time I did not get further than the words "He Leadeth Me." Those words took hold of me as they had never done before, and I saw in them a significance . . . of which I had never dreamed.

It was the darkest hour of the Civil War. I did not refer to that fact— that is, I don't think I did—but it may subconsciously have led me to realize that God's leadership is the one significant fact in human experience, that it makes no difference how we are led, or whither we are led, so long as we are sure God is leading us.

At the close of the meeting a few of us in the parlor of my host, Deacon Watson, kept on talking about the thought I had emphasized; and then and there, on a blank page of the brief from which I had intended to speak, I penciled the hymn, talking and writing at the same time, then handed it to my wife and thought no more about it. She sent it to *The Watchman and Reflector,* a paper published in Boston, where it was first printed. I did not know until 1865 that my hymn had been set to music by William B. Bradbury. I went to Rochester to preach as a candidate before the Second Baptist Church. Going into their chapel . . . I picked up a hymnal to see what they were singing, and opened it at my own hymn, "He Leadeth Me."

Revive Us Again

William P. MacKay   John J. Husband

1. We   praise Thee,   O   God,   For   the   Son   of   Thy   love;
2. We   praise Thee,   O   God,   For   Thy   Spir - it   of   light,
3. All   glo - ry   and   praise   To   the   Lamb that   was   slain,
4. Re - vive   us   a - gain;   Fill   each   heart with   Thy   love;

For   Je - sus, who   died And   is   now   gone   a - bove.
Who   has   shown us   our   Sav - ior And   scat - tered   our   night.
Who   has   borne   all   our   sins And   hath   cleansed ev - ery   stain.
May   each   soul   be   re - kin - dled With   fire   from   a - bove.

Hal - le -lu - jah! Thine the glo - ry! Hal - le - lu - jah!   A - men!

Hal - le -lu - jah! Thine the glo - ry!   Re - vive us   a - gain.

Revive Us Again
1863

Will You not revive us again, that Your people may rejoice in You? Psalm 85:6

I n his own words, here is the testimony of Scottish doctor, W. P. Mackay, author of "Revive Us Again."

My dear mother . . . had been a godly, pious woman, quite often telling me of the Savior, and many times I had been a witness to her wrestling in prayer for my soul's salvation. But nothing had made a deep impression on me. The older I grew the more wicked I became . . . .

One day a seriously injured (laborer) . . . was brought into the hospital. The case was hopeless . . . . He seemed to realize his condition, for he was fully conscious, and asked me how long he would last . . . . I gave him my opinion in as cautious a manner as I could. . . .

"Have you any relatives whom we could notify?" I continued.

The patient shook his head . . . . His only wish was to see his landlady, because he owed her a small sum, and also wished to bid her farewell. He also requested his landlady send him, "The Book . . . ."

I went to see him on my regular visits at least once a day. What struck me most was the quiet, almost happy expression constantly on his face . . . . After the man died, some things about the deceased's affairs were to be attended to in my presence.

"What shall we do with this?" asked the nurse, holding up a book in her hand.

"What kind of book is it?" I asked.

"The Bible of the poor man . . . . As long as he was able to read it, he did so, and when he was unable to do so anymore, he kept it under his bed cover."

I took the Bible and—could I trust my eyes? It was my own Bible! The Bible which my mother had given me when I left my parents' home, and which later, when short of money, I sold for a small amount. My name was still in it, written in my mother's hand . . . .

With a deep sense of shame I looked upon . . . the precious Book. It had given comfort and refreshing to the unfortunate man in his last hours. It had been a guide to him into eternal life, so that he had been enabled to die in peace and happiness. And this Book, the last gift of my mother, I had actually sold for a ridiculous price . . . .

Be it sufficient to say that the regained possession of my Bible was the cause of my conversion.

For the Beauty of the Earth

Folliott S. Pierpoint

Conrad Kocher

1. For the beau - ty of the earth, For the glo - ry
2. For the won - der of each hour Of the day and
3. For the joy of hu - man love, Broth - er, sist - er,
4. For Thy Church that ev - er - more Lift - eth ho - ly
5. For Thy - self, best gift di - vine, To our race so

of the skies, For the love which from our birth
of the night, Hill and vale and tree and flower,
par - ent, child; Friends on earth and friends a - bove;
hands a - bove, Of - fering up on ev - ery shore
free - ly given; For that great, great love of Thine,

O - ver and a - round us lies;
Sun and moon and stars of light:
For all gen - tle thoughts and mild:
Her pure sac - ri - fice of love:
Peace on earth and joy in heaven:

Lord of all, to Thee we raise This our hymn of grate - ful praise.

For the Beauty of the Earth

1864

Therefore You are great, O LORD God. For there is none like You, nor is there any God besides You, according to all that we have heard with our ears. 2 Samuel 7:22

olliot Sandford Pierpoint—that's the unlikely name of the author of this great hymn. Folliot was born October 7, 1835, in Bath, England. After graduating from Cambridge, he taught at Somersetshire College in his home area of Bath.

One day when he was 29, Folliot found himself walking in the countryside on a beautiful Spring day. He saw the ocean of green, the blue dome of heaven, and the winding Avon River cutting through the flowery landscape. Overwhelmed with God's creative brilliance, he wrote this poem. He intended it primarily for Communion services in the Anglican Church, but when it jumped the Atlantic, it quickly became associated with the American Thanksgiving holiday.

In Folliot's original version, each verse ended with: "Christ, Our God, to Thee we raise / This our sacrifice of praise." That line was eventually changed to, "Lord of all, to Thee we raise / This our hymn of grateful praise."

Little else is known about Folliot Sandford Pierpoint. He resigned from his position at Somersetshire, and apparently moved from place to place, teaching some, writing hymns, and publishing his poetry. He died in 1917.

"For the Beauty of the Earth" is one of only a few songs devoted purely to giving thanks. One of the strange things about the "attitude of gratitude" is that we tend to exhibit it in reverse proportion to the number of blessings received. The more we have, the less thankful we are.

Among the lessons Viktor Frankl learned in the Nazi death-camp, Auschwitz, was to take time to be thankful and to count your blessings. He wrote that prisoners in the camp dreamed at night about certain things more than others. Bread, cakes, and nice warm baths—the very things we take for granted every day.

Ralph Waldo Emerson observed that if the constellations appeared only once in a thousand years, imagine what an exciting event it would be. But because they're there every night, we barely give them a look.

One of the evidences of the Holy Spirit's work in our lives is a gradual reversal of that twisted pattern. God wants to make us people who exhibit a thankfulness in proper proportion to the gifts and blessings we've received.

Why not take time to sing this hymn to the Lord right now?

My Jesus, I Love Thee

William R. Featherston

Adoniram J. Gordon

1. My Je - sus I love Thee; I know Thou art mine.
2. I love Thee, Be - cause Thou hast first lov - ed me,
3. I'll love Thee in life, I will love Thee in death,
4. In man - sions of glo - ry And end - less de - light,

For Thee all the fol - lies Of sin I re - sign.
And pur - chased my par - don On Cal - va - ry's tree.
And praise Thee As long as Thou lend - est me breath;
I'll ev - er a - dore Thee In heav - en so bright.

My gra - cious Re - deem - er, My Sa - vior art Thou.
I love Thee For wear - ing the thorns On Thy brow,
And say when the death dew Lies cold on my brow,
I'll sing with the glit - ter - ing crown On my brow,

If ev - er I loved Thee, My Je - sus, 'tis now.
If ev - er I loved Thee, My Je - sus, 'tis now.
"If ev - er I loved Thee, My Je - sus 'tis now."
"If ev - er I loved Thee, My Je - sus, 'tis now."

My Jesus, I Love Thee

1864

We love Him because He first loved us. 1 John 4:19

*T*he young people of today are utterly dissolute and disorderly," fumed grumpy old Martin Luther in the sixteenth century. The philosopher Plato agreed. "The youth are rebellious, pleasure-seeking, and irresponsible," he wrote. "They have no respect for their elders." Socrates complained, "Children now love luxury. They have bad manners, contempt for authority. They show disrespect for elders, and love chatter."

A 6000-year-old Egyptian tomb bears this inscription: "We live in a decadent age. Young people no longer respect their parents. They are rude and impatient. They inhabit taverns and have no self-control."

The next time you think the "modern generation" is going from bad to worse, remember that God always has a rich handful of teenage heroes ready to change the world. In Bible times, we read of Joseph the dreamer, Daniel in Babylon, David the giant-killer, and the virgin Mary (likely still a teen).

As a teenager, Charles Spurgeon preached to great crowds, but when they referred to his youthfulness, he replied, "Never mind my age. Think of the Lord Jesus Christ and His preciousness."

In our own day, we've been deeply moved by young people like 17-year old Cassie Bernall of Littleton, Colorado, who was shot for her faith during the Columbine tragedy.

Some of our greatest hymns were also written by young adults. Isaac Watts wrote most of his most memorable hymns at about the age of nineteen. When poet John Milton was fifteen, he wrote the well-known, "Let Us with a Gladsome Mind." The hymn, "Work for the Night Is Coming," was written by an eighteen-year-old. And this hymn of deep devotion, "My Jesus, I Love Thee," was written William Ralph Featherston at age sixteen. Sixteen!

Featherston was born July 23, 1846, in Montreal. He died in the same city 26 years later. His family attended the Wesleyan Methodist Church, and it seems likely that William wrote this hymn as a poem celebrating his conversion to Christ. Reportedly, he sent it to an aunt living in California, and somehow it was published as an anonymous hymn in a British hymnal in 1864.

Little else is known about the origin of the hymn or its author, but that's all right. It's enough just to know that God can change the world through anyone—regardless of age—who will say, "My Jesus, I love Thee, I know Thou art mine. For Thee, all the follies of sin I resign."

151

Shall We Gather at the River?

Robert Lowry   Robert Lowry

1. Shall we gath-er at the riv-er, Where bright an-gel feet have trod;
2. On the mar-gin of the riv-er, Wash-ing up its sil-ver spray,
3. Ere we reach the shin-ing riv-er, Lay we ev-ery bur-den down;
4. Soon we'll reach the shin-ing riv-er, Soon our pil-grim-age will cease,

With its crys-tal tide for-ev-er Flow-ing by the throne of God?
We will walk and wor-ship ev-er, All the hap-py gold-en day.
Grace our spir-its will de-liv-er, And pro-vide a robe and crown.
Soon our hap-py hearts will quiv-er With the mel-o-dy of peace.

Yes, we'll gath-er at the riv-er, The beau-ti-ful, the beau-ti-ful riv-er;

Gath-er with the saints at the riv-er That flows by the throne of God.

Shall We Gather at the River?

<u>1864</u>

And he showed me a pure river of water of life, clear as crystal, proceeding from the throne of God and of the Lamb. Revelation 22:1

Often called the "Good Doctor," Robert Lowry was a cheerful man with a big beard and a quick mind. He pastored Baptist churches in the Eastern U.S. during the mid-1800s. One friend said, "Very few men had greater ability in painting pictures from imagination. He could thrill an audience with his vivid descriptions, inspiring them with the same thoughts that inspired him."

But he is best remembered for his hymns. Even in childhood he had composed tunes, and as he became acquainted with leaders in America hymnology—many of them based in New York—he realized he could reach more people through his songs than through his sermons.

He set many of Fanny Crosby's hymns to music, including the classic, "All the Way My Savior Leads Me." And he wrote both words and music to the popular gospel song: "What can wash away my sins? / Nothing but the blood of Jesus."

The doctor's best known hymn is "Shall We Gather at the River?" Though often used at baptisms, it's actually a song about heaven. It came to Lowry on a mid-summer's day in New York, when, in the sweltering heat, he began musing about the cool, crystal river that flows through the city of God as described in Revelation 22.

One afternoon in July, 1864, when I was pastor at Hanson Place Baptist Church, Brooklyn, the weather was oppressively hot, and I was lying on a lounge in a state of physical exhaustion. I felt almost incapable of bodily exertion, and my imagination began to take itself wings. Visions of the future passed before me with startling vividness. The imagery of the apocalypse took the form of a tableau. Brightest of all were the throne, the heavenly river, and the gathering of the saints. My soul seemed to take new life from that celestial outlook. I began to wonder why the hymn writers had said so much about the "river of death" and so little about the "pure water of life, clear as crystal, proceeding out of the throne of God and the Lamb." As I mused, the words began to construct themselves. They came first as a question of Christian inquiry, "Shall we gather?" Then they broke out in a chorus, "Yes, we'll gather." On this question and answer the hymn developed itself. The music came with the hymn.

153

Day by Day

Karolina Sandell-Berg

Oskar Ahnfelt

1. Day by day and with each pass-ing mo-ment, Strength I find to meet my tri-als here;
2. Ev - 'ry day the Lord Him-self is near me With a spe-cial mer-cy for each hour;
3. Help me then in ev - 'ry trib-u - la-tion, So to trust Your prom-is-es, O Lord;

Trust-ing in my Fa-ther's wise be - stow-ment, I've no cause for wor-ry or for fear.
All my cares He fain would bear and cheer me, He whose name is Coun - se - lor and Pow'r.
That I lose not faith's sweet con - so - la-tion, Of - fered me with - in Your ho - ly Word.

He whose heart is kind be-yond all mea-sure, Give un - to each day what He deems best;
The pro - tec - tion of His child and trea-sure, Is a charge that on Him-self He laid;
Help me, Lord, when toil and trou-ble meet-ing, E'er to take, as from a Fa-ther's hand,

Lov-ing -ly, its part of pain and plea-sure, Min-gling toil with peace and rest.
"As your days, your strength shall be in mea-sure," This the pledge to me He made.
One by one, the days, the mo-ments fleet-ing, Till I reach the prom - ised land.

Day by Day

1865

The LORD is my light and my salvation; whom shall I fear? the LORD is the strength of my life; of whom shall I be afraid?—Psalm 27:1

This is a Scandinavian hymn, written by the "Fanny Crosby of Sweden," Karolina W. Sandell-Berg.

Lina was born in Frvderyd on October 3, 1832, the daughter of Jonas Sandell, pastor of the village's Lutheran church. Though frail in body, she had a strong spirit, feasting on the artistic, literary, and religious influences of her home life.

But tragedy struck when she was twenty-six. Lina and her father were enjoying a boat trip on the east coast of Sweden near Gothenburg when the ship suddenly lurched. Before her eyes, Rev. Sandell pitched overboard and drowned. Returning home alone, Lina began processing her grief through the Scriptures and expressing her faith in poetry. Fourteen poems were published that year, 1858, one of which is sung to this day:

> *Children of the heavenly Father | Safely in His bosom gather; |*
> *Nestling bird nor star in heaven | Such a refuge e'er was given.*

Seven years later, her best-known hymn, "Day by Day," was published. In it, Lina spoke from personal experience about the daily strength the Lord provides for His struggling children.

> *Day by day, and with each passing moment, | Strength I find, to meet my trials here; |*
> *Trusting in my Father's wise bestowment, | I've no cause for worry or for fear.*

If you need strength for a particular trial, take this grand old hymn into the day with you, and claim some of the wonderful promises God has given:

- *The LORD is my strength and song, and He has become my salvation*—Exodus 15:2
- *As your days, so shall your strength be*—Deuteronomy 33:25
- *Do not sorrow, for the joy of the Lord is your strength*—Nehemiah 8:10
- *God is our refuge and strength, a very present help in trouble*—Psalm 46:1
- *Those who wait on the Lord shall renew their strength*—Isaiah 40:31
- *My grace is sufficient for thee: for my strength is made perfect in weakness*—2 Corinthians 12:9
- *I can do all things through Christ who strengthens me*—Philippians 4:13

Jesus Paid It All

Elvina M. Hall

John T. Grape

1. I   hear the Sav - ior   say, "Thy   strength in - deed   is   small;
2. Lord,   now in - deed   I   find, Thy   power and Thine   a - lone;
3. For   noth - ing good have   I, Where - by Thy grace to claim;
4. And   when be - fore the   throne, I   stand   in Him com - plete;

Child of weak - ness watch and   pray, Find in   Me thine all   in   all."
Can   change the   lep - er's   spots And   melt the heart of   stone.
I'll   wash my   gar - ments white, In the   blood of Cal - vary's Lamb.
"Je - sus died   my   soul to   save," My   lips shall still re - peat.

Je - sus paid it   all,   all   to Him I   owe;

Sin   had left a   crim - son stain, He   washed   it white as   snow.

Jesus Paid It All

1865

Not with the blood of goats and calves, but with His own blood He entered the Most Holy Place once for all, having obtained eternal redemption. Hebrews 9:12

I t was Sunday morning at Monument Street Methodist Church in Baltimore. Rev. George Schrick was droning on in a lengthy prayer while, up in the choir loft, Elvina Hall's mind was wandering. She thumbed quietly through the hymnbook, then began doodling on the flyleaf. By and by, these words came to her, which she scribbled on the front flap of her hymnal:

I hear my Savior say | Thy strength indeed is small, |
Thou hast naught My debt to pay, | Find in Me thy all in all.

Yea, nothing good have I, | Whereby Thy grace to claim; |
I'll wash my garments white | In the blood of Calvary's Lamb.

And now complete in Him, | My robe His righteousness, |
Close sheltered 'neath His side, | I am divinely blest,

When from my dying bed | My ransomed soul shall rise, |
Jesus paid it all | Shall rend the vaulted skies.

Elvina's poem fell into the hands of John T. Grape, a coal merchant and the church organist at Monument Street Methodist Church. As it happened, the church was being renovated, and the small organ had been taken to Grape's house for safekeeping. There he composed the music to "Jesus Paid It All."

Through the years, the words of this hymn have been edited and altered, but its great theme of redemption has remained untouched.

⌒

The colorful preacher, Rowland Hill, was once preaching to a crowd of people when the wealthy aristocrat, Lady Ann Erskine, drove up in her coach. Seeing her, Rev. Hill changed his sermon.

"I have something for sale," he suddenly declared. "Yes, I have something for sale. It is the soul of Lady Ann Erskine. Is there anyone here that will bid for her soul? Ah, do I hear a bid? Who bids? Satan bids. Satan, what will you give for her soul? 'I will give riches, honor, and pleasure.' But stop, do I hear another bid? Yes, Jesus Christ bids. Jesus, what will You give for her soul? 'I will give eternal life.' Lady Ann Erskine, you have heard the two bids—which will you take?"

Lady Erskine, realizing Christ had purchased her soul with His life's blood on the Cross, took Him.

Now the Day Is Over

Sabine Baring-Gould

Joseph Barnby

1. Now the day is o - ver,
2. Je - sus, give the wear - y
3. Grant to lit - tle chil - dren
4. Through the long night watch - es
5. When the morn - ing wak - ens,

Night is draw - ing nigh, Shad - ows of the
Calm and sweet re - pose; With Thy ten - derest
Vi - sions bright of Thee; Guard the sail - ors
May Thine an - gels spread Their white wings a -
Then may I a - rise Pure, and fresh, and

eve - ning Steal a - cross the sky.
bless - ing May mine eye - lids close.
toss - ing On the deep, blue sea.
bove me, Watch - ing round my bed.
sin - less In Thy ho - ly eyes.

Now the Day Is Over

1865

When you lie down, you will not be afraid; Yes, you will lie down and your sleep will be sweet. Proverbs 3:24

Highly productive people have one thing in common—they know how to plunge into their work. Basketball star Jerry West said, "You can't get much done in life if you only work on the days when you feel good."

That was the attitude of British pastor Sabine Baring-Gould, author of "Onward Christian Soldiers." In addition to shepherding his village church, teaching in the local college, dabbling in archaeology, publishing travelogues, and writing hymns, he wrote fiction. For many years he published a new novel annually. His novels have recently been republished in England and are finding a new generation of fans.

He also wrote "Lives of the Saints," "Curious Myths of the Middle Ages," and, "The Book of Werewolves: Being an Account of Terrible Superstition."

He is primarily remembered in southwest England for his work as a collector of local folk songs. For years, he traveled through the west of England, visiting old people and recording the songs they remembered from childhood. In 1889, he published a remarkable book, "Songs of the West" which established him as an authority in the field of British folk music.

No one really knows how many other books and publications he penned. It was an astonishing number—at one time, he was responsible for more books in the British Museum Library than any other author.

The ensuing income allowed him to travel, explore, compose poetry, raise a family of fifteen children, restore his vast family estate, rebuild the old village church, and pursue his multitude of hobbies.

Sabine Baring-Gould declared that he often did his best work when he felt least inclined to apply himself to the task. Rather than waiting for inspiration, he plunged into his work and plodded on until it was finished. "The secret is simply that I stick to a task when I begin it," he said. "It would never do to wait from day to day for some moments that might seem favorable for work."

Did his massive workload shorten his life? No, he lived to be ninety, and was buried in his own churchyard across the street from his estate.

"Now the Day is Over" is a fitting epitaph for this prodigious man. It was written for a vesper service in 1865, based on Proverbs 3:24, and is one of Church history's classic "bedtime prayers."

Onward Christian Soldiers

Sabine Baring-Gould   Arthur S. Sullivan

1. On-ward, Chris-tian sol - diers, March-ing as to war, With the cross of
2. At the sign of tri - umph, Sa - tan's host doth flee; On, then, Chris-tian

Je - sus   Go - ing on be - fore!   Christ, the roy - al   Mas - ter, Leads a-
sol - diers,   On to vic - to - ry!   Hell's foun - da - tions quiv - er   At the

gainst the   foe;   For - ward in - to bat - tle,   See His ban-ners   go!
shouts of   praise;   Broth - ers, lift your voi - ces,   Loud your an-thems raise!

On - ward,   Chris - tian sol - diers,   March - ing as to   war,

With   the   cross   of   Je - sus   Go - ing   on   be - fore!

Onward Christian Soldiers

1865

You will not need to fight in this battle. Position yourselves, stand still and see the salvation of the LORD, Who is with you . . . 2 Chronicles 20:17

R ev. Sabine Baring-Gould was born in Exeter in 1834. His father, an officer with the East India Company, had a disabling carriage accident and decided that if he couldn't work, he could at least travel. As a result, little Sabine was dragged from one end of Europe to the other, year after year. It gave him an unsettled childhood, spotty schooling, and a wanderlust he never outgrew. He later managed to scrape through Cambridge, but for the most part he is remembered as a brilliant, self-taught scholar. That helps explain why he developed certain eccentric habits. When he taught school, for example, he kept a pet bat on his shoulder.

From Sabine's original mind flowed an endless number of books, articles, poems, hymns, and tracts. This particular hymn, "Onward Christian Soldiers," was written on a Whitsunday's evening in the mid-1860s.

Whitsunday is better known as Pentecost Sunday. It got its "nickname" because it became a popular day for new Christians to be baptized. The baptismal candidates marched to the rivers or fonts wearing robes of white. Thus it came to be called "White Sunday" or Whitsunday.

It was on this day in 1865, in the little town of Horbury, England, that Sabine stayed up late searching through hymnbooks for a martial-type hymn for children. The next day, Monday, all the village children were marching to the neighboring town for a Sunday School rally. Sabine wanted to give them a "marching song" for the trip. Searching his hymnals and finding nothing, he began scribbling on a piece of paper, playing with words, dashing off lines until he had written a hymn of his own just for the occasion:

> *Onward, Christian soldiers, / Marching as to war, /*
> *With the cross of Jesus / Going on before.*

"It was written in great haste," he later said, "and I am afraid some of the rhymes are faulty. Certainly, nothing has surprised me more than its popularity."

Perhaps you've noticed that several of our greatest "adult" hymns were originally written or translated for children. See, for example, the stories behind "All Creatures of Our God and King," "I Sing the Mighty Power of God," "I Heard the Voice of Jesus Say," and "O Little Town of Bethlehem." Add "Onward, Christian Soldiers" to that list, and visualize this eccentric preacher, singing in step, marching alongside the children—perhaps with a pet bat on his shoulder.

Rejoice, Ye Pure in Heart

Edward H. Plumptre

Arthur H. Messiter

1. Re - joice ye pure in heart; Re -
2. Bright youth and snow crowned age, Strong
3. With all the an - gel choirs, With
4. Yes, on through life's long path, Still
5. Then on, ye pure in heart! Re -

joice, give thanks, and sing; Your fes - tal ban - ner
men and maid - ens meek, Raise high your free, ex -
all the saints of earth, Pour out the strains of
chant - ing as ye go; From youth to age, by
joice, give thanks and sing! Your glo - rious ban - ner

wave on high, The cross of Christ your King.
ul - tant song, God's won - drous prais - es speak.
joy and bliss, True rap - ture, no - blest mirth.
night and day, In glad - ness and in woe.
wave on high, The cross of Christ your King.

Re - joice, re - joice, re - joice, Give thanks and sing.
Re - joice, re - joice

Rejoice, Ye Pure in Heart

1865

Rejoice in the Lord always. Again I will say, rejoice! Philippians 4:4

*E*dward H. Plumptre was a Christian intellectual. Born in London in 1821, he became a well-known Anglican scholar, author, theologian, and preacher. For many years he served as chaplain of King's College, where he also taught pastoral theology and New Testament exegesis. He wrote books on the classics, history, theology, biblical criticism, and biography. He served on the Old Testament Company for the Revision of the Authorized Version of the Holy Scriptures, and for the last ten years of his life (1881-1891), he was the dean of Wells Cathedral.

Edward was also a poet. In May, 1865, he was preparing for the annual choir festival in the majestic, towering cathedral of Peterborough, England. Needing a long and celebratory processional to give the participating choirs time to proceed down the aisles, he focused his thoughts on two passages of Scripture:

- Psalm 20:5: *We will rejoice in your salvation, and in the name of our God we will set up our banners!*
- Philippians 4:4: *Rejoice in the Lord always. Again I will say, rejoice!*

Inspired by those verses, Edward, 44, began writing:

Rejoice ye pure in heart; | Rejoice, give thanks, and sing; |
Your glorious banner wave on high, | The cross of Christ your King. |
Rejoice, Rejoice, Rejoice, give thanks, and sing!

Edward composed eleven stanzas in all. Most hymnals today use only stanzas 1, 2, 7, and 10. Here are some of the omitted verses:

Yes onward, onward still | With hymn, and chant and song, |
Through gate, and porch and columned aisle, | The hallowed pathways throng. |
Rejoice, Rejoice, Rejoice, give thanks, and sing!

Your clear hosannas raise; | And alleluias loud; |
Whilst answering echoes upward float, | Like wreaths of incense cloud. |
Rejoice, Rejoice, Rejoice, give thanks, and sing!

Praise Him Who reigns on high, | The Lord Whom we adore, |
The Father, Son and Holy Ghost, | One God forevermore. |
Rejoice, Rejoice, Rejoice, give thanks, and sing!

Safe in the Arms of Jesus

Fanny J. Crosby

William H. Doane

1. Safe in the arms of Je - sus, safe on His gen-tle breast,
2. Safe in the arms of Je - sus, safe from cor-rod-ing care,
3. Je - sus, my heart's dear Ref - uge, Je - sus has died for me;

There by His love o'er - shad - ed, sweet - ly my soul shall rest.
Safe from the world's temp - ta - tions, sin can-not harm me there.
Firm on the Rock of A - ges, ev - er my trust shall be.

Hark! 'tis the voice of an - gels, borne in a song to me.
Free from the blight of sor - row, free from my doubts and fears;
Here let me wait with pa - tience, wait till the night is o'er;

O - ver the fields of glo - ry, o - ver the jas - per sea.
On - ly a few more tri - als, on - ly a few more tears!
Wait till I see the morn - ing break on the gold - en shore.

Safe in the Arms of Jesus
1868

And He took them up in His arms, laid His hands on them, and blessed them.
Mark 10:16

*O*n March 5, 1858, Fanny Crosby, the blind hymnist and America's "Queen of Gospel Songs," quietly married Alexander Van Alsteine. A year later, the couple suffered a tragedy that shook the deepest regions of Fanny's heart.

She gave birth to a child—no one knows if it was a boy or a girl. In later years, she never spoke about it except to say in her oral biography, "God gave us a tender babe," and "soon the angels came down and took our infant up to God and His throne."

One of Fanny's relatives, Florence Paine, lived with the poet for six years and could never get her to talk about this. The child's death seemed to have devastated her, and she privately bore the sadness all her life.

Years later, on April 30, 1868, musician Howard Doane knocked on the door of Fanny's apartment in Manhattan. "I have exactly forty minutes," he said, "before I must meet a train for Cincinnati. I have a tune for you. See if it says anything to you. Perhaps you can commit it to memory and then compose a poem to match it." He then hummed the tune.

Fanny clapped her hands and said, "Why, that says, 'Safe in the arms of Jesus!'" She retreated to the other room of her tiny apartment, knelt on the floor, and asked God to give her the words quickly. Within half an hour, she had composed the poem in her mind and dictated it to Doane, who dashed off to catch his train.

During her lifetime, "Safe in the Arms of Jesus" was among the most widely sung of Fanny's hymns, and she considered it in a class by itself. She claimed it was written for the bereaved, especially for mothers who had lost children. Often when comforting a grief-stricken mother, she would say, "Remember, my dear, your darling cherub is safe in the arms of Jesus." Rev. John Hall of New York's Fifth Avenue Presbyterian Church told Fanny that her hymn had given more "peace and satisfaction to mothers who have lost their children than any other hymn I have ever known."

It isn't hard to understand why.

Safe in the arms of Jesus, safe on His gentle breast;
There by His love o'ershaded, sweetly my soul shall rest.

165

O Little Town of Bethlehem

Phillips Brooks   Lewis H. Redner

1. O lit-tle town of Beth-le-hem, How still we see thee lie;
2. For Christ is born of Ma - ry And gath-ered all a-bove;
3. How si-lent-ly, how si-lent-ly, The won-drous gift is giv'n;
4. O, ho-ly child of Beth-le-hem, De-scend to us we pray;

A - bove thy deep and dream-less sleep, The si - lent stars go by.
While mor-tals sleep the an-gels keep Their watch of won-dering love.
So God im-parts to hu - man hearts, The bless-ings of His heaven.
Cast out our sin and en - ter in, Be born in us to - day.

Yet in thy dark streets shin - eth The ev - er - last - ing Light;
O, morn - ing stars to - geth - er Pro - claim the ho - ly birth;
No ear may hear His com - ing, But in this world of sin;
We hear the Christ-mas an - gels, The great glad tid - ings tell;

The hopes and fears of all the years, Are met in thee to-night.
And prais - es sing to God the King And peace to men on earth.
Where meek souls will Re - ceive Him still, The dear Christ en - ters in.
O, come to us a - bide with us, Our Lord, Em - man - u - el.

O Little Town of Bethlehem

1868

. . . Bethlehem . . . though you are little among the thousands of Judah, yet out of you shall come forth to Me the One to be Ruler in Israel . . . Micah 5:2

A t nearly six feet six, weighing three hundred pounds, Phillips Brooks cast a long shadow. He was a native Bostonian, the ninth generation of distinguished Puritan stock, who entered the Episcopalian ministry and pastored with great power in Philadelphia and in Boston. His sermons were topical rather than expositional, and he's been criticized for thinness of doctrine. Nonetheless he's considered one of America's greatest preachers. His delivery came in lightning bursts; he felt he had more to say than time in which to say it.

While at Philadelphia's Holy Trinity Church, Phillips, 30, visited the Holy Land. On December 24, 1865, traveling by horseback from Jerusalem, he attended a five-hour Christmas Eve service at the Church of the Nativity in Bethlehem. He was deeply moved. "I remember standing in the old church in Bethlehem," he later said, "close to the spot where Jesus was born, when the whole church was ringing hour after hour with splendid hymns of praise to God, how again and again it seemed as if I could hear voices I knew well, telling each other of the *Wonderful Night* of the Savior's birth."

Three years later, as he prepared for the Christmas season of 1867, he wanted to compose an original Christmas hymn for the children to sing during their annual program. Recalling his magical night in Bethlehem, he wrote a little hymn of five stanzas and handed the words to his organist, Lewis Redner, saying, "Lewis, why not write a new tune for my poem. If it is a good tune, I will name it 'St. Lewis' after you."

Lewis struggled with his assignment, complaining of no inspiration. Finally, on the night before the Christmas program, he awoke with the music ringing in his soul. He jotted down the melody, then went back to sleep. The next day, a group of six Sunday school teachers and thirty-six children sang "O Little Town of Bethlehem."

Brooks was so pleased with the tune that he did indeed name it for his organist, changing the spelling to ST. LOUIS, so as not to embarrass him. The fourth stanza, usually omitted from our hymnbooks, says:

> *Where children pure and happy pray to the blessèd Child,*
> *Where misery cries out to Thee, Son of the mother mild;*
> *Where charity stands watching and faith holds wide the door,*
> *The dark night wakes, the glory breaks, and Christmas comes once more.*

The King of Love My Shepherd Is

Henry W. Baker

John B. Dykes

1. The King of love my Shep - herd is, Whose good - ness fail - eth nev - er; I noth - ing lack if I am His, And He is mine for - ev - er.
2. Where streams of liv - ing wa - ter flow My ran - somed soul He lead - eth; And where the ver - dant pas - tures grow, With food ce - les - tial feed - eth.
3. Per - verse and fool - ish oft I strayed But yet in love He sought me. And on His shoul - der gent - ly laid, And home re - joic - ing brought me.
4. In death's dark vale I fear no ill With Thee, dear Lord be - side me; Thy rod and staff my com - fort still, Thy cross be - fore to guide me.
5. And so through all the length of days, Thy good - ness fail - eth nev - er. Good Shep - herd, may I sing Thy praise, With - in Thy house for - ev - er.

The King of Love My Shepherd Is

1868

Yea, though I walk through the valley of the shadow of death, I will fear no evil;
For You are with me; Your rod and Your staff, they comfort me. Psalm 23:4

This is among the most beautiful of all the renditions of the Twenty-third Psalm. It was written by Henry Williams Baker, born in London on May 27, 1821, the oldest son of a Vice Admiral in the British Navy. Henry attended Trinity College, Cambridge, and was ordained in 1844 at age 24. After serving as an assistant pastor for several years, he became the vicar of Monkland, Herefordshire, in 1851. That same year, upon his father's death, he was knighted and became a baronet.

For years Henry worked on a book of hymns that would reflect the grandeur of majestic worship. The first edition was published in 1861, entitled *Hymns Ancient and Modern*. On the British Isles, it was known by its initials: *H. A. and M.* Because Henry had labored so earnestly over every hymn, editing and changing and deleting words, some called it *Hymns Asked for and Mutilated*. But it became the leading hymnbook in the Anglican church, going through many revisions and selling over 150 million copies. "The King of Love" didn't appear until the 1868 revision, in the appendix.

When Henry passed away in 1877, his friend, John Ellerton, reported that his last words were from this great hymn:

> *Perverse and foolish oft I stayed, | But yet in love He sought me, |*
> *And on His shoulder gently laid, | And home, rejoicing, brought me.*

Henry wrote many other, lesser-known hymns. One of the finest is his morning hymn, to be recommended for all upon arising:

> *My Father, for another night of quiet sleep and rest,*
> *For all the joy of morning light, Thy holy Name be blest.*
>
> *Now with the newborn day I give myself anew to Thee,*
> *That as Thou willest I may live, and what Thou willest be.*
>
> *Whate'er I do, things great or small, whate'er I speak or frame,*
> *Thy glory may I seek in all, do all in Jesus' Name.*
>
> *My Father, for His sake, I pray thy child accept and bless;*
> *And lead me by Thy grace today in paths of righteousness.*

The Ninety and Nine

Elizabeth C. Clephane

Ira D. Sankey

The Ninety and Nine
1868

And if he should find it, assuredly, I say to you, he rejoices more over that sheep than over the ninety-nine that did not go astray. Matthew 18:13

Evangelist D. L. Moody enlisted Ira Sankey as the song leader and soloist at his great campaigns. The two became a renowned duo; but unfortunately, within a few years Sankey's magnificent voice was ruined by overuse. Later in life, exhausted and facing blindness, he was invited by Dr. J. H. Kellogg (of Kellogg's cereal fame) to Battle Creek, Michigan, for convalescence. There Sankey finished a long-anticipated book of hymn stories. But a fire at the sanitarium destroyed his manuscript and all his notes. He rewrote the book as well as memory would allow, and there we find the story of the "The Ninety and Nine."

In 1874, Moody and Sankey had just finished a series of meetings in Glasgow. At the station en route to Edinburgh, Sankey picked up a penny newspaper, hoping for news from America. Aboard the train, he perused the paper, finding in it a poem by a woman named Elizabeth C. Clephane.

Sankey wrote:

I called Mr. Moody's attention to it, and he asked me to read it to him. This I proceeded to do with all the vim and energy at my command. After I finished I looked at Moody to see what the effect had been, only to discover he had not heard a word, so absorbed was he in a letter he had received. I cut out the poem and placed it in my musical scrapbook.

At the meeting on the second day, the subject was the Good Shepherd. At the conclusion Moody turned to me with the question: "Have you a solo appropriate for this subject with which to close?" I was troubled to know what to do. At this moment I seemed to hear a voice saying: "Sing the hymn you found on the train!" But I thought this impossible, as no music had been written for it. Placing the newspaper slip on the organ, I lifted my heart in prayer, struck the key of A flat, and began to sing.

Note by note the tune was given, which has not been changed from that day to this. Mr. Moody was greatly moved. He came to where I was seated and said, 'Sankey, where did you get this hymn? I've never heard the like of it in my life.' Moved to tears, I replied, 'Mr. Moody, that's the hymn I read to you yesterday on the train, which you did not hear.'

Sweet By and By

Sanford F. Bennett

Joseph P. Webster

1. There's a land that is fair-er than day, And by faith we can see it a-far; For the Fa-ther waits o-ver the way, To pre-pare us a dwell-ing place there.

2. We shall sing on that beau-ti-ful shore The me-lo-di-ous songs of the blest, And our spir-its shall sor-row no more, Not a sigh for the bless-ing of rest.

3. To our boun-ti-ful Fa-ther a-bove We will of-fer our trib-ute of praise, For the glo-ri-ous gift of His love And the bless-ings that hal-low our days.

In the sweet by and by We shall meet on that beau-ti-ful shore. In the sweet by and by, We shall meet on that beau-ti-ful shore.

Sweet By and By

1868

In My Father's house are many mansions; if it were not so, I would have told you. I go to prepare a place for you. John 14:2

I n 1868, a pharmacist named Sanford Fillmore Bennett, 31, was filling prescriptions and handling sales at his apothecary in Elkhorn, Wisconsin. His friend Joseph Webster entered the store. Joseph was a local musician, vocalist, violinist, and amateur composer who suffered from periods of depression. The two men had occasionally collaborated on hymns and songs, Sanford writing the words and Joseph the music.

On this particular day, Joseph was unusually blue and his face was long. Looking up, Sanford asked, "What is the matter now?"

"It's no matter," Joseph replied, "it will be all right by and by."

An idea for a hymn hit Sanford like a flash of sunlight. Sitting at his desk, he began writing as fast as he could. The words came almost instantly. Two customers entered the drugstore, but no attempt was made to assist them—Sanford was too absorbed in his poem—so they sallied over to the stove and visited with Joseph. Finally, Sanford rose and joined them, handing a sheet of paper to his friend.

"Here is your prescription, Joe," he said. "I hope it works." Webster read the words aloud:

> There's a land that is fairer than day,
> And by faith we can see it afar;
> For the Father waits over the way,
> To prepare us a dwelling place there.
> In the sweet by and by,
> We shall meet on that beautiful shore.
> In the sweet by and by,
> We shall meet on that beautiful shore.

Instantly a tune suggested itself, and Joseph jotted down some notes. Picking up his fiddle, he played his melody over a time or two, then said to the others, "We four make a good male quartet. Let's try the new song and see how it sounds."

As "Sweet By and By" was being sung for the first time, another customer, R. R. Crosby, entered the store. "Gentlemen," he said, "I never heard that song before but it is immortal."

He was right. For over a hundred years we've been singing an immortal hymn that was written in less than thirty minutes in a drugstore.

Rescue the Perishing

Fanny J. Crosby

William H. Doane

1. Res - cue the per - ish - ing, Care for the dy - ing, Snatch them in
2. Tho' they are slight-ing Him, Still He is wait - ing, Wait - ing the
3. Down in the hu - man heart, Crushed by the tempt - er, Feel - ings lie
4. Res - cue the per - ish - ing, Du - ty de-mands it, Strength for thy

pit - y From sin and the grave; Weep o'er the err - ing one, Lift up the
pen - i - tent Child to re - ceive; Plead with them earn-est - ly, Plead with them
bur - ied That grace can re - store; Touched by a lov-ing heart, Wak-ened by
la - bor The Lord will pro - vide; Back to the nar-row way Pa - tient - ly

fall - en, Tell them of Je - sus, The might - y to save. Res-cue the
gent - ly, He will for-give, If they on - ly be - lieve.
kind - ness, Chords that are bro - ken Will vi - brate once more.
win them, Tell the poor wan-d'rer A Sav - ior has died.

per - ish-ing, Care for the dy-ing; Je-sus is mer-ci-ful, Je-sus will save.

Rescue the Perishing

1869

But others save with fear, pulling them out of the fire . . . Jude 23

While visiting her friend, Howard Doane, in Cincinnati, Fanny Crosby, the blind hymnist, was asked to speak to a group of blue collar workers. Near the end of her address, she had an overwhelming sense that "some mother's boy" before her "must be rescued that night or not at all." She mentioned this to the crowd, pleading, "If there is a dear boy here tonight who has perchance wandered away from his mother's home and his mother's teaching, would he please come to me at the close of the service?"

Afterward a young man of about eighteen approached her. "Did you mean me?" he asked. "I promised my mother to meet her in heaven, but the way I have been living, I don't think that will be possible now." Fanny had the joy of leading him to Christ.

Returning to her room that night, all she could think about was the theme "rescue the perishing," and when she retired that night she had written the complete hymn. The next day, Howard Doane wrote the music, and it was published the following year in his *Songs of Devotion.*

Many years later, Fanny was speaking at the YMCA in Lynn, Massachusetts, and she recounted the story behind "Rescue the Perishing." After the service, a man approached her, his voice quivering. "Miss Crosby," he said, "I was that boy who told you more than thirty-five years ago that I had wandered from my mother's God. That evening you spoke, I sought and found peace, and I have tried to live a consistent Christian life ever since. If we never meet again on earth, we will meet up yonder." He turned and left, unable to say another word. But Fanny later described it as one of the most gratifying experiences of her life.

This song served as a prelude to Fanny Crosby's second career. About age sixty, she began working in downtown rescue missions, spending several days a week in lower Manhattan, witnessing to the down-and-out. Despite her fame as a hymnwriter, she chose to live in near poverty in New York's ghettos, for she felt a calling to minister to the needy. Just a few blocks from her little tenement apartment was the Bowery, a haunt for alcoholics and where every kind of vice flourished. There Fanny would go day after day to rescue the perishing.

Jesus Loves Even Me

Philip P. Bliss

Philip P. Bliss

1. I am so glad that our Fa - ther in heaven Tells of His
2. Tho' I for - get Him and wan - der a - way, Still He doth
3. Oh, if there's on - ly one song I can sing, When in His

love in the book He has giv'n. Won - der - ful things in the
love me wher - ev - er I stray. Back to His dear lov - ing
beau - ty I see the great King, This shall my song in e -

Bi - ble I see. This is the dear - est that Je - sus loves me.
arms would I flee When I re - mem - ber that Je - sus loves me.
ter - ni - ty be. "Oh what a won - der that Je - sus loves me!"

I am so glad that Je - sus loves me, Je - sus loves me, Je - sus loves me.

I am so glad that Je - sus loves me, Je - sus loves e - ven me.

Jesus Loves Even Me

About 1870

Now hope does not disappoint, because the love of God has been poured out in our hearts by the Holy Spirit who was given to us. Romans 5:5

hilip Bliss was born in a Pennsylvania log cabin where his father led in daily prayer and where music was the primary entertainment. As a result, the lad found himself drawn to both the Lord Jesus and to music at an early age.

When he was ten, Philip sold vegetables door to door. Approaching an elegant home, he heard a sort of music he'd never heard before. Dropping his vegetables, he scaled the fence and slipped unseen into the parlor. A woman was playing something new and strange to Philip—a piano. He was enthralled. When she stopped, he exclaimed, "O lady, please play some more!"

Spinning on her stool, the alarmed woman saw the little urchin standing there. "Get out of here with your big, bare feet!" she cried. Philip beat a fast retreat, but the sounds of that piano stayed with him and deepened his desire to become a musician.

The next year, he left home to work in lumber camps, earning nine dollars a month as assistant cook. Later he became a log cutter and sawmill worker, but he never lost his burden for music.

In 1859, Philip married Lucy Young and spent a year working her father's farm. Lucy encouraged his dreams, and her grandmother provided funds for classes at a nearby music school. The next year, armed with a melodeon, Philip mounted his horse, Old Fanny, and began traveling place to place, teaching music and leading singing schools. In 1864, he sold his first song to a publishing company. Within a remarkably short time, he was one of America's foremost writers of gospel hymns. Among his songs: "Wonderful Words of Life," "Almost Persuaded," "Dare to Be a Daniel," "Hallelujah, What a Savior," "The Light of the World is Jesus," and "I Will Sing of My Redeemer."

In 1870, Philip joined the staff of the First Congregational Church in Chicago. One evening, very weary, Philip found inner refreshment while meditating on Romans 5:5: "The love of God has been poured out in our hearts by the Holy Spirit." Picking up pen and paper, he began writing: "I am so glad that my Father in heaven / tells of His love in the book He has given . . . ."

As he taught that song to his children the next Sunday, perhaps his mind went back to that elegant parlor where he wasn't welcome, and to the strains of music that had defined his life.

177

I Need Thee Every Hour

Annie S. Hawks; Robert Lowry, Refrain

Robert Lowry

1. I need Thee ev - 'ry hour, Most gra - cious Lord;
2. I need Thee ev - 'ry hour, Stay Thou near by;
3. I need Thee ev - 'ry hour In joy or pain;
4. I need Thee ev - 'ry hour, Most Ho - ly One.

No ten - der voice like Thine Can peace af - ford.
Temp - ta - tions lose their power When Thou art nigh.
Come quick - ly and a - bide Or life is vain.
Oh, make me Thine in - deed, Thou bless - ed Son!

I need Thee, O I need Thee; Ev - 'ry hour I need Thee;

O bless me now, my Sav - ior, I come to Thee!

I Need Thee Every Hour

1872

Not that we are sufficient of ourselves to think of anything as being from ourselves, but our sufficiency is from God. 2 Corinthians 3:5

I n his book, *The Practice of the Presence of God,* Brother Lawrence claimed to be as close to God while working in the kitchen as when praying the chapel. The Lord, after all, is *always* near us, thus wherever we are is holy ground. That was the experience of Annie Hawks, a housewife and mother of three in Brooklyn, New York.

As a child, Annie Sherwood had dabbled in poetry, her first verse being published when she was fourteen. In 1857, she married Charles Hawks and they established their home in Brooklyn, joining Dr. Robert Lowry's Hanson Place Baptist Church.* With the good doctor's encouragement, she began writing Sunday school songs for children, and he set many of them to music.

"I Need Thee Every Hour" was written on a bright June morning in 1872. Annie later wrote, "One day as a young wife and mother of 37 years of age, I was busy with my regular household tasks. Suddenly, I became so filled with the sense of nearness to the Master that, wondering how one could live without Him, either in joy or pain, these words, 'I Need Thee Every Hour,' were ushered into my mind, the thought at once taking full possession of me."

The next Sunday, Annie handed these words to Dr. Lowry, who wrote the tune and chorus while seated at the little organ in the living room of his Brooklyn parsonage. Later that year, it was sung for the first time at the National Baptist Sunday School Association meeting in Cincinnati, Ohio, and published in a hymnbook the following year.

When Annie's husband died sixteen years later, she found that her own hymn was among her greatest comforts. "I did not understand at first why this hymn had touched the great throbbing heart of humanity," Annie wrote. "It was not until long after, when the shadow fell over my way, the shadow of a great loss, that I understood something of the comforting power in the words which I had been permitted to give out to others in my hour of sweet serenity and peace."

Some time after Charles' death, Annie moved to Bennington, Vermont, to live with her daughter and son-in-law. All in all, she wrote over four hundred hymns during her eighty-three years, though only this one is still widely sung.

---

*See story of "Shall We Gather at the River."

Lord, Speak to Me

Frances Ridley Havergal

Robert Schumann

1. Lord, speak to me, that I may speak
2. O teach me, Lord, that I may teach
3. O fill me with Thy full - ness, Lord,
4. O use me, Lord, use e - ven me,

In liv - ing ech - oes of Thy tone;
The pre - cious things Thou dost im - part;
Un - til my ver - y heart o'er - flow
Just as Thou wilt, and when, and where,

As Thou hast sought, so let me seek Thine
And wing my words that let they may reach The
In kin - dling thought and glow - ing reach word, Thy
Un - til Thy bless - ed face I see Thy

err - ing chil - dren lost and lone.
hid - den depths of many a heart.
love to tell, Thy praise to show.
rest, Thy joy, Thy glo - ry share.

Lord, Speak to Me
1872

... that in it I may speak boldly, as I ought to speak. Ephesians 6:20

rances Ridley Havergal came by her love of hymnology naturally. Her father, Rev. William Henry Havergal, was an Anglican clergyman who devoted his life to improving the music of the Church of England, writing over 100 hymns himself.

Frances, born in the rectory at Astley, Worcestershire, on December 14, 1836, was a delightful child who began reading and memorizing the Bible at age four. By age seven, she was already writing poems. At age nine, her family moved to the rectory of St. Nicholas, Worcester, and there she had her own room. "Dear child," her mother told her, "you have your own little bedroom now, it ought to be a little Bethel."

"I could not then make head or tail of what she meant," Frances later wrote, "and often wondered, till some months later, when reading in Genesis, I came to the chapter; and then I understood it. Having that small room to myself developed me much as a child; it was mine, and to me it was the coziest little nest in the world."

A deep sadness fell on her at age eleven, however, when her mother became ill. Calling Frances to her bedside, she said, "You are my youngest little girl, and I feel more anxious about you than the rest. I do pray for the Holy Spirit to lead and guide you. And remember, nothing but the precious blood of Christ can make you clean and lovely in God's sight."

"Oh, mamma, I am sure you will get better and go to church again."

"No, dear child; the church mamma is going to is the general assembly and the church of the Firstborn in heaven. How glorious to know I shall soon see my Savior face to face! Now go and play and sing some of your little hymns for me."

When her mother died shortly afterward, Frances crept again and again into the room when no one was near, drawing aside the curtain, looking at the stilled form. But she never forgot her mother's last words to her, and soon thereafter she gained assurance of her salvation.

Frances Ridley Havergal went on to become a deeply spiritual writer of hymns and devotional books. This hymn, originally entitled "A Worker's Prayer," was written on April 28, 1872, at Winterdyne, Bewdley, England, for the use of lay helpers in the church.

Blessed Assurance

Fanny J. Crosby

Phoebe P. Knapp

1. Bless-ed as - sur-ance, Je - sus is   mine!   Oh, what a   fore-taste of
2. Per - fect sub - mis-sion, per-fect de - light!   Vi - sions of   rap-ture now
3. Per - fect sub - mis-sion, all is at   rest.   I   in my Sav - ior am

glo - ry di   -vine!   Heir of sal - va - tion, pur - chase of God,
burst at my   sight!   An - gels de - scend - ing bring from a - bove
hap - py and   blest;   Watch - ing and   wait - ing, look - ing a - bove,

Born of His Spir - it, washed in His blood!   This is my sto - ry,
Ech - oes of   mer - cy, whis - pers of love.
Filled with His good - ness, lost in His love.

this is my   song,   Prais-ing my Sav - ior all the day long.   This is my

sto - ry, this is my   song,   Prais-ing my Sav - ior all the day long.

Blessed Assurance

1873

... nevertheless I am not ashamed, for I know whom I have believed and am persuaded that He is able to keep what I have committed to Him until that Day.
2 Timothy 1:12

rances Ridley Havergal and Frances (Fanny) Crosby never met, but they became dear pen pals—the two most famous women hymnists of their age, the former in England and the latter in America. Havergal once wrote a poem about her American counterpart:

Sweet, blind singer over the sea, | Tuneful and jubilant! How can it be, |
That the songs of gladness, which float so far, | As if they fell from the evening star |
Are the notes of one who may never see | 'Visible music' of flower and tree . . . . |
Oh, her heart can see, her heart can see! | And its sight is strong and swift and free . . . .

Another of Fanny's dearest friends was Phoebe Knapp. While Fanny lived in the Manhattan slums and worked in rescue missions, Phoebe lived in the Knapp Mansion, a palatial residence in Brooklyn, where she entertained lavishly. She was an extravagant dresser with a wardrobe full of elaborate gowns and diamond tiaras. Her music room contained one of the finest collections of instruments in the country, and Fanny was a frequent houseguest.

One day in 1873, while Fanny was staying at the Knapp Mansion, Phoebe said she had a tune she wanted to play. Going to the music room, she sat at the piano and played a new composition of her own while the blind hymnist listened. Fanny immediately clapped her hands and exclaimed, "Why, that says, 'Blessed Assurance!'" She quickly composed the words, and a great hymn was born.

Many years later, D. L. Moody was preaching in New York at the 23rd Street Dutch Reformed Church. The Moody/Sankey meetings had popularized Fanny Crosby's hymns around the world and had made the blind poetess a household name. But whenever she attended a Moody/Sankey meeting, she refused to be recognized, disavowing acclaim.

This day the church was so crowded she could find nowhere to sit. Moody's son, Will, seeing her, offered to find her a seat. To her bewilderment, he led her onto the platform just as the crowd was singing "Blessed Assurance." Moody, Sr., jumped to his feet, raised his hand, and interrupted the singing. "Praise the Lord!" he shouted. "Here comes the authoress!"

Fanny took her seat amid thunderous ovation, humbly thanking God for making her a blessing to so many.

It Is Well with My Soul

Horatio G. Spafford

Philip P. Bliss

1. When peace like a riv-er, At-tend-eth my way, When sor-rows, Like
2. My sin, O the bliss Of this glo-ri-ous tho't, My sin not in
3. O, Lord haste the day When my faith shall be sight, The clouds be rolled

sea bil-lows roll; What-ev-er my lot, Thou hast taught me to say,
part But the whole Is nailed to the cross And I bear it no more.
back As a scroll; The trump shall re-sound And the Lord shall de-scend,

"It is well, It is well, with my soul." It is well,
Praise the Lord, Praise the Lord, O my soul! It is well
"E-ven so" it is well With my soul.

with my soul, It is well, It is well, with my soul.
with my soul,

It Is Well with My Soul

1873

Many are the afflictions of the righteous, but the LORD delivers him out of them all. Psalm 34:19

When the great Chicago fire consumed the Windy City in 1871, Horatio G. Spafford, an attorney heavily invested in real estate, lost a fortune. About that time, his only son, age 4, succumbed to scarlet fever. Horatio drowned his grief in work, pouring himself into rebuilding the city and assisting the 100,000 who had been left homeless.

In November of 1873, he decided to take his wife and daughters to Europe. Horatio was close to D. L. Moody and Ira Sankey, and he wanted to visit their evangelistic meetings in England, then enjoy a vacation.

When an urgent matter detained Horatio in New York, he decided to send his wife, Anna, and their four daughters, Maggie, Tanetta, Annie, and Bessie, on ahead. As he saw them settled into a cabin aboard the luxurious French liner *Ville du Havre,* an unease filled his mind, and he moved them to a room closer to the bow of the ship. Then he said good-bye, promising to join them soon.

During the small hours of November 22, 1873, as the *Ville du Havre* glided over smooth seas, the passengers were jolted from their bunks. The ship had collided with an iron sailing vessel, and water poured in like Niagara. The *Ville du Havre* tilted dangerously. Screams, prayers, and oaths merged into a nightmare of unmeasured terror. Passengers clung to posts, tumbled through darkness, and were swept away by powerful currents of icy ocean. Loved ones fell from each other's grasp and disappeared into foaming blackness. Within two hours, the mighty ship vanished beneath the waters. The 226 fatalities included Maggie, Tanetta, Annie, and Bessie. Mrs. Spafford was found nearly unconscious, clinging to a piece of the wreckage. When the 47 survivors landed in Cardiff, Wales, she cabled her husband: "Saved Alone."

Horatio immediately booked passage to join his wife. En route, on a cold December night, the captain called him aside and said, "I believe we are now passing over the place where the *Ville du Havre* went down." Spafford went to his cabin but found it hard to sleep. He said to himself, "It is well; the will of God be done."

He later wrote his famous hymn based on those words.

〜〜

The melody for "It Is Well," titled VILLE DU HAVRE, was written by Philip Bliss who was himself soon to perish, along with his wife, in a terrible train wreck in Ohio.*

---

*See the story of "I Will Sing of My Redeemer."

Another Year Is Dawning

Frances R. Havergal

Samuel S. Wesley

1. An - oth - er year is dawn - ing: Dear Fa - ther, let it be,
2. An - oth - er year of mer - cies, Of faith - ful - ness and grace;
3. An - oth - er year of ser - vice, Of wit - ness for Thy love;

In work-ing or in wait - ing, An - oth - er year with Thee;
An - oth - er year of glad-ness In the shin-ing of Thy face;
An - oth - er year of train - ing For ho - lier work a - bove.

An - oth - er year of pro - gress, An - oth - er year of praise;
An - oth - er year of lean - ing Up - on Thy lov - ing breast;
An - oth - er year is dawn - ing: Dear Fa - ther, let it be,

An - oth-er year of prov - ing Thy pres-ence all the days.
An - oth - er year of trust - ing, Of qui - et, hap - py rest.
On earth or else in heav - en, An - oth - er year for Thee.

Another Year Is Dawning

1874

Create in me a clean heart, O God, and renew a steadfast spirit within me. Psalm 51:10

I n many churches, the first Sunday of the year wouldn't be complete without singing Frances Ridley Havergal's great "Another Year is Dawning." Its words reflect the deep consecration that marked her poems. Frances considered every New Year's Day a never-to-be-missed opportunity of rededication to Christ, and several New Year's hymns came from her pen.

This particular poem, "Another Year is Dawning," was written as a prayer for the beginning of 1874. Frances composed it near the end of the old year and had it printed on a specially designed greeting card to be sent to friends. The caption said, "A Happy New Year! Ever Such May It Be!"

As it turned out, Frances herself needed that prayer, because just a few days later she suffered a stunning disappointment. She was hoping to be launched as an author in America, and her agent in New York had made reassuring promises. Then came a letter she thought would bear the first of many royalty checks. Instead it reported that her publisher had gone bankrupt in the Stock Market crash of 1873.

But as Frances had only recently turned all her affairs over to the Lord, she bore the crisis with peace, writing to a friend:

I have just had such a blessing in the shape of what would have been only two months ago a really bitter blow to me. . . . I was expecting a letter from America, enclosing thirty-five pounds now due me, and possibly news that [my book] was going on like steam. The letter has come, and, instead of all this, my publisher has failed in the universal crash. He holds my written promise to publish only with him as the condition of his launching me, so this is not simply a little loss, but an end of all my American prospects . . . .

I really had not expected that He would do for me so much above all I asked, as not merely to help me to acquiesce in this, but positively not to feel it at all, and only to rejoice in it as a clear test of the reality of victorious faith which I do find brightening almost daily. Two months ago this would have been a real trial to me, for I had built a good deal on my American prospects; now "Thy will be done" is not a sigh but only a song.

Bringing in the Sheaves

Knowles Shaw

George A. Minor

Bringing in the Sheaves

1874

. . . The harvest truly is plentiful, but the laborers are few. Matthew 9:37

nowles Shaw, the "Singing Evangelist," wrote this gospel song in 1874. Four years later, on June 7, 1878, he and Elder Kirk Baxter boarded a train in Dallas, en route to McKinney, Texas, where Shaw was beginning an evangelistic campaign. As the train chugged across Texas, the two men fell into conversation with a Methodist minister named Malloy. Baxter later wrote:

> Malloy asked him to tell the secret of his success in protracted meetings, which Brother Shaw proceeded to do in an earnest manner, saying he depended much on the power of song; preached Christ; always kept Jesus before the people; made them feel that they were sinners and needed just such a Savior as he preached; that he never became discouraged; had confidence in the gospel truth as the power of God; that he loved his work, and became wholly absorbed in it; and added: "Oh, it is a grand thing to rally people to the Cross of Christ."
>
> At that moment, I felt the car was off the track, bouncing over the ties. I saw Brother Shaw rise from his seat and realized at once the car was going over. All became dark as night. When I came to myself, the coach was at the bottom of the embankment. I looked round, but all were gone. When I got out, I saw the passengers on the railroad track above me, and made my way up to them. The first one I met was Mr. Malloy. I said, "Have you seen Brother Shaw?" "No," said he, "I fear he is under the wreck; but he saved my life by pushing me from the position in which he himself fell."
>
> I waited to hear no more, but ran down to the wreck, looked in, and saw a man's hand pointing upward out of the water. It was Brother Shaw's. I called for help, and in about fifteen minutes he was taken lifeless from the water.
>
> I sent a telegram to Dallas, telling the sad news. In a short time, a deep gloom pervaded the whole city, as from house to house passed the sad words, "Brother Shaw is dead."

But his life proved his song. According to records found in his diary, Shaw recorded more than 11,400 conversions to Christ under his nineteen years of preaching. He entered heaven rejoicing, bringing in the sheaves.

Take My Life and Let It Be

Frances R. Havergal

Henri A. Cesar Malan

Take My Life and Let It Be

1874

Yet indeed I also count all things loss for the excellence of the knowledge of Christ Jesus my Lord, for whom I have suffered the loss of all things, and count them as rubbish, that I may gain Christ. Philippians 3:8

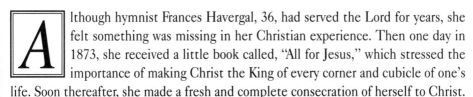

Although hymnist Frances Havergal, 36, had served the Lord for years, she felt something was missing in her Christian experience. Then one day in 1873, she received a little book called, "All for Jesus," which stressed the importance of making Christ the King of every corner and cubicle of one's life. Soon thereafter, she made a fresh and complete consecration of herself to Christ.

Years later when asked about it, she replied, "Yes, it was on Advent Sunday, December 2, 1873, I first saw clearly the blessedness of true consecration. I saw it as a flash of electric light, and what you see you can never un-see. There must be full surrender before there can be full blessedness."

Not long afterward, she found herself spending several days with ten people in a house, some of them unconverted. Others were Christians, but not fully surrendered to Christ. "Lord, give me all in this house," she prayed. She went to work witnessing, and before she left, all ten were yielded Christians. On the last night of her visit, Frances—too excited to sleep—wrote this great consecration hymn, "Take My Life . . . ."

In the years that followed, Frances frequently used this hymn in her own devotions, especially every December 2, on the anniversary of her consecration.

On one occasion, as she pondered the words, "Take my voice and let me sing / Always only for my King," she felt she should give up her secular concerts. Her beautiful voice was in demand, and she frequently sang with the Philharmonic. But from that moment, her lips were exclusively devoted to the songs of the Lord.

On another occasion she was praying over the stanza that says, "Take my silver and my gold / Not a mite would I withhold." She had accumulated a great deal of jewelry, but she now felt she should donate it to the Church Missionary Society. Writing to a friend, she said, "I retain only a brooch for daily wear, which is a memorial to my dear parents; also a locket with the holy portrait I have of my niece in heaven. Evelyn, I had no idea I had such a jeweler's shop; nearly fifty articles are being packed off. I don't think I need to tell you I never packed a box with such pleasure."

Have you given your whole life—everything—over to Jesus? Why not make this the date of your own complete consecration?

I Will Sing of My Redeemer

Philip P. Bliss

James McGranahan

1. I will sing of my Re - deem-er, And His won - drous love to me.
2. I will tell the won - drous sto - ry, How my lost es - tate to save,
3. I will praise my dear Re - deem-er; His tri - um - phant power I'll tell,

On the cru - el cross He suffered, From the curse to set me free.
In His boundless love and mer-cy He the ran - som free - ly gave.
How the vic - to - ry He giv-eth O - ver sin and death and hell.

Sing, oh sing, of my Re - deem-er. With His blood He pur - chased

me. On the cross He sealed my par-don, Paid the debt and made me free.

I Will Sing of My Redeemer

1874

For you were bought at a price; therefore glorify God in your body and in your spirit, which are God's. 1 Corinthians 6:20

A s a ten-year-old boy, when Philip Paul Bliss heard the sounds of a piano for the first time, his imagination was deeply stirred.* Later, riding his horse, Old Fanny, he had become a traveling musician. In 1870, he joined the staff of a Chicago church as music director and Sunday school superintendent. In March, 1874, he became the song leader and children's director for the evangelistic campaigns of Major Daniel W. Whittle. All the while, Philip was penning some of America's favorite gospel songs.

By the end of 1876, Philip needed a break. He had just written the music to "It is Well With My Soul," and finished a whirlwind tour of meetings with Major Whittle. While he and his wife Lucy were spending the Christmas holidays with his family in Pennsylvania, a telegram arrived requesting they come to Chicago to sing at Moody's Tabernacle on the last Sunday of the year.

On December 29, 1876, leaving their two small children with Philip's mother, they boarded the *Pacific Express.* The snow was blinding, and the eleven-coach train was running about three hours late. About eight o'clock that night as the train creaked over a chasm near Ashtabula, Ohio, the trestle bridge collapsed. The engine reached solid ground on the other side of the bridge, but the other cars plunged 75 feet into the ravine.

Philip survived the crash and crawled out through a window. But within moments, fire broke out, and Lucy was still inside, pinned under the twisted metal of the iron seats. The other survivors urged Philip not to crawl back into the flaming wreckage. "If I cannot save her, I will perish with her," he shouted, plunging into the fiery car. Both Philip and Lucy died. He was thirty-eight.

Philip's trunk finally arrived in Chicago safely. In it were found the words to the last hymns he had written, one of which was:

> *I will sing of my Redeemer,*
> *And His wondrous love to me;*
> *On the cruel cross He suffered,*
> *From the curse to set me free.*
>
> *Sing, oh sing, of my Redeemer,*
> *With His blood, He purchased me.*
> *On the cross, He sealed my pardon,*
> *Paid the debt, and made me free.*

---

*See the story behind "Jesus Loves Even Me."

All the Way My Savior Leads Me

Fanny J. Crosby

Robert Lowry

1. All the way my Sav-ior leads me; What have I to ask be - side?
2. All the way my Sav-ior leads me, Cheers each wind-ing path I tread,
3. All the way my Sav-ior leads me O, the full-ness of His love!

Can I doubt His ten-der mer - cy, Who thro' life has been my guide?
Gives me grace for ev-'ry tri - al, Feeds me with the liv - ing bread.
Per - fect rest to me is prom-ised In my Fa-ther's house a - bove.

Heav'n-ly peace, di - vin - est com-fort, Here by faith in Him to dwell!
Tho' my wea - ry steps may fal - ter, And my soul a - thirst may be,
When my spir - it, clothed im - mor-tal, Wings its flight to realms of day,

For I know, what-e'er be - fall me, Je-sus do - eth all things well;
Gush-ing from the Rock be - fore me, Lo! A spring of joy I see;
This my song thro' end-less a - ges: Je-sus led me all the way;

All the Way My Savior Leads Me

1875

. . . that you may be filled with the knowledge of His will in all wisdom and spiritual understanding. Colossians 1:9

When Fanny Crosby wrote, "All the way my Savior leads me, / What have I to ask beside?" she was expressing her own testimony of God's guidance. Even her blindness, she realized, was part of His plan.

When Fanny was about six weeks old, her parents had realized with alarm that something was wrong with her eyes. The local doctor was away, but the Crosbys found a man—no one afterward recalled his name—who claimed to be a physician. He put hot poultice on the baby's inflamed eyes, insisting it would draw out the infection. The infection did clear up, but white scars appeared, and in the months that followed the baby registered no response to objects held before her. As it turned out, Fanny was not totally blind. Even in old age she could discern day from night. But her vision was gone.

Yet this stimulated other gifts, such as her phenomenal memory. As a child, Fanny memorized whole sections of the Bible, including most of the Pentateuch, the four Gospels, all of Proverbs, and vast portions of other books. Whenever she wanted to "read" a passage, she just turned there in her mental "Bible" and read it verbatim. "This Holy Book," she said when eighty-five, "has nurtured my entire life."

Years later, Fanny viewed her blindness as a special gift from God, believing He had given her a particular "soul-vision" which equipped her for a special work. "It was the best thing that could have happened to me," she declared. "How in the world could I have lived such a helpful life had I not been blind?"

"Don't blame the doctor," Fanny said on another occasion. "He is probably dead by this time. But if I could meet him, I would tell him that he unwittingly did me the greatest favor in the world."

⌒⊃

Though this hymn expressed Fanny Crosby's lifelong testimony, it was prompted by a specific incident in 1874. One day she didn't have enough money to pay her rent. Just as she committed the matter to God in prayer, a stranger appeared at her door and pressed a ten-dollar bill in her hand before disappearing. It was the very amount needed. That night, she wrote the words to "All the Way My Savior Leads Me."

O the Deep, Deep Love of Jesus

Samuel Trevor Francis

Thomas J. Williams

1. O the deep, deep love of Je - sus, Vast, un - mea - sured, bound - less, free!
2. O the deep, deep love of Je - sus, Spread His praise from shore to shore!
3. O the deep, deep love of Je - sus, Love of ev - 'ry love the best!

Roll - ing as a might - y o - cean In its full - ness o - ver me!
How He lov - eth, ev - er lov - eth, Chang - eth nev - er, nev - er - more!
'Tis an o - cean full of bless - ing, 'Tis a ha - ven giv - ing rest!

Un - der - neath me, all a - round me, Is the cur - rent of Thy love,
How He watch - es o'er His loved ones, Died to call them all His own;
O the deep, deep love of Je - sus, 'Tis a heav'n of heav'ns to me;

Lead - ing on - ward, lead - ing home - ward, To my glo - rious rest a - bove!
How for them He in - ter - ced - eth, Watch - eth o'er them from the throne!
And it lifts me up to glo - ry, For it lifts me up to Thee!

O the Deep, Deep Love of Jesus

1875

For I am persuaded that neither death nor life, nor angels nor principalities nor powers, nor things present nor things to come, nor height nor depth, nor any other created thing, shall be able to separate us from the love of God which is in Christ Jesus our Lord. Romans 8:38–39

F ew hymns paint such a vivid picture of God's love as this one by Samuel Trevor Francis: . . . *vast, unmeasured, boundless free; / rolling as a mighty ocean in its fullness over me. / Underneath me, all around me, is the current of Thy love . . . .* It helps us visualize the immensity of Christ's liquid-love, overwhelming and submerging us in the depths of His tender, triumphant heart.

Samuel was born on November 19, 1834, in a village north of London, but his parents soon moved to the city of Hull midway up the English coast. His father was an artist. As a child, Samuel enjoyed poetry and even compiled a little hand-written volume of his own poetry. He also developed a passion for music, joining the church choir at age nine. But as a teenager, he struggled spiritually, and when he moved to London to work, he knew things weren't right in his heart.

One day, as he later wrote, "I was on my way home from work and had to cross Hungerford Bridge to the south of the Thames. During the winter's night of wind and rain and in the loneliness of that walk, I cried to God to have mercy on me. I stayed for a moment to look at the dark waters flowing under the bridge, and the temptation was whispered to me: 'Make an end of all this misery.' I drew back from the evil thought, and suddenly a message was borne into my very soul: 'You do believe in the Lord Jesus Christ?' I at once answered, 'I do believe,' and I put my whole trust in Him as my Savior."

Francis went on to become a London merchant, but his real passion was Kingdom work—especially hymn writing and open-air preaching—which occupied his remaining seventy-three years. He traveled widely and preached around the world for the Plymouth Brethren. He died on December 28, 1925, at age ninety-two.

⌒⌒

EBENEZER, the ponderous, rolling melody for this hymn is traditionally called "Ton-Y-Botel" ("Tune in a Bottle") because of a legend that it was found in a bottle along the Welsh Coast. It was actually composed by Thomas J. Williams and first appeared as a hymn tune in 1890 in a Welsh hymnal entitled *Llawlyfn Moliant.*

197

Jesus, I Am Resting, Resting

Jean S. Pigott   James Mountain

1. Je - sus, I am rest - ing, rest - ing, In the joy of what Thou art;
2. O, how great Thy lov - ing kind - ness, Vast - er, broad - er than the sea!
3. Sim - ply trust - ing Thee, Lord Je - sus, I be - hold Thee as Thou art,
4. Ev - er lift Thy face up - on me As I work and wait for Thee;

I am find - ing out the great - ness Of Thy lov - ing heart.
O, how mar - ve - lous Thy good - ness, Lav - ished all on me!
And Thy love, so pure, so change - less, Sa - tis - fies my heart;
Rest - ing 'neath Thy smile, Lord Je - sus, Earth's dark sha - dows flee.

Thou hast bid me gaze up - on Thee, And Thy beau - ty fills my soul,
Yes, I rest in Thee, Be - lov - èd, Know what wealth of grace is Thine,
Sa - tis - fies its deep - est long - ings, Meets, sup - plies its ev - ery need,
Bright - ness of my Fa - ther's glo - ry, Sun - shine of my Fa - ther's face,

For by Thy trans - form - ing pow - er, Thou hast made me whole.
Know Thy cer - tain - ty of prom - ise, And have made it mine.
Com - pass - eth me round with bless - ings: Thine is love in - deed!
Keep me ev - er trust - ing, rest - ing, Fill me with Thy grace.

Jesus, I Am Resting, Resting

1876

Abide in Me, and I in you. As the branch cannot bear fruit of itself, unless it abides in the vine, neither can you, unless you abide in Me. John 15:4

T his poem, written by an Irish woman named Jean Sophia Pigott, became the favorite hymn of J. Hudson Taylor, the great missionary to China. Often, taking a break from his crushing load of work, Hudson would sit at his little reed organ and sing this hymn. It perfectly expressed his greatest life-lesson.

Hudson had envisioned a missionary task greater than any since the days of Paul—the evangelization of China. He had established the China Inland Mission in 1865, but it almost proved his undoing. Overwhelmed by worry, work, and responsibility, he was near a breakdown when he received a letter from a fellow missionary, John McCarthy. In it, McCarthy spoke from John 15 about abiding in Christ.

"Abiding, not striving or struggling," wrote McCarthy, "looking off unto Him; trusting Him for present power . . . This is not new, and yet 'tis new to me. . . . Christ literally all seems to me now the power, the only power for service; the only ground for unchanging joy."

As Hudson read this letter at his mission station in Chin-kiang on Saturday, September 4, 1869, his eyes were opened. "As I read," he recalled, "I saw it all. I looked to Jesus, and when I saw, oh how the joy flowed!"

Writing to his sister in England, he said: "As to work, mine was never so plentiful, so responsible, or so difficult; but the weight and strain are all gone. The last month or more has been perhaps the happiest of my life, and I long to tell you a little of what the Lord has done for my soul. . . . When the agony of soul was at its height, a sentence in a letter from dear McCarthy was used to remove the scales from my eyes, and the Spirit of God revealed the truth of our oneness with Jesus as I had never known it before. McCarthy, who had been much exercised by the same sense of failure, but saw the light before I did, wrote: 'But how to get faith strengthened? Not by striving after faith but by resting on the Faithful One.'

"As I read, I saw it all! . . . . As I thought of the Vine and the branches, what light the blessed Spirit poured into my soul!"

Like a River Glorious

Frances R. Havergal

James Mountain

1. Like a riv-er glo-rious Is God's per-fect peace, O - ver all vic - to-rious
2. Hid-den in the hol-low Of His bless-ed hand, Nev - er foe can fol-low,
3. Ev - ery joy or tri - al Fall-eth from a - bove, Traced up-on our di - al

In its bright in - crease; Per-fect, yet it flow - eth Full-er ev - ery day,
Nev-er trai - tor stand; Not a surge of wor - ry, Not a shade of care,
By the Sun of Love. We may trust Him ful - ly All for us to do;

Per - fect, yet it grow-eth Deep - er all the way.
Not a blast of hur - ry Touch the Spir - it there. Stayed up - on Je - ho - vah,
They who trust Him whol - ly Find Him whol - ly true.

Hearts are ful - ly blest; Find-ing, as He prom-ised, Per-fect peace and rest.

Like a River Glorious

1876

. . . I will extend peace to her like a river . . . Isaiah 66:12

I n 1876, while vacationing in the south of Wales, Frances Havergal caught a severe cold and suffered inflammation of the lungs. Told she might die, her response was: "If I am really going, it is too good to be true." Her friends were amazed at how peacefully she faced the prospect of dying. That same year, she wrote the hymn:

> *Like a river glorious, is God's perfect peace,*
> *Over all victorious, in its bright increase;*
> *Perfect, yet it floweth, fuller every day,*
> *Perfect, yet it groweth, deeper all the way.*
> *Stayed upon Jehovah, hearts are fully blest*
> *Finding, as He promised, perfect peace and rest.*

Three years later, while meeting some boys to talk with them about the Lord, she ran into cold, wet weather and became chilled. As her fever grew worse, her family became alarmed. It gradually became apparent that Frances, 42, was dying. On Whitsunday, as one of her doctors left the room, he said, "Goodbye, I shall not see you again."

"Then you really think I am going?" asked Frances.

"Yes."

"Today?"

"Probably."

"Beautiful," said Frances. "Too good to be true."

Soon afterward she looked up smiling and said, "Splendid to be so near the gates of heaven!" She asked her brother to sing some hymns to her, then he said to her, "You have talked and written a great deal about the King, and you will soon see Him in His beauty."

"It's splendid!" she replied. "I thought He would have left me here a long while; but He is *so* good to take me now."

A little later she whispered, "Come, Lord Jesus, come and fetch me."

A terrible rush of convulsions seized her, and when they ceased, the nurse gently laid her back on her pillows. Frances' sister later wrote: "Then she looked up steadfastly, as if she saw the Lord. Surely nothing less heavenly could have reflected such a glorious radiance upon her face. For ten minutes we watched that almost visible meeting with her King, and her countenance was so glad, as if she were already talking to Him! Then she tried to sing, but after one sweet, high note, "HE—," her voice failed and her brother commended her soul into the Redeemer's hand."

O Master, Let Me Walk with Thee

Washington Gladden

H. Percy Smith

1. O Mas - ter, let me walk with Thee
2. Help me the slow of heart to move
3. Teach me Thy pa - tience still with Thee
4. In hope that sends a shin - ing ray

In low - ly paths of ser - vice free;
By some clear, win - ning word of love;
In clos - er, dear - er com - pa - ny,
Far down the fu - ture's broad - 'ning way,

Tell me Thy se - cret; Help me bear
Teach me the way - ward feet to stay,
In work that keeps faith sweet and strong,
In peace that on - ly Thou canst give,

the strain of toil, The fret of care.
And guide them in the home - ward way.
In trust that tri - umphs o - ver wrong.
With Thee, O Mas - ter, let me live.

O Master, Let Me Walk with Thee
1879

Therefore you shall keep the commandments of the LORD your God, to walk in His ways and to fear Him. Deuteronomy 8:6

Washington Gladden (so named because his great-grandfather served as George Washington's bodyguard during the Revolutionary War) was a Congregational pastor. He served in New York, Massachusetts, and Ohio during the post-Civil War industrial era when racial and economic injustice was rampant. People everywhere were searching for a new American ethic.

Washington wanted to give them one, and he is remembered today as the father of the Social Gospel in America, an activist who crusaded tirelessly for political and moral reform in industry, commerce, and politics. He was a champion of the "working man," a strong supporter of union rights, and he was unafraid to attack corruption in politics.

Unfortunately, Washington advanced the liberal-leaning biblical criticism that undercut conservative theology at the turn of the century. He was more concerned with applied Christianity than with biblical Christianity. He wrote thirty-eight books on such themes. In one of them he said: "The Bible is not an infallible Book, in the sense in which it is popularly supposed to be infallible . . . . The Book is not infallible historically . . . It is not infallible scientifically . . . It is not infallible morally . . . ."

He embraced evolution and opposed the outreach efforts of evangelists like Billy Sunday. He infuriated his own denomination by railing against a large gift to foreign missions because it was donated by the Standard Oil Company. Not surprisingly, conservative Christians opposed Washington's liberal theology. During a period of heavy criticism, he sat alone in his church and wrote this hymn.

Dr. Charles H. Richards later saw it in a magazine, and, while loving the poem, was troubled by the second verse:

> *O Master, let me walk with Thee | Before the taunting Pharisee; |*
> *Help me to bear the sting of spite, | The hate of men who hide Thy light, |*
> *The sore distrust of souls sincere | Who cannot read Thy judgments clear, |*
> *The dullness of the multitude, | Who dimly guess that Thou art good.*

After discarding that verse, Richards selected music for the remaining stanzas and included them in his book *Christian Praise*.

Ironically, Christians of all stripes have embraced this as a prayer of their own while laboring for the Master in a world desperately needing the transformation of Christ.

God Be with You

Jeremiah E. Rankin

William G. Tomer

1. God be with you 'til we meet a-gain; By His coun-sels guide, up-hold you,
2. God be with you 'til we meet a-gain; 'Neath His wings pro-tect-ing hide you,
3. God be with you 'til we meet a-gain; Keep love's ban-ner float-ing o'er you,
4. God be with you 'til we meet a-gain; When life's per-ils thick con-found you,

With His sheep se-cure-ly fold you; God be with you 'til we meet a-gain.
Dai-ly man-na still pro-vide you; God be with you 'til we meet a-gain.
Smite death's threat'ning wave be-fore you; God be with you 'til we meet a-gain.
Put His arms un-fail-ing round you; God be with you 'til we meet a-gain.

'Til we meet, 'til we meet, 'Til we meet at Je-sus' feet;

'Til we meet, 'til we meet, God be with you 'til we meet a-gain.

God Be with You

1880

Grace, mercy, and peace will be with you from God the Father and from the Lord Jesus Christ, the Son of the Father, in truth and love. 2 John 3

On September 19, 1945, missionary Darlene Deibler was liberated from the Japanese Prison Camp at Kampili, seventeen days after Japan had signed the Instrument of Surrender aboard the USS *Missouri*. She was in bad shape, having been subjected to years of physical suffering and mental torture.

Eight years before, Darlene and her husband, Russell, had landed as missionaries in New Guinea. Plunging into the work, they were making solid progress in building a growing church, aided by Darlene's dear friend and mentor, Dr. Robert Jaffray. Now both Russell and Dr. Jaffray were dead, and Darlene was leaving behind two lonely white crosses on the hillside. As a 28-year-old widow, she was returning home without a single possession. All her mementos and private keepsakes were gone, her loved ones were dead, and her body was debilitated by exhaustion, starvation, malaria, beriberi, and dysentery.

For over four years, she had witnessed atrocities that can scarcely be described. Prisoners all around her had suffered horrible deaths, and she herself had seen the inside of death cells. During that time, not one letter or package had reached her.

As the boat carried her from her island prison, she prayed a bitter prayer: "Lord, I'll never come to these islands again. They've robbed me of everything that was most dear to me."

Suddenly she heard voices, Indonesian voices ringing from the distance. There on the shore were those who had come to know the Lord through her mission, raising their voices, singing: "God be with you till me meet again. / By His counsels guide, uphold you, / With His sheep securely fold you; / God be with you till we meet again."

Darlene later wrote in her autobiography, *Evidence Not Seen:* "This song released the waters of bitterness that had flooded my soul, and the hurt began to drain from me as my tears flowed in a steady stream. The healing had begun. I knew then that some day, God only knew when, I would come back to these my people and my island home."

"God Be With You Till We Meet Again," was written by Jeremiah Rankin, pastor of Washington's First Congregational Church and president of Howard University, the great African-American college in the nation's capital. He wrote it, he said, after discovering that the term "good-bye" meant "God be with you."

O Love That Wilt Not Let Me Go

George Matheson   Albert L. Peace

1. O love that wilt not let me go, I rest my wea-ry soul in Thee. I give Thee back the life I owe, That in Thine o-cean depths its flow, May rich-er, full-er be.

2. O light that fol-low'st all my way, I yield my flick-'ring torch to Thee. My heart re-stores its bor-rowed ray, That in Thy sun-shine's blaze its day, May bright-er, fair-er be.

3. O joy that seek-est me through pain, I can-not close my heart to Thee. I trace the rain-bow through the rain, And feel the prom-ise is not vain, That morn shall tear-less be.

4. O cross that lift-est up my head, I dare not ask to fly from Thee. I lay in dust life's glo-ry dead, And from the ground there blos-soms red, Life that shall end-less be.

O Love That Wilt Not Let Me Go

1882

. . . Let me fall into the hand of the Lord, for His mercies are very great . . .
1 Chronicles 21:13

G eorge Matheson was only a teenager when he learned that his poor eyesight was deteriorating further. Not to be denied, he continued straightaway with his plans to enroll in Glasgow University, and his determination led to his graduating at age nineteen. But as he pursued graduate studies for Christian ministry he became totally blind. His sisters joined ranks beside him, learning Greek and Hebrew to assist him in his studies, and he pressed faithfully on. But his spirit collapsed when his fiancée, unwilling to be married to a blind man, broke their engagement and returned his ring.

George never married, and the pain of that rejection never totally left him. Years later, his sister came to him, announcing her engagement. He rejoiced with her, but his mind went back to his own heartache. He consoled himself in thinking of God's love which is never limited, never conditional, never withdrawn, and never uncertain. Out of this experience it is said he wrote the hymn, *O Love That Wilt Not Let Me Go*, on June 6, 1882.

George Matheson became a powerful and popular preacher pastoring in the Scottish village of Innellan. Despite his flourishing ministry, there was one winter's evening when the Sunday night crowd was miserably small. George had worked hard on his sermon, but the empty chairs nearly defeated him. Nevertheless he did his best, not knowing that in the congregation was a visitor for the large St. Bernard's Church in Edinburgh, which was seeking a pastor. As a result, in 1886, he was called to St. Bernard's where he became one of Scotland's favorite preachers.

"Make every occasion a great occasion," Matheson later said. "You can never tell when somebody may be taking your measure for a larger place."

Recently while in Edinburgh, I tracked down George Matheson's old church, St. Bernard's, in a lovely residential neighborhood not far from Princess Street. The doors were locked shut, and this curious notice was posted to the front door:

Public Entertainment License
The premises will be used as a concert and dance hall,
and for no other purpose without written permission from the council.

Take Time to Be Holy

William D. Longstaff   George C. Stebbins

1. Take time to be ho - ly. Speak oft with thy Lord;
2. Take time to be ho - ly. The world rush - es on;
3. Take time to be ho - ly. Let Him be thy Guide;
4. Take time to be ho - ly, Be calm in thy soul;

A - bide in Him al - ways, And feed on His Word.
Spend much time in se - cret With Je - sus a - lone.
And run not be - fore Him, What - ev - er be - tide.
Each tho't and each mo - tive Be - neath His con - trol;

Make friends with God's chil - dren; Help those who are weak,
By look - ing to Je - sus, Like Him thou shalt be;
In joy or in sor - row, Still fol - low thy Lord,
Thus led by His Spir - it To foun - tains of love,

For - get - ting in noth - ing His bless - ing to seek.
Thy friends in thy con - duct His like - ness shall see.
And, look - ing to Je - sus, Still trust in His Word.
Thou soon shalt be fit - ted For ser - vice a - bove.

Take Time to Be Holy

1882

Because it is written, "Be holy, for I am holy." 1 Peter 1:16

T he words to "Take Time to Be Holy" were written about 1882 by William Longstaff, a wealthy Englishman who served as treasurer of the Bethesda Free Chapel in Sunderland, a port city in Northeast England. His church hosted the first meetings held by D. L. Moody and Ira Sankey in that area, and Longstaff became a great supporter of the two.

In his book of hymn stories, Ira Sankey said that "Take Time to Be Holy" was prompted by a sermon William heard in New Brighton on the text "Be holy, for I am holy" (1 Peter 1:16). George C. Stebbins, who composed the music, said Longstaff was inspired to write this poem after hearing a missionary to China quoted as saying, "Take time to be holy." There's no reason why both stories can't be true.

The tune, HOLINESS, was composed by George C. Stebbins, who cast a long shadow over gospel music. In his book, *Reminiscences and Gospel Hymn Stories,* Mr. Stebbins told of his travels and ministries with people like D. L. Moody, Major Daniel Whittle, Philip P. Bliss, Ira Sankey, William Doane, and Fanny Crosby.

In 1890, Stebbins spent time in India working with evangelist George Pentecost. Someone mentioned the need for a hymn on holiness. Stebbins had a habit of making notebooks of poems and hymns by cutting and pasting.* Searching through his pages, he found a poem previously clipped and saved—Longstaff's "Take Time to Be Holy." He composed music for the stanzas and sent the words and music to Ira Sankey in New York where it was published. This hymn has not only aged well; it has become more and more relevant. If people in the 1880s needed to slow down and be holy, how much more now!

George Stebbins aged well, too. He lived to be nearly 100 years old, dying in 1945. When he was 95, living in a house in the Catskills, he received a visit from George Beverly Shea, who was just beginning the ministry of sacred song. Shea later described him as hard-of-hearing, but alert, "a tall man with whiskers" who "exuded great dignity and warmth."

Shea was persuaded to sing for the old man, but he had to sing loudly—and right into his ear.

---

*Over one hundred of these notebooks are now in the The George C. Stebbins Memorial Collection, housed in the rare book library of Washington's National Cathedral.

'Tis So Sweet to Trust in Jesus

Louisa M. R. Stead

William J. Kirkpatrick

1. 'Tis so sweet to trust in Je - sus, Just to take Him at His word;
2. O how sweet to trust in Je - sus, Just to trust His cleans-ing blood;
3. Yes, 'tis sweet to trust in Je - sus, Just from sin and self to cease;
4. I'm so glad I learned to trust Thee, Pre-cious Je - sus, Sav - ior friend;

Just to rest up - on His prom - ise; Just to know "Thus saith the Lord."
Just in sim - ple faith to plunge me, Neath the heal - ing, cleans-ing flood!
Just from Je - sus sim - ply tak - ing Life and rest and joy and peace.
And I know that Thou art with me, Wilt be with me to the end.

Je - sus, Je - sus how I trust Him! How I've proved Him o'er and o'er!

Je - sus, Je - sus, pre - cious Je - sus! O for grace to trust Him more!

'Tis So Sweet to Trust in Jesus

1882

In God I have put my trust; I will not be afraid. Psalm 56:11

How fitting that a missionary should write this hymn about faith and trust. Louisa M. R. Stead was born about 1850 in Dover, England, and became a Christian at age nine. She felt a burden to become a missionary in her teenage years. When she was 21 or so, she immigrated to the United States and attended a revival meeting in Urbana, Ohio. There the Lord deeply impressed her with a ringing missionary call.

She made plans to go to China, but her hopes were dashed when her health proved too frail for the climate there. Shortly afterward, she married a man named Stead. But sometime around 1879 or 1880, Mr. Stead drowned off the coast of Long Island. Some accounts say that he saved a boy who was drowning, and other accounts say both Mr. Stead and the boy perished. Other records suggest it was his own four-year-old daughter, Lily, that he saved. In any event, the family's beach-side picnic ended in tragedy for Louisa.

Shortly afterward, taking little Lily, Louisa went to South Africa as a missionary, and it was there during those days she wrote, "'Tis So Sweet to Trust in Jesus."

Louisa served in South Africa for fifteen years, and while there she married Robert Wodehouse. When her health forced a return to America, Robert pastored a local Methodist Church. In 1900, her health restored, Robert and Louisa attended a large missionary conference in New York, and were so enthused by the experience they again offered themselves as missionary candidates.

They arrived as Methodist missionaries in Rhodesia on April 4, 1901. "In connection with this whole mission there are glorious possibilities," she wrote. "One cannot in the face of the peculiar difficulties help saying, 'Who is sufficient for these things?' but with simple confidence and trust we may and do say, 'Our sufficiency is of God.'"

Louisa retired in 1911, and passed away in 1917; but her daughter, Lily, married missionary D. A. Carson and continued the work for many years at the Methodist mission station in southern Rhodesia (Zimbabwe).

How Great Thou Art

Carl Boberg

Swedish Folk Melody

1. O Lord, my God, When I in awe - some won - der, Con - sid - er all the worlds Thy hands have made; I see the stars, I hear the roll - ing thun - der, Thy pow'r through - out The u - ni - verse dis - played.

2. When thru the woods and for - est glades I wan - der, And hear the birds sing sweet - ly in the trees; When I look down from loft - y moun - tain gran - deur And hear the brook and feel the gent - le breeze.

3. And when I think that God, His Son not spar - ing, Sent Him to die, I scarce can take it in; That on the cross my bur - den glad - ly bear - ing, He bled and died To take a - way my sin.

4. When Christ shall come With shout of ac - cla - ma - tion And take me home, What joy shall fill my heart! Then I shall bow In hum - ble ad - o - ra - tion, And there pro - claim, "My God, how great Thou art!"

Then sings my soul, My Sav - ior God, to Thee, How great Thou art! How great Thou art!

Then sings my soul, My Sav - ior God, to Thee, How great Thou art! How great Thou art!

How Great Thou Art

1885

For thus says the LORD, Who created the heavens, Who is God, Who formed the earth and made it, Who has established it, Who did not create it in vain, Who formed it to be inhabited: "I am the LORD, and there is no other." Isaiah 45:18

arl Boberg, a 26-year-old Swedish minister, wrote a poem in 1885 which he called "O Store Gud"—"O Mighty God." The words, literally translated to English, said:

> *When I the world consider | Which Thou has made by Thine almighty Word*
> *And how the webb of life Thou wisdom guideth | And all creaion feedeth at Thy board.*
> *Then doth my soul burst forth in song of praise | Oh, great God, Oh, great God!*

His poem was published and "forgotten"—or so he thought. Several years later, Carl was surprised to hear it being sung to the tune of an old Swedish melody; but the poem and hymn did not achieve widespread fame.

Hearing this hymn in Russia, English missionary, Stuart Hine, was so moved he modified and expanded the words and made his own arrangement of the Swedish melody. He later said his first three verses were inspired, line upon line, by Russia's rugged Carpathian Mountains. The first verse was composed when he was caught in a thunderstorm in a Carpathian village, the second as he heard the birds sing near the Romanian border, and the third as he witnessed many of the Carpathian mountain-dwellers coming to Christ. The final verse was written after Dr. Hine returned to Great Britain.

Some time later, Dr. J. Edwin Orr* heard "How Great Thou Art" being sung by Naga Tribespeople in Assam, in India, and decided to bring it back to America for use in his own meetings. When he introduced it at a conference in California, it came to the attention of music publisher, Tim Spencer, who contacted Mr. Hine and had the song copyrighted. It was published and recorded.

During the 1954 Billy Graham Crusade in Harringay Arena, George Beverly Shea was given a leaflet containing this hymn. He sang it to himself and shared it with other members of the Graham team. Though not used in London, it was introduced the following year to audiences in Toronto.

In the New York Crusade of 1957, it was sung by Bev Shea ninety-nine times, with the choir joining the majestic refrain:

> *Then sings my soul, my Savior God to Thee,*
> *How great Thou art! How great Thou art!*

---

*See the story behind the hymn "Search Me, O God."

Standing on the Promises

R. Kelso Carter

R. Kelso Carter

1. Stand-ing on the prom-is-es Of Christ my King, Thro' e-ter-nal a-ges Let His
2. Stand-ing on the prom-is-es That can-not fail, When the howl-ing storms Of doubt and
3. Stand-ing on the prom-is-es Of Christ the Lord, Bound to Him e-ter-nal-ly By
4. Stand-ing on the prom-is-es I can-not fall, Lis-t'ning ev-ery mo-ment To the

prais-es ring, Glo-ry in the high-est I will shout and sing, Stand-ing on the
fear as-sail, By the liv-ing Word of God I shall pre-vail, Stand-ing on the
love's strong cord, Ov-er-com-ing dai-ly with The Spir-it's sword, Stand-ing on the
Spir-it's call, Rest-ing in my Sav-ior, As my all in all, Stand-ing on the

prom-is-es of God. Stand - ing, stand - ing,

Stand-ing on the prom-is-es Of God my Sav-ior. Stand - ing,

stand - ing, I'm stand-ing on the prom-is-es of God.

Standing on the Promises

__1886__

For all the promises of God in Him are Yes, and in Him Amen, to the glory of God through us. 2 Corinthians 1:20

Russell Kelso Carter, author of this hymn, was an athlete, educator, rancher, preacher, and physician. Here is his condensed testimony:

From my birth in 1849, I was surrounded by Christian influences. My father stood for nearly half a century in the rank of Christian workers in Baltimore; by his side I had the example of a patient, loving mother. I cannot remember when I was not subject to deep convictions of sin; yet as a school-boy, I wandered from the truth until age fifteen, when, under the influence of the cadet prayer-meeting in the Pennsylvania Military Academy, I made a profession of faith in Jesus.

But I made a common mistake; I didn't forsake my old companions and habits, and for fourteen years I lived the up-and-down experience so familiar to the average church member. I never enjoyed myself so much as when working in Mr. Moody's meetings in Baltimore; yet even up to that time I was continually slipping and falling. My soul cried for deliverance, and God's *unlimited promises* stood out like stars above me. But I wasn't willing to pay the price.

In the summer of 1879, my heart, which had been chronically diseased for seven years, resisting the remedies of physicians, and, refusing to grow better even after three years of sheep-ranching in California, suddenly broke down so seriously as to bring me to the verge of the grave. I had heard of the "prayer of faith" for healing, but I felt persuaded it would border on blasphemy to ask God for a strength which I didn't propose to use wholly for Him.

Kneeling in my mother's room in Baltimore, I made a consecration that covered everything. All doubtful things were swept aside. I meant every word, and I have never had any doubts about it since. A quietness came over me and I found the Bible wonderfully open and marvelously satisfying, as it had never been before.

Feeling all the more impressed with God's healing promises, I concluded to go to Boston and ask prayer and anointing at the hands of Dr. Cullis. I was terribly weak, but I went. I will only add that I returned in three days, walking by faith, and not by feeling, resumed my college work in September, and at once engaged in all kinds of religious work. I was healed by the power of God alone. Praise the Lord!

When They Ring the Golden Bells

Daniel (Dion) de Marbelle   Daniel (Dion) de Marbelle

1. There's a land be - yond the riv - er, that we
2. We shall know no sin or sor - row, in that
3. When our days shall know their num - ber, and in

call the sweet for - ev - er, And we on - ly reach that shore by faith's de - cree;
ha - ven of to - mor-row, When our barque shall sail be - yond the sil - ver sea;
death we sweet-ly slum-ber, When the King com-mands the spir - it to be free;

One by one we'll gain the por - tals, there to dwell with the im - mor-tals,
We shall on - ly know the bless-ing of our Fa - ther's sweet ca - ress-ing,
Nev - er -more with an-guish lad - en, we shall reach that love - ly E - den,

When they ring the gold - en bells for you and me.
When they ring the gold - en bells for you and me.
When they ring the gold - en bells for you and me.

you and me.

When They Ring the Golden Bells

1887

. . . Having been justified by His grace we should become heirs according to the hope of eternal life. Titus 3:7

s a child, I remember my mother scurrying around the house, dusting, cleaning, working, and singing a hymn that became quite popular in the early to mid-twentieth century:

> *There's a land beyond the river, that we call the sweet forever,*
> *And we only reach that shore by faith's decree;*
> *One by one we'll gain the portals, there to dwell with the immortals,*
> *When they ring the golden bells for you and me.*

Many hymns were written by pastors and theologians. Some by homemakers and merchants. This one was written by a clown. His name was Daniel (Dion) de Marbelle. He was born in France in 1818, and spent his youth sailing the Arctic on whaling ships. When he was about 30, he joined the American Navy and fought in the Mexican War. Later, during the Civil War, he was a musician with the sixth Michigan infantry regiment.

During Reconstruction, he joined an opera troupe and traveled across America, singing, acting, entertaining in theaters, barns, auditoriums—wherever crowds would gather.

He was 69 when he became one of the first clowns hired by James A. Bailey who took over P. T. Barnum's Circus following the latter's death in 1891. Under Bailey's leadership, the Barnum & Bailey Circus rode the rails on 85 cars and employed more than 1,000 people.

Daniel later organized his own circus. When a fire in Canada destroyed his big top and all his equipment, he came back to the U.S. to assist Buffalo Bill Cody in his famous Wild West Show.

De Marbelle was a multi-talented performer—a magician, actor, ventriloquist, soloist, writer; he was a musician who could play virtually any instrument and a public speaker who said he could make an eloquent speech on any subject at a moment's notice.

But he wasn't a businessman. Despite his many talents, his last years were spent in poverty, and he lived in an abandoned schoolroom. At the local Methodist church in Elgin, Illinois, he sang in the choir and sometimes gave this testimony: "For years I was so busy I didn't have time for God and so rich I didn't need Him. God had to slow me down and take my success away so that He could talk to me about the home beyond the river."

Leaning on the Everlasting Arms

Elisha A. Hoffman

Anthony J. Showalter

1. What a fel-low-ship, what a joy di - vine, Lean-ing on the ev - er - last-ing arms!
2. Oh how sweet to walk in this pil-grim way, Lean-ing on the ev - er - last-ing arms!
3. What have I to dread, what have I to fear, Lean-ing on the ev - er - last-ing arms?

What a bless - ed-ness, what a peace is mine, Lean-ing on the ev - er - last-ing arms!
Oh how bright the path Grows from day to day, Lean-ing on the ev - er - last-ing arms.
I have bless - ed peace with my Lord so near, Lean-ing on the ev - er - last-ing arms.

Lean - ing, lean - ing, Safe and se-cure from all a - larms;
Lean-ing on Je - sus, lean-ing on Je - sus,

Lean - ing, lean - ing, Lean-ing on the ev - er - last-ing arms.
Lean-ing on Je - sus, lean-ing on Je - sus,

Leaning on the Everlasting Arms

<u>1887</u>

The eternal God is your refuge, and underneath are the everlasting arms . . .
Deuteronomy 33:27

The idea for this song came from Anthony Showalter, principal of the Southern Normal Musical Institute in Dalton, Georgia. Showalter, a Presbyterian elder, was a well-known advocate of gospel music. He published over 130 music books with combined sales of two million copies, and he became known through the South for his singing schools in local churches.

Showalter took a personal interest in his students and enjoyed keeping up with them as the years passed. One evening in 1887, he was leading a singing school in a local church in Hartselle, Alabama. After dismissing the class for the evening, he gathered his materials and returned to his boardinghouse.

Two letters had arrived, both from former pupils. Each of the young men was heartbroken, having just lost his wife. Professor Showalter went to the Bible, looking for a verse to comfort them. He selected Deuteronomy 33:27—"The eternal God is your refuge, And underneath are the everlasting arms. . . ." As he pondered that verse, these words came to mind:

> *Leaning, leaning, safe and secure from all alarms;*
> *Leaning, leaning, leaning on the everlasting arms.*

He scribbled replies to his bereaved friends, then, reaching for another piece of paper, he wrote to his friend, hymnist Elisha Hoffman. "Here is the chorus for a good hymn from Deuteronomy 33:27," his letter said, "but I can't come up with any verses." Hoffman wrote three stanzas and sent them back. Showalter set it all to music, and ever since, these words have cheered us in adversity:

> *What have I to dread, what have I to fear, / Leaning on the everlasting arms. /*
> *I have blessed peace with my Lord so near, / Leaning on the everlasting arms.*

God, the eternal God, is our support at all times, especially when we are sinking into deep trouble. There are seasons when we sink quite low . . . . Dear child of God, even when you are at your lowest, underneath are the everlasting arms.—Charles Spurgeon

However low the people of God are at any time brought, everlasting arms are underneath them to keep the spirit from fainting and the faith from failing, even when they are pressed above measure . . . everlasting arms with which believers have been wonderfully sustained and kept cheerful in the worst of times. Divine grace is sufficient.—Matthew Henry

Trust and Obey

John H. Sammis

Daniel B. Towner

Trust and Obey

1887

*Trust in the LORD with all your heart, and lean not on your own understanding;
In all your ways acknowledge Him, and He shall direct your paths.* Proverbs 3:5–6

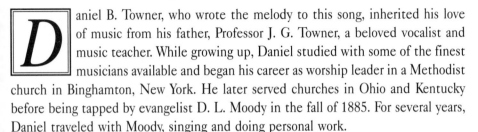 aniel B. Towner, who wrote the melody to this song, inherited his love of music from his father, Professor J. G. Towner, a beloved vocalist and music teacher. While growing up, Daniel studied with some of the finest musicians available and began his career as worship leader in a Methodist church in Binghamton, New York. He later served churches in Ohio and Kentucky before being tapped by evangelist D. L. Moody in the fall of 1885. For several years, Daniel traveled with Moody, singing and doing personal work.

He once explained how this hymn came to be written:

> Mr. Moody was conducting a series of meetings in Brockton, Massachusetts, and I had the pleasure of singing for him there. One night a young man rose in a testimony meeting and said, "I am not quite sure—but I am going to trust, and I am going to obey." I just jotted that sentence down, and sent it with the little story to Rev. J. H. Sammis, a Presbyterian minister.

Sammis wrote a poem based on the phrase "trust and obey," and sent it back to Towner, who went to work on the music.

Alfred Smith, in his *Treasury of Hymn Histories,* adds that while working on the music to "Trust and Obey," Dr. Towner grew discouraged. That evening in his home, he crumpled up the paper and threw the manuscript into the wastebasket. The next morning, as his wife was straightening his office, she retrieved the crumpled paper and sang over the words and melody to herself. She left it on the organ and encouraged her husband to work on it some more, telling him, "I feel the melody you have written is just what is needed to carry the message." She was right.

In 1893, Dr. Towner became head of the Music Department of the Moody Bible Institute of Chicago where he trained hundreds of young people to lead worship and minister to the Lord in music. He wrote the melodies of some of our favorite hymns, including: "At Calvary," "My Anchor Holds," and "Grace Greater Than All Our Sins." He also compiled fourteen hymnbooks and wrote several textbooks.

At age 70, while leading singing in revival meetings at Longwood, Missouri, he suffered a seizure and died.

Sunshine in My Soul

Eliza E. Hewitt

John R. Sweney

1. There is sun - shine in my soul to - day, More glo - ri - ous and bright
2. There is mu - sic in my soul to - day, A car - ol to my King;
3. There is spring - time in my soul to - day, For when the Lord is near
4. There is glad - ness in my soul to - day, And hope and praise and love,

Than glows in an - y earth - ly sky, For Je - sus is my light.
And Je - sus, lis - ten - ing can hear The songs I can - not sing.
The dove of peace sings in my heart, The flow'rs of grace ap - pear.
For bless - ings which He gives me now, For joys "laid up" a - bove.

O there's sun - shine, bless - ed sun - shine, When the peace - ful hap - py mo - ments

roll. When Je - sus shows His smil - ing face, There is sun - shine in my soul.

Sunshine in My Soul
1887

But the path of the just is like the shining sun, That shines ever brighter unto the perfect day. Proverbs 4:18

Edmunds Rhoad, account executive for an information systems company, has spent many hours researching his family tree. In the process, he discovered the diary that his great grandmother, Zeruiah Edmunds, started keeping at age nineteen, and it reveals a passionate love for Christ.

Zeruiah married James S. Hewitt, a young sailor who also kept a journal that tells of harrowing storms, shipwrecks, near escapes—and an earnest faith. One entry, for example, tells of a voyage to China in which he was surrounded by "a rough irreligious body of men who paid no attention or any duty to God on the Sabbath or on any other day. Oaths, card-playing, etc. marked their conduct when at leisure." James, deeply saddened, would slip off to quiet spots to read his Bible and pray.

It was into this Christian home that a daughter was born in 1851, in a house on Christian Street in Philadelphia. Little Eliza grew up in the nurture of the Lord. She was a teenager during the Civil War, but she managed to concentrate on school well enough to graduate valedictorian of her class. She displayed an unusual love for children, and after further study she became a schoolteacher.

In 1887, while teaching at the Northern Home for Friendless Children, Eliza, 35, was struck by an unruly student. He slammed his slate across her, severely injuring her back. The doctor placed her in a heavy cast for six months, and Eliza was virtually immobile, perhaps wondering if she would every walk again. When the cast was removed in early 1887, the doctor told her to talk a short walk in nearby Fairmont Park. It was a warm spring day, and she was overcome with joy. Returning home, she picked up her pen and immediately wrote the hymn:

> *There's sunshine in my soul today*
> *More glorious and bright,*
> *Than glows in any earthly sky,*
> *For Jesus is my light.*

Her injuries were severe enough to preclude school teaching, so she devoted herself Bible study and hymn-writing. Eliza lived many more years and wrote scores of hymns, including "My Faith Has Found a Resting Place," "When We All Get To Heaven," and "Will There Be Any Stars In My Crown?"

Eliza died in 1920, and her grave at Woodlands Cemetery in Philadelphia, reads simply: "Eliza Edmunds Hewitt, Hymnwriter, author of Sunshine in My Soul."*

---

*Edmunds Rhoad is available for presentations on the life of his great aunt, and can be reached at 285 67th Street, Avalon, New Jersey 08202.

Yesterday, Today, Forever

Albert B. Simpson

James H. Burke

Yes-ter-day, to - day, for-ev - er, Je-sus is the same.

All may change but Je-sus nev - er! Glo-ry to His name!

Glo - ry to His name! Glo - ry to His name!

All may change but Je - sus nev-er! Glo-ry to His name!

Yesterday, Today, Forever

1890

Jesus Christ is the same yesterday, today, and forever. Hebrews 13:8

Many people complain that A. B. Simpson's hymns are hard to sing. Well, maybe. But give them a good try anyway.

Albert Benjamin Simpson was born in 1843, of Scottish parents on Prince Edward Island. Despite his father's misgivings, young Albert announced his call to the ministry as a teenager, and it was arranged for him to preach at the local church. The appointed Sunday came, and the Simpson family was seated nervously in a row. When the moment for the sermon came, Albert rose, announced his text, and spoke so smoothly and powerfully that no one could believe it was his first sermon.

He went on to become a great preacher, a missionary advocate, and the founder of the Christian and Missionary Alliance. His famous four-fold message was Jesus Christ as Savior, Sanctifier, Healer, and Coming King. He wrote more than seventy books, opened a Bible and missionary training school at Nyack on the Hudson, and composed hymns.

A. W. Tozer, in *Wingspread*, his classic little biography of Simpson, wrote: "Simple truth requires us to state that A. B. Simpson does not rate high as a writer of hymns. The effort on the part of some of his admirers to place him along with Watts and Wesley is simply absurd. A hymn, to be great—to be a hymn at all—must meet with certain simple requirements. It must have literary excellence; it must be compact enough to be sung easily; it must express the religious feeling of the Universal Church; the music must have dignity and reserve.

"On none of these counts could Mr. Simpson's compositions qualify . . . His singing heart sometimes betrayed him into attempting to sing things that simply were not lyrical and could not be sung . . ."

But Tozer continues: "After saying all this, I would yet confess that hardly a day goes by that I do not kneel and sing, in a shaky baritone comfortably off key, the songs of Simpson. They feed my heart and express my longings, and I can find no other's songs that do this in as full a measure . . . . It is my sober judgment that Simpson has put into a few of his songs more of awful longing, of tender love, of radiant trust, of hope and worship and triumph than can be found in all the popular gospel songs of the last hundred years put together."

My Faith Has Found a Resting Place

Lidie H. Edmunds

Norwegian Folk Melody arr. by William J. Kirkpatrick

1. My faith has found a rest-ing place, Not in de-vice or creed;
2. E-nough for me that Je-sus saves, This ends my fear and doubt;
3. My heart is lean-ing on the Word, The writ-ten Word of God,
4. My great Phy-si-cian heals the sick, The lost He came to save;

I trust the Ev-er-liv-ing One, His wounds for me shall plead.
A sin-ful soul, I come to Him, He'll nev-er cast me out.
Sal-va-tion by my Sav-ior's name, Sal-va-tion through His blood.
For me His pre-cious blood He shed, For me His life He gave.

I need no oth-er ar-gu-ment, I need no oth-er plea,

It is e-nough that Je-sus died, And that He died for me.

My Faith Has Found a Resting Place

1891

Who through Him believe in God, who raised Him from the dead and gave Him glory, so that your faith and hope are in God. 1 Peter 1:21

This hymn was written by the mysterious Lidie H. Edmunds. For years no one seemed to know who she was. As it turns out, this was a pseudonym for a popular hymnwriter named Eliza Edmunds Hewitt.

In those days, hymnists often used pen names because publishers were nervous about having too many hymns from one author in their books. Fanny Crosby, for example, published under the names Carrie Hawthorne, Maud Marion, Louise W. Tilden, Lillian G. Frances, Mrs. Edna Forest, Eleanor Craddock—and 198 others!

The music for "My Faith Has Found a Resting Place" was written by the prolific William J. Kirkpatrick, who was born in Pennsylvania in 1838. His father was his earliest music teacher, and William edited his first hymnbook, *Devotional Melodies*, at age 21. He went on to write the melodies of some of our favorite hymns, including:

- COMING HOME—"I've Wandered Far Away from God" (music and words).
- DUNCANNON—"King of My Life, I Crown Thee Now."
- JESUS SAVES—"We Have Heard the Joyful Sound."
- KIRKPATRICK—"A Wonderful Savior is Jesus My Lord"
- TRUST IN JESUS—"'Tis So Sweet to Trust in Jesus"
- REDEEMED—"Redeemed, How I Love to Proclaim It"
- And this one, LÅNDES, a traditional Norwegian melody—"My Faith Has Found a Resting Place."

On the evening of September 21, 1921, Professor Kirkpatrick huddled away in his study in Germantown, Pennsylvania, working on a poem he was planning to put to music. His wife, sleeping in a nearby bedroom, awoke and noticed his study light was on. "Professor," she called, "it's very late, don't you think you'd better come to bed?"

"I'm all right, dear," he replied. "I have a little work I want to finish. Go back to sleep, everything is all right."

Mrs. Kirkpatrick went back to sleep, but awakened again later. The study light was still on, and again she called. This time there was no response. She found the Professor slumped over, his last hymn on the desk before him. It said:

*Just as Thou wilt, Lord, this is my cry | Just as Thou wilt, to live or die. |
I am Thy servant, Thou knowest best, | Just as Thou wilt, Lord, labor or rest.*

America, the Beautiful

Katharine Lee Bates

Samuel A. Ward

1. O beau - ti - ful for spa - cious skies, For am - ber waves of grain,
2. O beau - ti - ful for pil - grim feet, Whose stern, im - pas - sioned stress
3. O beau - ti - ful for he - roes proved In lib - er - at - ing strife,
4. O beau - ti - ful for pa - triot dream That sees be - yond the years

For pur - ple moun - tains maj - es - ties A - bove the fruit - ed plain!
A thor - ough - fare for free - dom beat A - cross the wil - der - ness!
Who more than self their coun - try loved, And mer - cy more than life!
Thine al - a - bas - ter cit - ies gleam, Un - dimmed by hu - man tears!

A - mer - i - ca! A - mer - i - ca! God shed His grace on thee,
A - mer - i - ca! A - mer - i - ca! God mend thine ev - 'ry flaw.
A - mer - i - ca! A - mer - i - ca! May God thy gold re - fine
A - mer - i - ca! A - mer - i - ca! God shed His grace on thee,

And crown thy good with broth - er - hood From sea to shin - ing sea!
Con - firm thy soul in self - con - trol, Thy lib - er - ty in law!
Till all suc - cess be no - ble - ness And ev - ery gain di - vine!
And crown thy good with broth - er - hood From sea to shin - ing sea.

America the Beautiful

1893

The heavens are Yours, the earth also is Yours; The world and all its fullness, You have founded them. Psalm 89:11

I n 1892, the United States observed the 400th anniversary of the discovery of America by Christopher Columbus.

As part of the celebration, the city of Chicago sponsored a World's Fair, which carried over to the next year. It was in the early summer of 1893, that a group of professors from Wellesley College visited the Exposition on their way to teach summer school in Colorado. The women later compared the wonders of the man-made Fair with the glory of God's handiwork in the Rockies.

At the close of school, the teachers decided to visit Pike's Peak, elevation 14,000 feet. One of them, Katharine Lee Bates, later wrote, "We hired a prairie wagon. Near the top we had to leave the wagon and go the rest of the way on mules. I was very tired. But when I saw the view, I felt great joy. All the wonder of America seemed displayed there, with the sea-like expanse . . . .

> It was then and there, as I was looking out over the sea-like expanse of fertile country spreading away so far under those ample skies, that the opening lines of the hymn floated into my mind. When we left Colorado Springs the four stanzas were penciled in my notebook . . . . The Wellesley work soon absorbed time and attention again, the notebook was laid aside, and I do not remember paying heed to these verses until the second summer following, when I copied them out and sent them to *The Congregationalist*, where they first appeared in print July 4, 1895. The hymn attracted an unexpected amount of attention . . . In 1904, I rewrote it, trying to make the phraseology more simple and direct.

> The new version first appeared in the *Boston Evening Transcript*, November 19, 1904.

There are two stories about the melody, MATERNA, which was written by Samuel A. Ward, originally for a hymn entitled, "O Mother Dear, Jerusalem." Ward's son-in-law said that the tune was composed in memory of Ward's oldest daughter. One of the employees at Ward's music store in Newark insisted that he composed the tune in 1882 while crossing New York harbor after spending the day at Coney Island. The notes came to him so quickly he jotted them on the cuff of his shirt. Perhaps both stories are true.

When the Roll Is Called Up Yonder

James M. Black   James M. Black

1. When the trum - pet of the Lord shall sound, and
2. On that bright and cloud - less morn - ing when the
3. Let us la - bor for the Mas - ter from the

time shall be no more, And the morn-ing breaks e - ter - nal bright and fair.
dead in Christ shall rise, And the glo - ry of His res - ur - rec - tion share;
dawn 'til set - ting sun, Let us talk of all His won-drous love and care;

When the saints on earth shall gath - er o - ver on the oth - er shore,
When the cho - sen ones shall gath - er to their home be-yond the skies,
And when all of life is o - ver and our work on earth is done,

And the roll is called up yon - der I'll be there.
And the roll is called up yon - der I'll be there.
And the roll is called up yon - der I'll be there.

When the Roll is Called Up Yonder

1893

I am the resurrection and the life. He who believes in Me, though he may die, he shall live. John 11:25

This old favorite was inspired by disappointment. James Black was calling roll one day for a youth meeting at his Methodist church in Williamsport, Pennsylvania. One name didn't answer—young Bessie, the daughter of an alcoholic. Crestfallen at her absence, James commented, "O God, when my own name is called up yonder, may I be there to respond!" Returning home, a thought struck him while opening the gate. Entering the house, he went to the piano and wrote the words and music effortlessly.

Years later, this song comforted a group of traumatized children in a Japanese concentration camp. In his book, *A Boy's War*, David Mitchell, tells of being in boarding school in Chefoo, China, during the Japanese invasion. On November 5, 1942, the students and faculty were marched from their campus and eventually ended up in Weihsien Concentration Camp.

Among the students was Brian Thompson, a lanky teenager. One evening about a year before the war ended, Brian was restless, waiting for the evening roll call which was long overdue. A bare wire from the searchlight tower was sagging low, and some of the older boys were jumping up and touching it with their fingers. "Whew, I got a shock off that," said one.

Brian decided to try. Being taller than the others, his hand was drawn into the wire, and it came down with him. When his bare feet hit the damp ground, the electricity shot through him like bolts of lightning. His mother, who had been interred with the students, tried to reach him, but the others held her back or she, too, would have been electrocuted. Finally someone found an old wooden stool and managed to detach the electrical wire, but it was too late.

At roll call that night, when the name "Brian Thompson" was called, there was no answer. David Mitchell later wrote: "Our principal and Mr. Houghton led a very solemn yet triumphant funeral service the next day. The shortness of life and the reality of eternity were brought home to us with force as Paul Bruce related that Brian had missed the roll call in camp but had answered one in Heaven. How important it was for us to sing and know, 'When the Roll is called up yonder, I'll be there.'"

I Must Tell Jesus

Elisha A. Hoffman

Elisha A. Hoffman

1. I must tell Jesus All of my tri - als, I can-not bear These
2. I must tell Jesus All of my trou-bles, He is a kind, Com -
3. O how the world to e - vil al - lures me. O how my heart Is

bur - dens a - lone. In my dis - tress He kind - ly will help me.
pas - sion-ate friend. If I but ask Him, He will de - liv - er,
tempt - ed to sin. I must tell Je - sus And He will help me,

He ev - er loves And cares for His own.
Make of my trou - bles Quick - ly an end. I must tell Je - sus!
O - ver the world The vic - t'ry to win.

I must tell Je - sus! I can-not bear My bur-dens a - lone.

I must tell Je-sus! I must tell Je-sus! Je-sus can help me, Je-sus a - lone.

I Must Tell Jesus

1894

Cast your burden on the LORD, and He shall sustain you; He shall never permit the righteous to be moved. Psalm 55:22

Many New Testament promises have corresponding verses in the Old Testament that reinforce their power. When Peter, for example, said, "Therefore humble yourselves under the mighty hand of God, that He may exalt you in due time, casting all your care upon Him, for He cares for you" (1 Peter 5:6–7), he was but restating David's words in Psalm 55:22: "Cast your burden on the Lord, and He shall sustain you; He shall never permit the righteous to be moved."

Elisha A. Hoffman loved those verses. He was born May 7, 1839, in Orwigsburg, Pennsylvania. His father was a minister, and Elisha followed Christ at a young age. He attended Philadelphia public schools, studied science, then pursued the classics at Union Seminary of the Evangelical Association. He worked for eleven years with the association's publishing house in Cleveland, Ohio. Then, following the death of his young wife, he returned to Pennsylvania and devoted 33 years to pastoring Benton Harbor Presbyterian Church.

Hoffman's pastime was writing hymns, many of which were inspired by pastoral incidents. One day, for example, while calling on the destitute of Lebanon, Pennsylvania, he met a woman whose depression seemed beyond cure. She opened her heart and poured on him her pent-up sorrows. Wringing her hands, she cried, "What shall I do? Oh, what shall I do?" Hoffman knew what she should do, for he had himself learned the deeper lessons of God's comfort. He said to the woman, "You cannot do better than to take all your sorrows to Jesus. You must tell Jesus."

Suddenly the lady's face lighted up. "Yes!" she cried, "That's it! I must tell Jesus." Her words echoed in Hoffman's ears, and he mulled them over as he returned home. He drew out his pen and started writing

> *I must tell Jesus! I must tell Jesus!*
> *I cannot bear my burdens alone;*
> *I must tell Jesus! I must tell Jesus!*
> *Jesus can help me, Jesus alone.*

Hoffman lived to be 90, telling Jesus his burdens and giving the church such hymns as "What A Wonderful Savior," "Down at the Cross," "Are You Washed in the Blood?," "Leaning on the Everlasting Arms," and a thousand more.*

---

*Taken from the author's book, *On This Day* (Nashville: Thomas Nelson Publishers, 1997), installment for May 7th.

At Calvary

William R. Newell

Daniel B. Towner

1. Years I spent in van - i - ty and pride, Car - ing not my Lord was cru - ci - fied, Know-ing not it was for me He died On Cal - va - ry.
2. By God's Word at last my sin I learned; Then I trem - bled at the law I'd spurned, Till my guilt - y soul im - plor-ing turned To Cal - va - ry.
3. Now I've giv'n to Je - sus ev - 'ry - thing; Now I glad - ly own Him as my King; Now my rap - tured soul can on - ly sing Of Cal - va - ry.
4. O the love that drew sal - va - tion's plan! O the grace that brought it down to man! O the might - y gulf that God did span At Cal - va - ry!

Mer - cy there was great and grace was free; Par - don there was mul - ti - plied to me; There my bur - dened soul found lib - er - ty, At Cal - va - ry.

At Calvary

1895

But God demonstrates His own love toward us, in that while we were still sinners, Christ died for us. Romans 5:8

When Dr. R. A. Torrey was president of the Moody Bible Institute of Chicago, he received a letter from a distressed father. The man, a pastor, had a prodigal son named Bill who was breaking his heart. Would Dr. Torrey let the boy enroll at Moody? Dr. Torrey replied that while he sympathized with the man, it wasn't possible to admit the boy. Moody was a Bible school, not a reformatory. The man wrote back, doubling his entreaties. Finally Dr. Torrey agreed, provided the boy meet with him daily and abide by the rules.

The arrangement didn't go well at first, and Dr. Torrey thought the experiment was hopeless. The boy had serious problems and seemed torn apart by turbulence. But he did keep the rules, and day by day he ventilated his frustrations to Dr. Torrey and—as it turned out—was more attentive to Torrey's answers than it appeared.

To make a long story short, several years later that boy, William R. Newell, himself, was a beloved professor at Moody Bible Institute.

In 1895, William began thinking of putting his testimony into verse form. The idea rolled around in the back of his mind for several weeks, then one day on his way to lecture, the lines came to him. Ducking into an empty classroom, he jotted down the words on the back of an envelope. As he hurried on to class, he happened to meet Dr. Daniel Towner, director of music at the Institute. Handing him the verses, William gently suggested they could use a good melody. By the time Dr. Newell finished his lecture, the completed tune was ready.

"Bill," said Dr. Towner, "I was so taken with the poem you gave me that I went immediately to my studio and composed a tune. I feel that it could be the best song that either of us will ever write in our lifetime."

The two men sang it together, and it was published shortly after.

Bill Newell went on to become a well-known Bible teacher throughout the Midwest and the author of a popular series of Bible commentaries. He once said that had he not gone through his troubled years, he might never have fully understood the importance of Calvary's grace

Mercy there was great, and grace was free;
Pardon there was multiplied to me;
There my burdened soul found liberty at Calvary.

Jesus Loves the Little Children

C. H. Woolston and Joseph Barlowe

George F. Root

1. Je-sus calls the chil-dren dear, "Come to me and nev-er fear, For I
2. Je-sus is the Shep-herd true, And He'll al-ways stand by you, For He
3. I am com-ing, Lord, to Thee, And Your sol-dier I will be, For You

love the lit-tle chil-dren of the world; I will take you by the hand, Lead you
loves the lit-tle chil-dren of the world; He's a Sav-ior great and strong, And He'll
love the lit-tle chil-dren of the world; And Your cross I'll al-ways bear, And for

to the bet-ter land, For I love the lit-tle chil-dren of the world."
shield you from the wrong, For He loves the lit-tle chil-dren of the world.
You I'll do and dare, For You love the lit-tle chil-dren of the world.

Je-sus loves the lit-tle chil-dren, All the chil-dren of the world. Red and yel-low, black and

white, They are pre-cious in His sight, Je-sus loves the lit-tle chil-dren of the world.

Jesus Loves the Little Children

Before 1895

Let the little children come to Me, and do not forbid them; for of such is the kingdom of God. Luke 18:16

Almost everyone knows "Jesus Loves the Little Children," but few of us have sung the three verses that go along with that chorus. Nor do many people realize this was originally a Civil War ballad.

George Frederick Root was born into a large family in Sheffield, Massachusetts, in 1820, and showed signs of musical genius. By age thirteen, he boasted that he could play thirteen different instruments. As a young adult, he taught music in Boston and New York, and he also composed music and served as church organist.

In 1855, he offered a song called "Rosalie, the Prairie Flower" to his publisher for the hefty sum of $100. Root's publisher, not thinking it worth that much, offered Root a royalty plan instead. In time, Root grossed *thousands* of dollars from "Rosalie," which helped establish him financially.

The outbreak of the Civil War deeply affected George, and he immediately began using his gifts to advance the Union war effort, writing a host of patriotic songs to rally the moral of the North. As a serious, classical composer, he was embarrassed at the simple martial music coming from his pen, so he signed them with the name "Wurzel," the German word for "Root." Among his most popular pieces was a ballad entitled, "Tramp! Tramp! Tramp!"

In the prison cell I sit,
Thinking, mother, dear of you,
And our bright and happy home so far away,
And the tears, they fill my eyes,
'Spite of all that I can do,
Tho' I try to cheer my comrades and be gay.

CHORUS:
Tramp! Tramp! Tramp! The boys are marching,
Cheer up, comrades, they will come,
And beneath the starry flag
We shall breathe the air again
Of the free land in our own beloved home.

After the Civil War, the melody remained popular but the words were dated. A minister named Clare Herbert Woolston, a lyricist whom Root occasionally used, wrote new verses and a chorus. And that's how a Civil War ballad about a soldier in prison became one of the most popular children's choruses in history.

I Surrender All

Judson W. Van De Venter

Winfield S. Weeden

1. All to Je-sus I sur-ren-der, All to Him I free-ly give;
2. All to Je-sus I sur-ren-der, Hum-bly at His feet I bow,
3. All to Je-sus I sur-ren-der, Make me Sav-ior whol-ly Thine;
4. All to Je-sus I sur-ren-der, Lord, I give my-self to Thee.

I will ev-er love and trust Him, In His pres-ence dai-ly live.
World-ly pleas-ures all for-sak-en, Take me, Je-sus, take me now.
Let me feel the Ho-ly Spir-it, Tru-ly know that Thou art mine.
Fill me with Thy love and pow-er; Let Thy bless-ings fall on me.

I sur-ren-der all, I sur-ren-der all.

I sur-ren-der all, I sur-ren-der all.

All to Thee my bless-ed Sav-ior, I sur-ren-der all.

I Surrender All

1896

But now, O LORD, You are our Father; we are the clay, and You our potter; and all we are the work of Your hand. Isaiah 64:8

S omeone once said, "Only in the Christian life does surrender bring victory." Judson Wheeler Van De Venter learned that for himself.

Born on a farm in Monroe Country, Michigan, in 1855, Judson grew up interested in art and music. He was converted to Christ at age 17. After graduating from college in Hillsdale, Michigan, Judson became an art teacher and then supervisor of art for the high school in Sharon, Pennsylvania. In 1885, he toured Europe, visiting art galleries and museums and studying painting. He was also a musician, having studied in numerous singing schools.

All the while, Judson was heavily involved in his local Methodist Episcopal Church where he sang in the choir. He found himself especially fulfilled when participating in evangelistic rallies and revivals in which people received Christ as their personal Savior. Friends encouraged him to resign from the school system to enter fulltime music evangelism, but for five years he struggled with the decision.

Finally falling to his knees, he said, "Lord, if you want me to give my full time to Thy work, I'll do it, I surrender all to Thee." For the next several years he traveled extensively through the United States, England, and Scotland, assisting in evangelistic work, leading the singing for Wilber Chapman and other evangelists, and winning men and women to Christ.

While engaged in meetings in East Palestine, Ohio, Judson stayed in the home of George Sebring (whose family founded Sebring, Ohio, and who himself later founded Sebring, Florida). It was there that he wrote the hymn, "I Surrender All," while recalling his own personal submitting to full-time ministry.

Moving to Tampa in 1923, he began teaching hymnology at Florida Bible Institute. He retired after several years, but still occasionally showed up on campus to lecture or to speak in chapel. In the 1930s, a student at Florida Bible Institute sat wide-eyed, listening to Judson Van De Venter. That student, Billy Graham, later wrote: "One of the evangelists who influenced my early preaching was also a hymnist who wrote 'I Surrender All,' the Rev. J. W. Van De Venter. He was a regular visitor at the Florida Bible Institute (now Trinity Bible College) in the late 1930s. We students loved this kind, deeply spiritual gentleman and often gathered in his winter home at Tampa, Florida, for an evening of fellowship and singing."

Under His Wings

William O. Cushing

Ira D. Sankey

1. Un-der His wings I am safe-ly a-bid-ing, Tho the night
2. Un-der His wings, What a ref-uge in sor-row! How the heart
3. Un-der His wings, O what pre-cious en-joy-ment! There will I

deep-ens And tem-pests are wild; Still I can trust Him I
yearn-ing-ly Turns to His rest! Of-ten when earth has no
hide 'Til life's tri-als are o'er! Shel-tered, pro-tect-ed, No

know He will keep me, He has re-deemed me And I am His child.
balm for my heal-ing, There I find com-fort And there I am blest.
e-vil can harm me, Rest-ing in Je-sus I'm safe ev-er-more.

Un-der His wings, Un-der His wings Who from His love can sev-er?

Un-der His wings My soul shall a-bide, Safely a-bide for-ev-er.

Under His Wings

<u>1896</u>

He shall cover you with His feathers, and under His wings you shall take refuge . . .
Psalm 91:4

n the days following World War II, when Communists were overrunning China, the endangered missionaries found comfort knowing that in a world dominated by the "Iron Curtain" and the "Bamboo Curtain" they could rest under the "Feather Curtain" of God.*

Psalm 91:4 says, "He shall cover you with His feathers, and under His wings you shall take refuge." The biblical patriarch, Boaz, referred to Ruth as a woman who had come under the Lord's wings for refuge (Ruth 2:12). Later Ruth's great-grandson, King David, perhaps recalling that story, asked the Lord in Psalm 17:8: "Keep me as the apple of Your eye; hide me under the shadow of Your wings." And in Psalm 57, he cried, "Be merciful to me, O God, be merciful to me! For my soul trusts in You; and in the shadow of Your wings I will make my refuge, until these calamities have passed by."

A thousand years later, David's great descendant, Jesus of Nazareth, said to the people of Jerusalem, "O Jerusalem, Jerusalem, the one who kills the prophets and stones those who are sent to her! How often I wanted to gather your children together, as a hen gathers her chicks under her wings . . ."

All these comforting word-pictures were woven together in the hymn, "Under His Wings," written by William Orcutt Cushing, who was born into a Unitarian home in 1823. He labored for over twenty years as a Christian pastor in New York with the Disciples of Christ, but the death of his wife and severe problems with his voice forced him out of the pastorate. In near despair, he asked God to give him something to do for the kingdom. It came into his heart to begin writing hymns, and in subsequent years, he produced more than 300 of them, including "Ring the Bells of Heaven," "When He Cometh," "Down in the Valley," and "Under His Wings."

If you find yourself in near despair with the worries and fears of life, close your eyes and visualize the warm safety of the "Feather Curtain of God."

Under His wings I am safely abiding,
Though the night deepens and tempests are wild,
Still I can trust Him; I know He will keep me,
He has redeemed me, and I am His child.

---

*See Isobel Kuhn, *Green Leaf in Drought* (Singapore: 1997), p. 37.

241

Count Your Blessings

Johnson Oatman, Jr.

Edwin O. Excell

1. When up - on life's bil - lows You are tem - pest tossed,
2. Are you ev - er bur-dened With a load of care,
3. When you look at oth - ers With their lands and gold,
4. So a - mid the con - flict Wheth - er great or small,

When you are dis - cour-aged Think - ing all is lost,
Does the cross seem heav - y You are called to bear.
Think that Christ has prom-ised You His wealth un - told.
Do not be dis - cour-aged God is o - ver all.

Count your man - y bless-ings Name them one by one,
Count your man - y bless-ings Ev - 'ry doubt will fly,
Count your man - y bless-ings Mon - ey can - not buy,
Count your man - y bless-ings An - gels will at - tend,

And it will sur - prise you What the Lord hath done.
And you will be sing - ing As the days go by.
Your re - ward in heav - en Nor your home on high.
Help and com - fort give you To your jour - ney's end.

Count Your Blessings

<u>1897</u>

Every good gift and every perfect gift is from above, and comes down from the Father of lights, with whom there is no variation or shadow of turning. James 1:17

I t's impossible to be thankful and, at the same time, grumpy, cantankerous, critical, or ill-tempered. That's a lesson Johnson Oatman wanted to teach young people in his song, "Count Your Blessings."

Johnson was born in New Jersey just before the Civil War. His father had a powerful voice which some people claimed was the best singing voice in the East. That's why, as a boy, Johnson, Jr., always wanted to stand beside his father in church.

When Johnson was a young man, he stood alongside his father in another way. He became a partner in Johnson Oatman & Son, his dad's mercantile business. At age 19, Johnson joined the Methodist Episcopal Church and was ordained into the ministry. He often preached, but Johnson never entered the fulltime pastorate, for he enjoyed the business world and found it paid his bills, giving him freedom to minister without cost.

In 1892, with his father's voice undoubtedly ringing in his memory, Johnson began writing hymns. He averaged 200 hymns and gospel songs a year—5,000 during the course of his lifetime, among them: "Higher Ground," "No, Not One," "The Last Mile of the Way," and this one, "Count Your Blessings," which was published in a song book for young people in 1897. It reflected Johnson's optimistic faith, and has been a lesson to many ever since.

Martin Luther wrote in his book, *Table Talk:* "The greater God's gifts and works, the less they are regarded." We tend to exhibit a degree of thanksgiving in reverse proportion to the amount of blessings we've received. A hungry man is more thankful for his morsel than a rich man for his heavily-laden table. A lonely woman in a nursing home will appreciate a visit more than a popular woman with a party thrown in her honor.

If the birds only burst into song once a year, we'd all pay close attention. But because they are singing every morning, we scarcely bother to listen.

Now is a good time to lay this book aside and deliberately thank God for something you've never before mentioned in thanksgiving. Count your blessings. Name them one by one.

And it will surprise you what the Lord has done.

Face to Face

Carrie E. Breck

Grant C. Tullar

1. Face to face with Christ my Sav - ior, Face to face what will it be
2. On - ly faint - ly now I see Him, With the dark - ling veil be - tween;
3. What re - joic - ing in His pres - ence When are ban - ished grief and pain;
4. Face to face! O bliss - ful mo - ment! Face to face to see and know;

When with rap - ture I be - hold Him, Je - sus Christ who died for me?
But a bless - ed day is com - ing When His glo - ry shall be seen.
When the crook - ed ways are straight - ened And the dark things shall be plain.
Face to face with my Re - deem - er, Je - sus Christ who loves me so.

Face to face I shall be - hold Him, Far be - yond the star - ry sky;

Face to face in all His glo - ry, I shall see Him by and by!

Face to Face

<u>1898</u>

Behold, He is coming with clouds, and every eye will see Him . . . Revelation 1:7

T his hymn came about because of a rocking chair, a jar of jelly, and a timely coincidence.

Grant Colfax Tullar was so named because he was born in 1869, when Ulysses S. Grant and Schuyler Colfax were President and Vice-President of the United States. He was raised by an austere set of relatives, his mother having died when he was two, and he spent his youth working in woolen mills and shoe stores. When he was 19, he was converted at a Methodist camp meeting and eventually became the music leader for evangelistic campaigns and a successful music publisher.

One Sunday in the late 1890s, Grant was leading the music for a revival in Rutherford, New Jersey. After spending the afternoon in visitation, he returned to the pastor's house where Rev. and Mrs. Charles Mead had spread leftovers on the table so everyone could make a hurried supper before the evening service. A nearly empty jar of jelly was on the table, and, knowing how Grant loved jelly, it was passed straight to him.

"So, this is all for me, is it?" he said, smiling. That little phrase, "all for me," prompted an idea. He rose, went over the piano, and on the spot composed the words and melody of a hymn entitled "All for me the Savior suffered; / All for me He bled and died." Rev. Mead reportedly sang it at church that very night.

The next morning, Grant received a packet of poems in the mail from Mrs. Frank A. Breck. Among them was a poem that said: "Face to face with Christ my Savior; / Face to face what will it be?"

As Grant read and reread the poem, he realized that the words perfectly fit the music he had written the day before. He sensed the Hand of God in this "coincidence," and, discarding his own poem, replaced it with the one by Mrs. Breck.

Carrie Elizabeth (Mrs. Frank) Breck was a homemaker and mother of five in Portland, Oregon, who wrote hymns in the midst of housework. "I penciled verses under all conditions," she once explained, "over a mending basket, with a baby on my arm, and sometimes even when sweeping or washing dishes, my mind moved in poetic meter." Frail in health, however, she often recorded her poems in a notebook while resting in her favorite rocking chair.

When We All Get to Heaven

Eliza E. Hewitt

Emily D. Wilson

1. Sing the won-drous love of Je - sus, Sing His mer - cy and His grace;
2. While we walk the pil - grim path - way, Clouds will o - ver - spread the sky;
3. Let us then be true and faith - ful, Trust - ing, serv - ing ev - ery day;
4. On - ward to the prize be - fore us! Soon His beau - ty we'll be - hold;

In the man - sions bright and bless - ed, He'll pre - pare for us a place.
But when trav - 'ling days are o - ver, Not a shad - ow, not a sigh.
Just one glimpse of Him in glo - ry Will the toils of life re - pay.
Soon the pearl - y gates will o - pen, We shall tread the streets of gold.

When we all get to heav - en, What a day of re -
When we all What a

joic - ing that will be! When we all see
day of re - joic - ing that will be! When we all

Je - sus, We'll sing and shout the vic - tor - y.
shout, and shout the vic - to - ry.

When We All Get to Heaven

<u>**1898**</u>

"And I will give you the keys of the kingdom of heaven, and whatever you bind on earth will be bound in heaven, and whatever you loose on earth will be loosed in heaven." Matthew 16:19

Eliza Edmunds Hewitt was one of the premier women hymnwriters of the late 1800s and the early 1900s. She wrote the popular hymn, "Singing I Go Along Life's Road," which was to have such a profound influence of soloist George Beverly Shea.* She is also the author of "Will There Be Any Stars in My Crown?" "My Faith Has Found a Resting Place," "Sunshine in My Soul," "More About Jesus," and this hymn, "When We All Get To Heaven."

It came to her as she studied John 14, where Jesus told His disciples, "Let not your heart be troubled; you believe in God, believe also in Me. In My Father's house are many mansions; if it were not so, I would have told you. I go to prepare a place for you."

But this wasn't Eliza's only hymn about heaven. Though now seldom-sung, one of her most unique songs is entitled, "The Everlasting Hymn," in which she imagines the majesty of worshipping the Lord as we gather around Him in the heavenly places, vibrantly echoing the biblical song of the angels:

> *Holy, holy, holy; / Angel voices singing;*
> *Holy, holy, holy, / Through high heaven ringing.*
> *From that temple, pure and bright, / Bathed in streams of crystal light,*
> *Hear the everlasting hymn, / Holy, holy, holy.*
>
> *Holy, holy, holy; / Grandest music swelling;*
> *Holy, holy, holy, / All sweet notes excelling.*
> *Those who conquered by His might, / Wearing now their crowns of light,*
> *Join the everlasting hymn, / Holy, holy, holy.*
>
> *Holy, holy, holy; / Come, let us adore Him;*
> *Holy, holy, holy, / Humbly bow before Him.*
> *Wisdom, glory, love and might, / With the seraphim unite*
> *In the everlasting hymn, / Holy, holy, holy.*

That's what we'll be singing—when we all get to heaven.

---

*See the story behind "I'd Rather Have Jesus."

There Is Power in the Blood

Lewis E. Jones

Lewis E. Jones

1. Would you be free From your bur-den of sin? There's pow'r in the blood,
2. Would you be free, From your pas-sion and pride? There's pow'r in the blood,
3. Would you be whit-er, Much whit-er than snow? There's pow'r in the blood,
4. Would you do ser-vice For Je-sus your King? There's pow'r in the blood,

Pow'r in the blood; Would you o'er ev-il a vic-tor-y win? There's
Pow'r in the blood; Come for a cleans-ing To Cal-va-ry's tide; There's
Pow'r in the blood; Sin stains are lost In its life giv-ing flow; There's
Pow'r in the blood; Would you live dai-ly, His prais-es to sing? There's

won-der-ful pow'r in the blood. There is pow'r, pow'r, Won-der work-ing pow'r,
There is pow'r, there is pow'r, Won-der work-ing pow'r,

In the blood of the Lamb; There is pow'r, pow'r,
In the blood of the Lamb. There is pow'r, there is pow'r,

Won-der work-ing pow'r, In the pre-cious blood of the Lamb.

There Is Power in the Blood

1899

Inasmuch as there is none like You, O LORD (You are great, and Your name is great in might). Jeremiah 10:6

Both the words and music of this old hymn were written during a camp meeting at Mountain Lake Park, Maryland by Lewis Jones. Jones, a California native, graduated from Moody Bible Institute and spent his vocational life with the Young Men's Christian Association (YMCA). On the side, he wrote hymns. This, his best known, is particularly effective in resisting the "wiles of the devil."

One day as missionary Dick Hillis preached in a Chinese village, his sermon was suddenly interrupted by a piercing cry. Everyone rushed toward the scream, and Dick's coworker, Mr. Kong, whispered that an evil spirit had seized a man. Dick, having not previously encountered demon possession, didn't believe him.

Just then, a woman rushed toward them. "I beg you help me!" she cried. "An evil spirit has again possessed the father of my children and is trying to kill him."

The two evangelists entered the house, stepping over a filthy old dog lying in the doorway. The room was charged with a sense of evil. "An evil spirit has possessed Farmer Ho," Kong told the onlookers. "Our God, the 'Nothing-He-Cannot-Do One' is more powerful than any spirit, and He can deliver this man. First, you must promise you will burn your idols and trust in Jesus, son of the Supreme Emperor."

The people nodded. Kong asked Dick to begin singing the hymn, "There is Power in the Blood." With great hesitation, Dick began to sing, "Would you be free from your burden of sin. . . ."

"Now," continued Kong, "in the name of Jesus we will command the evil spirit to leave this man." Kong began praying fervently. Suddenly, the old dog in the doorway vaulted into the air, screeching, yelping, whirling in circles snapping wildly at his tail. Kong continued praying, and the dog abruptly dropped over dead.

Instantly Dick remembered Luke 8, the demons of the Gadarenes who invisibly flew into the herd of swine. As Kong finished praying, Farmer Ho seemed quiet and relaxed, and soon he was strong enough to burn his idols. At his baptism shortly afterward, he testified, "I was possessed by an evil spirit who boasted he had already killed five people and was going to kill me. But God sent Mr. Kong at just the right moment, and in Jesus I am free."*

---

*This story is related in *Steel in His Soul: The Dick Hillis Story* by Jan Winebrenner (Chicago: Moody Press, 1985), chapter 6, "The Day the Dog Died."

O That Will Be Glory

Charles H. Gabriel   Charles H. Gabriel

1. When all my la-bors And tri-als are o'er, And I am safe On that
2. When by the gift Of His in-fi-nite grace, I am ac-cord-ed In
3. Friends will be there I have loved long a-go; Joy like a riv-er A-

beau-ti-ful shore, Just to be near The dear Lord I a-dore
heav-en a place, Just to be there And to look on His face
round me will flow. Yet, just a smile From my Sav-ior I know,

Will through the a-ges Be glo-ry for me. O that will be
                                              O   that will

glo-ry for me, Glo-ry for me, glo-ry for me! When by His grace
be glo-ry for me, Glo-ry for me, glo-ry for me!

I shall look on His face. That will be glo-ry, Be glo-ry for me.

O That Will Be Glory

1900

For in this we groan, earnestly desiring to be clothed with our habitation which is from heaven. 2 Corinthians 5:2

T his song came from the pen of Charles H. Gabriel, who was one of America's most prolific writers of gospel songs at the turn of the century. Charles had grown up in a musical family in Iowa, and his mom encouraged his musical inclinations. When Charles told her he was going to write a song that would one day be world-famous, she replied, "My boy, I would rather have you write a song that will help somebody than see you President of the United States."

Several decades later, in 1900, Charles, 44, wrote a song inspired by his friend Ed Card, director of the Sunshine Rescue Mission in Saint Louis. Ed often punctuated his sermons with the word, "Glory!", and at the end of his prayers, he usually said, "And that will be glory for me!"

Using those expressions, Gabriel wrote "O, That Will Be Glory for Me."

Not long afterward, this song came to the attention of the famous music director, Charles M. Alexander. Alexander and J. Wilber Chapman had been the first men to entirely circle the globe holding evangelistic campaigns. He was a gifted, popular, and enthusiastic worship leader, beloved around the world. His blessing on a song could make it a "hit."

But when Alexander saw "O, That Will Be Glory," he didn't think too highly of it. "That man has wasted a page for I do not believe that song will be sung much," he said to himself as he tossed it aside.

Several months later, Alexander attended a Convention where "The Glory Song" was sung with great vivacity. It affected him so deeply that he was soon teaching it to his friends and co-workers. When he joined Dr. R. A. Torrey for a series of evangelistic rallies in Australia, this became their theme song.

Alexander was surprised to hear telephone operators and hotel maids singing this song, even workmen in the streets and executive in their offices. It was translated into a myriad of languages. In Great Britain, it was sung again and again in Alexander's evangelistic rallies. Other evangelists such as Gipsy Smith caught on and started using it. It became enormously popular around the world, the most popular gospel song of its era.

And Charles Gabriel . . . well, he couldn't have been happier if he had been elected President of the United States.

Does Jesus Care?

Frank E. Graeff

J. Lincoln Hall

Does Jesus Care?

1901

Casting all your care upon Him, for He cares for you. 1 Peter 5:7

I n his book, *Lectures to My Students*, Charles Haddon Spurgeon devoted a chapter to "The Minister's Fainting Fits," warning his students of the dangers of discouragement and depression in the ministry. The chapter begins: "Fits of depression come over the most of us . . . The strong are not always vigorous, the wise not always ready, the brave not always courageous, and the joyous not always happy."

That observation is perfectly illustrated by Rev. Frank Graeff, the Methodist minister who wrote this hymn. Frank was born in 1860, in northeastern Pennsylvania. When he entered the ministry, one of his greatest assets was his cheerful disposition. While pastoring in the Philadelphia area, he was dubbed the "Sunshine Minister" because of his radiant personality. He had a special way with children, who were drawn to his simple faith and perpetual smile.

But as Spurgeon said, "the joyous are not always happy." A series of heartbreaks shattered his spirits, and Frank Graeff found himself in the unfamiliar valley of deep depression and despondency. His gloom became as great as the bliss he had previously enjoyed. At length, he collapsed into the Everlasting Arms and found himself singing Joseph Scriven's old hymn:

> *What a friend we have in Jesus, / All our sins and griefs to bear /*
> *What a privilege to carry, / Everything to God in prayer . . .*

The truth of 1 Peter 5:7 suddenly took hold of him: ". . . casting all your care upon Him, for He cares for you." Out of that experience, Frank wrote "Does Jesus Care?" with its series of commonly asked questions, followed by this resounding reply:

> *O yes, He cares; I know He cares; / His heart is touched with my grief;*
> *When the days are weary, the long nights dreary, / I know my Savior cares.*

How *do* we cast our cares on the One who cares for us? The secret is found in the word CAST:

- Commit your burden to the Lord. Give it over to Him who cares even more than you do, and who has the power to do what you cannot.
- Ask for His help in prayer. Philippians 4 tells us to be anxious about nothing, but in everything, by prayer and supplication, to let our needs be known to the Lord.
- Search the Scriptures. God has a promise for every need.
- Trust Him. For He *does* care for you.

This Is My Father's World

Maltbie D. Babcock

Traditional English Melody

1. This is my Fa-ther's world, And to my lis-t'ning ears;
2. This is my Fa-ther's world; The birds their car-ols raise.
3. This is my Fa-ther's world, O let me ne'er for-get

All na-ture sings and round me rings The mu-sic of the spheres.
The morn-ing light, the lil-y white, De-clare their Mak-er's praise;
That though the wrong seems oft so strong, God is the Rul-er yet.

This is my Fa-ther's world; I rest me in the thought
This is my Fa-ther's world; He shines in all that's fair;
This is my Fa-ther's world; The bat-tle is not done;

Of rocks and trees, of skies and seas; His hand the won-ders wrought.
In the rust-ling grass I hear Him pass, He speaks to me ev-ery-where.
Je-sus, who died, shall be sat-is-fied, And earth and heav'n be one.

This Is My Father's World

1901

... For the world is Mine, and all its fullness. Psalm 50:12b

Maltbie Babcock was arguably the most remarkable student Syracuse University had ever seen. Hailing from an aristocratic family, he was a brilliant scholar with a winning personality. Tall and steel-muscled, he was an outstanding athlete, expert swimmer, and captain of the baseball team. He also directed the university's orchestra, played several instruments, and composed original compositions. A proficient vocalist, he directed the university glee club. He entertained other students by drawing and doing impersonations. On the side, he was an avid fisherman.

He would have been successful in any profession, but God called him to the ministry; and after further training at Auburn Theological Seminary, he became pastor of the First Presbyterian Church in Lockport, New York. It was a beautiful area—midway between Lake Erie and Lake Ontario, not far from Niagara Falls—and Maltbie enjoyed hiking and running in the hills outside town. Telling his secretary, "I'm going out to see my Father's world," he would run or hike a couple of miles into the countryside where he'd lose himself in nature.

It was during his pastorate at Lockport that he wrote a sixteen-stanza poem, each verse beginning with the words, "This is My Father's World."

In 1886, Maltbie was called to the Brown Memorial Church in Baltimore. While there, he traveled widely and was in great demand on college campuses. He was a fresh, engaging speaker who never failed to stimulate students. In 1899, he moved to the Brick Presbyterian Church in New York City. Here he found it more difficult to take off on his hikes. The work load was enormous, but Maltbie faced it stoically, writing:

> *Be strong! We are not here to play, to dream, to drift,*
> *We have hard work to do and loads to lift;*
> *Shun not the struggle. Face it. 'Tis Gods gift. Be strong!*

When he was 42, his church presented him with a special gift—a pilgrimage to the "Holy Land." With great excitement, Maltbie departed by ship. While enroute at Naples, Italy, he was seized with a deadly bacterial fever and died at the International Hospital on May 18, 1901.

After his death, his wife compiled his writings into a book entitled *Thoughts for Everyday Living,* published in 1901. Included was Maltbie's "This Is My Father's World."

Near to the Heart of God

Cleland B. McAfee

Cleland B. McAfee

1. There is a place of qui - et rest, Near to the heart of God;
2. There is a place of com - fort sweet, Near to the heart of God;
3. There is a place of full re - lease, Near to the heart of God;

A place where sin can - not mo - lest, Near to the heart of God.
A place where we our Sav - ior meet, Near to the heart of God.
A place where all is joy and peace, Near to the heart of God.

O Je - sus, blest Re - deem - er, Sent from the heart of God,

Hold us, who wait be - fore Thee, Near to the heart of God.

Near to the Heart of God
1903

. . . He will gather the lambs with His arm, and carry them in His bosom . . .
Isaiah 40:11

Park University in Parkville, Missouri, with 38 campuses across the United States, boasts of an enrollment of over 17,000 students. It was begun in 1875, with only 17 students, by John A. McAfee, and by Colonel George Park, the colorful founder of Parkville, who donated the land.

McAfee had five sons and a daughter who all became involved in the college. The fourth son, Cleland, graduated from what was then Park College; after studying at Union Theological Seminary, he returned to Park as chaplain and choir director. Cleland's daughter, Katharine, later told how her father came to write the great hymn, "Near to the Heart of God":

My father's father, John A. McAfee, was one of the founders and the first president of Park College in Missouri. In the last years of the past century, his five sons (Lowell, Howard, Lapsley, Cleland, Ernest) and his only daughter (Helen) were all living in Parkville, serving the college. My father was the college preacher and director of the choir, and it was his custom, when communion services came, to write the words and music of a response which his choir could sing and which would fit into the theme of his sermon.

One terrible week, just before a communion Sunday, the two little daughters of my Uncle Howard and Aunt Lucy McAfee died of diphtheria within twenty-four hours of each other. The college family and town were stricken with grief. My father often told us how he sat long and late thinking of what could be said in word and song on the coming Sunday . . .

So he wrote ("Near to the Heart of God"). The choir learned it at the regular Saturday night rehearsal, and afterward they went to the Howard McAfee's home and sang it as they stood under the sky outside the darkened, quarantine house. It was sung again on Sunday morning at the communion service.

"Near to the Heart of God" was published in October, 1903, in *The Choir Leader.*

In later years, Cleland pastored in the Presbyterian denomination, taught at McCormick Theological Seminary in Chicago, and helped direct the Presbyterian foreign missions program. He is the author of a number of textbooks including, *The Greatest English Classic: A Study of the King James Version and Its Influence,* and *Ministerial Practices: Some Fraternal Suggestions,* published in 1928.

God Will Take Care of You

Civilla D. Martin

W. Stillman Martin

1. Be not dis-mayed what-e'er be-tide, God will take care of you;
2. Thro' days of toil, when heart doth fail, God will take care of you;
3. All you may need He will pro-vide, God will take care of you;
4. No mat-ter what may be the test, God will take care of you;

Be - neath His wings of love a - bide, God will take care of you.
When dan - gers fierce your path as - sail, God will take care of you.
Noth - ing you ask will be de - nied, God will take care of you.
Lean, wea - ry one, up - on His breast, God will take care of you.

God will take care of you. Thro' ev-ery day, o'er all the way,

He will take care of you; God will take care of you.

God Will Take Care of You

1904

Bless the LORD, O my soul, and forget not all His benefits: who forgives all your iniquities, who heals all your diseases. Psalm 103:2–3

J. C. Penney, who descended from a long line of Baptist preachers, was well on his way to establishing a successful career when the 1929 Great Depression threw him into crisis. His business deals turned sour, and Penney became overwhelmed with anxiety and insomnia. He developed a painful case of shingles and was hospitalized, but tranquilizers and drugs only made things worse. His mental state deteriorated until, as he later said, "I was broken nervously and physically, filled with despair, unable to see even a ray of hope. I had nothing to live for. I felt I hadn't a friend left in the world, that even my family turned against me."

But one morning he heard singing coming from the little hospital chapel. The words of the song said, "Be not dismayed whate'er betide / God will take care of you."

Entering the chapel, he listened to the song, to the Scripture reading, and to the prayer. "Suddenly—something happened. I can't explain it. I can only call it a miracle. I felt as if I had been instantly lifted out of the darkness of a dungeon into warm, brilliant sunlight." All worry left him as he realized more fully than he had ever imagined just how much the Lord Jesus Christ cared for him. From that day J. C. Penney was never plagued with worry, and he later recalled those moments in the chapel as, "the most dramatic and glorious twenty minutes of my life." He later became one of America's greatest retail merchants.

On a Sunday in 1904, Civilla Martin was in Lestershire, New York, where her husband, Walter, was compiling a collection of hymns for the Practical Bible Training School. They were planning to travel to another town that day, for Martin had a preaching assignment. Civilla woke up sick, and Martin was about to cancel his plans, when their young child piped up and said: "Oh, Daddy, you don't have to stay home because of mother—God will take care of us."

Martin proceeded to the train station and fulfilled his appointment. When he returned, Civilla handed him the words of "God Will Take Care of You," which she had written in his absence. Going to his little organ, Martin composed the music, and it was first published in the songbook he was compiling for the school.

His Eye Is on the Sparrow

His Eye Is on the Sparrow

1905

Are not two sparrows sold for a copper coin? And not one of them falls to the ground apart from your Father's will. Matthew 10:29

Most people have a hobby of some sort to provide a healthy diversion from the rigors of work. Long ago, there was a woodworker in Nazareth who counted bird-watching among His diversions. We can make that assumption, because Jesus later referred frequently to bird-life in His sermons, saying things like:

- "Are not two sparrows sold for a copper coin? And not one of them falls to the ground apart from your Father's will" (Matthew 10:29).
- "Look at the birds of the air, for they neither sow nor reap nor gather into barns; yet your heavenly Father feeds them. Are you not of more value than they?" (Matthew 6:26)
- "Consider the ravens . . ." (Luke 12:26).
- "Do not fear . . . you are of more value than many sparrows" (Luke 12:7).

It was this theme that caused the author of "God Will Take Care of You," to write, a year later, another great hymn on God's care: "His Eye Is on the Sparrow."

Civilla Durfee Martin was a Canadian by birth, born on August 21, 1869, in Nova Scotia. She became a school and music teacher, but when she married Dr. Walter Martin, an evangelist, she gave up teaching to travel with him and assist in his meetings.

This is her account of the writing of this song:

Early in the spring of 1905, my husband and I were sojourning in Elmira, New York. We contracted a deep friendship for a couple by the name of Mr. and Mrs. Doolittle—true saints of God. Mrs. Doolittle had been bedridden for nigh twenty years. Her husband was an incurable cripple who had to propel himself to and from his business in a wheel chair. Despite their afflictions, they lived happy Christian lives, bringing inspiration and comfort to all who knew them. One day while we were visiting with the Doolittles, my husband commented on their bright hopefulness and asked them for the secret of it. Mrs. Doolittle's reply was simple: "His eye is on the sparrow, and I know He watches me." The beauty of this simple expression of boundless faith gripped the hearts and fired the imagination of Dr. Martin and me. The hymn "His Eye Is on the Sparrow" was the outcome of that experience.

The day after writing the song, she mailed it to the famous Gospel composer, Charles Gabriel, who penned the music.

Have Thine Own Way, Lord

Adelaide A. Pollard

George C. Stebbins

1. Have Thine own way, Lord! Have Thine own way!
2. Have Thine own way, Lord! Have Thine own way!
3. Have Thine own way, Lord! Have Thine own way!
4. Have Thine own way, Lord! Have Thine own way!

Thou art the Pot - ter, I am the clay.
Search me and try me, Mas - ter, to - day!
Wound - ed and wea - ry, help me, I pray!
Hold o'er my be - ing ab - so - lute sway!

Mold me and make me af - ter Thy will,
Whit - er than snow, Lord, wash me just now,
Pow - er, all pow - er sure - ly is Thine!
Fill with Thy Spir - it till all shall see,

While I am wait - ing, yield - ed and still.
As in Thy pres - ence hum - bly I bow.
Touch me and heal me, Sav - ior di - vine!
Christ on - ly, al - ways, liv - ing in me!

Have Thine Own Way, Lord

<u>1907</u>

. . . as the clay is in the potter's hand, so are you in My hand . . . Jeremiah 18:6

Hope differed makes the heart sick," says Proverbs 13:12. Yet *"dis*appointments are *His* appointments." God uses setbacks to renew our focus on Him, to strengthen our faith, and to divert us to other opportunities. In this case, a bitter disappointment led to one of our greatest invitational hymns.

Its author, Adelaide Pollard, was born in Iowa during the Civil War. Her parents named her Sarah, but when she was old enough, she changed her name to "Adelaide," not liking the name "Sarah." After attending the Boston School of Oratory (Emerson College), she moved to Chicago to teach in a girls' school.

While in Chicago and struggling with frail health, she was attracted to the strange ministry of John Alexander Dowie, a Scottish-born faith healer who was drawing international attention. In 1901, Dowie announced he was the Elijah who would precede the Coming of Christ. Purchasing 6,800 acres of land outside Chicago, he began building "Zion City," which, despite a strong start, ended in failure. Adelaide, however, was apparently healed of diabetes through Dowie's ministry.

Afterward, she became very involved in the work of an evangelist named Sanford, who was predicting the imminent return of Christ. In New England, where she had moved to assist Sanford, she felt God was calling her to Africa as a missionary. But, to her intense disappointment, she was unable to raise her financial support. Heartsick, Adelaide, in her forties at the time, attended a prayer meeting. That night an elderly woman prayed, "It doesn't matter what you bring into our lives, Lord. Just have your own way with us."

That phrase rushed into Adelaide's heart, and the verses began shaping in her mind. At home that evening, she read again the story of the potter and the clay in Jeremiah 18. By bedtime she had written out the prayer, "Have Thine Own Way."

Adelaide did eventually make it to Africa, but the outbreak of World War I sent her to Scotland and, later, back to America where she wrote poems, spoke to groups, and ministered freely.

In the middle of December, 1934, Adelaide, 72, purchased a ticket at New York's Penn Station. She was heading to Pennsylvania for a speaking engagement. While waiting for the train, she was stricken with a seizure and shortly thereafter died.

Joyful, Joyful, We Adore Thee

Henry van Dyke

Ludwig van Beethoven

1. Joy - ful, joy - ful, we a - dore Thee, God of glo - ry Lord of love;
2. All Thy works with joy sur-round Thee, Earth and heaven re - flect Thy rays;
3. Thou art giv - ing and for - giv - ing. Ev - er bless - ing, ev - er blest,
4. Mor - tals join the might - y cho - rus, Which the Morn - ing Stars be - gan.

Hearts un - fold like flow'rs be - fore Thee, Open - ing to the sun a - bove.
Stars and an - gels sing a - round Thee, Cen - ter of un - bro - ken praise.
Well - spring of the joy of liv - ing, O - cean depth of hap - py rest!
Fa - ther love is reign-ing o'er us, Broth - er love binds man to man.

Melt the clouds of sin and sad - ness; Drive the dark of doubt a - way;
Field and for - est, vale and moun-tain, Flow - ery mea-dow, flash - ing sea,
Thou our Fa - ther, Christ our Broth - er, All who live in love are Thine.
Ev - er sing - ing, march we on - ward, Vic - tors in the midst of strife;

Giv - er of im - mor - tal glad-ness, Fill us with the light of day!
Chant - ing bird and flow - ing foun-tain, Call us to re - joice in Thee.
Teach us how to love each oth - er; Lift us to the joy di - vine.
Joy - ful mu - sic lifts us sun-ward, In the tri - umph song of life.

Joyful, Joyful, We Adore Thee

1907

For I know the thoughts that I think toward you, says the LORD, thoughts of peace and not of evil, to give you a future and a hope. Jeremiah 29:11

Once when recovering from a bout of depression, I found this hymn very therapeutic. "Melt the clouds of sin and sadness, drive the dark of doubt away," it says. "Giver of immortal gladness, fill us (me) with the light of day." Notice how every phrase of this prayer is bursting with exuberance: The Lord is our "wellspring of the joy of living," our "ocean depth of happy rest," and we ask Him to, "Lift us to the joy divine."

The author of the hymn, Henry Jackson van Dyke, was born in Pennsylvania in 1852, and became pastor of the Brick Presbyterian Church in New York City.* Henry later became professor of English literature at Princeton, and the author of a number of books, including the still popular "The Other Wise Man." He went on to occupy a number of eminent positions, including:

- American Ambassador to the Netherlands and Luxenbourg (appointed by his friend, Woodrow Wilson)
- Lieutenant Commander in the United States Navy Chaplains Corps during World War I
- Moderator of the General Assembly of the Presbyterian Church
- Commander of the Legion of Honor
- President of the National Institute of Arts and Letters
- Chairman of the committee that compiled the Presbyterian *Book of Common Worship*

In 1907, Henry van Dyke was invited to preach at Williams College in Massachusetts. At breakfast one morning, he handed the college president a piece of paper, saying, "Here is a hymn for you. Your mountains (the Berkshires) were my inspiration. It must be sung to the music of Beethoven's 'Hymn of Joy.'"

When he was later asked about his hymn, van Dyke replied: "These verses are simple expressions of common Christian feelings and desires in this present time—hymns of today that may be sung together by people who know the thought of the age, and are not afraid that any truth of science will destroy religion, or any revolution on earth overthrow the kingdom of heaven. Therefore this is a hymn of trust and joy and hope."

---

*His resignation from Brick Church in 1899 paved the way for Maltbie Babcock to be called as pastor. See the story behind "This Is My Father's World."

He Keeps Me Singing

Luther B. Bridgers

Luther B. Bridgers

1. There's with-in my heart a mel-o-dy. Je-sus whis-pers sweet and low:
2. All my life was wrecked by sin and strife; Dis-cord filled my life with pain.
3. Feast-ing on the rich-es of His grace, Rest-ing 'neath His shel-t'ring wing,
4. Tho' some-times He leads thro' wa-ters deep, Tri-als fall a-cross my way,
5. Soon He's com-ing back to welcome me Far be-yond the star-ry sky.

"Fear not, I am with thee; peace, be still," In all of life's ebb and flow.
Je-sus swept a-cross the bro-ken strings, Stirred the slumb-'ring chords a-gain.
Al-ways look-ing on His smil-ing face, That is why I shout and sing.
Tho' some-times the path seems rough and steep, See His foot-prints all the way.
I shall wing my flight to worlds un-known; I shall reign with Him on high.

Je-sus, Je-sus, Je-sus, Sweet-est name I know,

Fills my ev-'ry long-ing, Keeps me sing-ing as I go.

He Keeps Me Singing

<u>1910</u>

And the ransomed of the Lord shall return, and come to Zion with singing, with everlasting joy on their heads. . . . Isaiah 35:10

T hough battered by life, the patriarch Job declared that God is able to give us "songs in the night" (Job 35:10). When the Psalmist, Asaph, felt overwhelmed, he consoled himself with God's "song in the night" (Psalm 77:6). God is strong enough to keep us singing, even in the night seasons.

North Carolina native Luther Bridgers began preaching at age seventeen while attending Asbury College in Kentucky. Afterward, he developed a reputation as an effective pastor/evangelist/church planter. The Lord gave him a wonderful wife and three precious boys.

In 1910, when Luther was twenty-six and the future seemed bright, he took his family to his wife's home in Harrodsburg, Kentucky, southwest of Lexington. They were going to stay with her parents while Luther was on a preaching trip.

One evening a nearby neighbor, unable to sleep, rose in the night and glanced out his window. He was horrified to see flames. Racing across the field, he gave the alarm, but by that time the house was fully engulfed. Luther's in-laws evidently escaped, but his wife and sons perished.*

During the long, slow recovery from overwhelming grief, Luther suffered deep and almost suicidal depression, according to some sources. But he recalled the Bible's promise of "songs in the night," and several months later he wrote both the words and the music for this gospel song about God's ability to keep him singing. Notice how he alludes to his tragedy in verse 4:

Though sometimes He leads through waters deep, | Trials fall across the way,
Though sometimes the path seems rough and steep, | See His footprints all the way.

Jesus, Jesus, Jesus, Sweetest Name I know,
Fills my every longing, Keeps me singing as I go.

In 1914, Luther married again and became a general evangelist for the Methodist Episcopal Church South, a ministry that kept him occupied for the next eighteen years (with a brief interruption after World War I when he traveled to Belgium, Czechoslovakia, and Russia, doing evangelistic work).

After 1932, he served as pastor in churches in Georgia and North Carolina, and retired in Gainesville, Georgia, in 1945. He passed away in Atlanta in 1948.

---

*Dr. Alfred B. Smith, the "Dean of Gospel Music," says that Luther himself was at his in-laws that night and had to be restrained by neighbors from re-entering the collapsing inferno.

Our Great Savior

J. Wilbur Chapman

Rowland W. Prichard

1. Je - sus! What a friend for sin - ners! Je - sus lov - er of my soul!
2. Je - sus! What a strength in weak - ness! Let me hide my - self in Him;
3. Je - sus! What a help in sor - row! While the bil - lows o'er me roll,
4. Je - sus! What a guide and keep - er! While the tem - pest still is high,
5. Je - sus! I do now re - ceive Him; More than all in Him I find.

Friends may fail me, foes as - sail me; He, my Sav - ior, makes me whole.
Tempt - ed tried and some-times fail - ing, He, my strength my vic - tory wins.
E - ven when my heart is break - ing, He, my Com - fort helps my soul.
Storms a - bout me, night o'er - takes me, He, my pi - lot hears my cry.
He hath grant - ed me for - give - ness; I am His and He is mine.

Hal - le - lu - jah! what a Sav - ior! Hal - le - lu - jah! what a Friend!

Sav - ing, help - ing, keep - ing, lov - ing, He is with me to the end.

Our Great Savior

1910

. . . you shall know no God but Me; For there is no Savior besides Me. Hosea 13:4

D uring his teen years, John Wilbur Chapman attended two Sunday schools each week in his hometown of Richmond, Indiana. He went to one church each Sunday morning, and in the afternoon he would go to Grace Methodist Episcopal Church. It was in the latter that he first publicly professed Christ as His Savior at age seventeen. A guest speaker gave the lesson that afternoon, then asked for those to stand who wanted to become Christians. Chapman later wrote:

> I think every boy in my class rose to his feet with the exception of myself . . .
> My Sunday School teacher (Mrs. C. C. Binkley), with tears in her eyes,
> leaned around back of the other boys, and looking straight at me, as I turned
> toward her, said, "Would it not be best for you to rise?" And when she saw
> I still hesitated, she put her hand under my elbow and lifted me up just a
> little bit, and I stood on my feet. I can never describe my emotions . . .
> Through all these years I have never forgotten it was my teacher who influ-
> enced me thus to take a stand—it was her personal touch that gave me
> courage to rise before the church and confess my Savior.

Wilber Chapman went on to become an outstanding pastor, writer, hymnist, and denominational leader. But he is best remembered for his evangelism. Multitudes of people were converted in his crusades (with songleader Charles M. Alexander) in the United States, Canada, Hawaii, the Fiji Islands, Australia, Tasmania, New Zealand, the Philippines, China, Japan, Ceylon, England, Scotland, Ireland, and Wales. It was in 1910 in the midst of his endeavors that he wrote the hymn "Our Great Savior," celebrating the varied and wonderful roles Christ plays in our lives: "Jesus! What a friend of sinners . . . . Jesus! What a Strength in weakness . . . . Jesus! What a Help in Sorrow . . . . Jesus! What a Guide and Keeper . . . Hallelujah! What a Savior."

This hymn is sung to the exhilarating tune HYFRYDOL, which is a Welsh word meaning "good cheer." It was composed around 1830 by Rowland W. Pritchard, a choir director born in north Wales, and has since become widely used with a number of hymn texts. It was Robert Harkness, the gifted pianist in Chapman's evangelistic campaigns, who took Chapman's words and wedded them to Pritchard's music.

In the Garden

C. Austin Miles

C. Austin Miles

1. I come to the gar - den a - lone, While the dew is still on the
2. He speaks, and the sound of His voice is so sweet, the birds hush their
3. I'd stay in the gar - den with Him, Though the night a - round me be

ros - es; And the voice I hear, fall - ing on my ear, The
sing - ing, And the mel - o - dy that He gave to me, With -
fall - ing, But He bids me go; through the voice of woe, His

Son of God dis - clos - es.
in my heart is ring - ing. And He walks with me, And He
voice to me is call - ing.

talks with me, And He tells me I am His own; And the

joy we share as we tar - ry there, None oth - er has ev - er known.

In the Garden

1912

. . . she turned around and saw Jesus standing there . . . John 20:14

T he art of meditating on Scripture involves using one's imagination. Instead of simply reading a passage, we must read it, close our eyes, and visualize the scene, perhaps even putting ourselves in the picture. That's what the author of this hymn did.

C. Austin Miles was a pharmacist who began writing gospel songs and eventually became an editor of hymnals and songbooks, as well as a popular music director at camp meetings, conventions, and churches. His hobby was photography, and he found his darkroom perfect for developing, not just his photographs, but his devotional life. In its privacy and strange blue glow, Miles could read his Bible in total privacy.

One day in March, 1912, while waiting for some film to develop, he opened the Bible to his favorite chapter, John 20, the story of the first Easter. Miles later said: "As I read it that day, I seemed to be part of the scene . . . My hands were resting on the Bible while I stared at the light blue wall. As the light faded, I seemed to be standing at the entrance of a garden, looking down a gently winding path, shaded by olive branches. A woman in white, with head bowed, hand clasping her throat as if to choke back her sobs, walked slowly into the shadows. It was Mary. As she came to the tomb, upon which she placed her hand, she bent over to look in and hurried away. John, in flowing robe, appeared, looking at the tomb; then came Peter, who entered the tomb, followed slowly by John.

"As they departed, Mary reappeared, leaning her head upon her arm at the tomb. She wept. Turning herself, she saw Jesus standing; so did I. I knew it was He. She knelt before Him, with arms outstretched and looking into his face, cried, 'Rabboni!'

"I awakened in full light, gripping my Bible, with muscles tense and nerves vibrating. Under the inspiration of this vision I wrote as quickly as the words would be formed the poem exactly as it has since appeared. That same evening I wrote the music."

In addition to "In the Garden," Austin Miles is the author of several other gospel songs, including "A New Name in Glory," "Dwelling in Beulah Land," and "If Jesus Goes with Me I'll Go Anywhere."

Brighten the Corner Where You Are

Ina Duley Ogdon

Charles H. Gabriel

1. Do not wait un - til some deed of great-ness you may do, Do not
2. Just a - bove are cloud - ed skies that you may help to clear, Let not
3. Here for all your tal - ent you may sure - ly find a need, Here re-

wait to shed your lights a - far; To the man - y du - ties Ev - er near you
nar - row self your way de - bar; Tho' in - to one heart a - lone may fall your
flect the Bright and Morn-ing Star, E - ven from your hum-ble hand The bread of

Now be true, Bright-en the cor - ner Where you are.
song of cheer, Bright-en the cor - ner Where you are. Bright-en the cor - ner
life may feed. Bright-en the cor - ner where you are.

Where you are! Bright-en the cor - ner Where you are! Some-one far from

har-bor You may guide A - cross the bar, Bright-en the cor - ner Where you are.

Brighten the Corner
Where You Are

1913

You are the light of the world. Matthew 5:14a

I n August, 1874, a Methodist minister named John Heyl Vincent organized a Sunday school training camp beside beautiful Lake Chautauqua in upstate New York. Families came for two-week summer camps that combined recreation, entertainment, and Sunday school training sessions. It was an enormous hit, and over the next several decades, the "Chautauqua Circuit" spread to other areas and quickly outgrew its Sunday school origins.

Performers, musicians, lecturers, and motivational speakers traveled the country, staying about a week in these summer camps. Enormous audiences gathered to enjoy Broadway hits, popular plays, and stars from the Metropolitan Opera. Speakers like William Jennings Bryan drew thousands, and Theodore Roosevelt called the Chautauqua Circuit, "the most American thing in America."*

In 1912, Ina Duley Ogdon received an invitation to be a Chautauqua Circuit speaker. Having long felt God's calling on her life, she was tremendously excited by the possibilities of motivating thousands of people for the cause of Christ. But as she was packing for the tour, her father was seriously injured in a wreck in one of the new-fangled "horseless carriages." Ina, deeply distressed, cancelled her travel plans to care for him.

Though bitterly disappointed, she was able to surrender the disappointment to God and trust His purposes. Making up her mind to be a blessing wherever she was, she concluded that even if she couldn't minister to thousands, she could be a blessing to one—her father—and to those around him. She sat down and wrote:

Do not wait until some deed of greatness you may do, / Do not wait to shed your light afar,
To the many duties ever near you now be true, / Brighten the corner where you are.

After this poem was set to music by Charles H. Gabriel, it was discovered by Homer Rodeheaver, the song director for Billy Sunday's evangelistic campaigns. He was so taken by the song that he made it the theme song of his ministry, and for twenty-two years, "Brighten the Corner" opened every Billy Sunday meeting. In the process, it became one of gospel music's most popular and uplifting songs.

Instead of speaking to thousands, Ina Duley Ogdon has ministered to millions.

---

*Today, the Library of Congress has a collection of 7,949 publicity brochures, promotional advertisements, and talent circulars for some 4,546 performers who were part of the Chautauqua Circuit.

The Old Rugged Cross

George Bennard   George Bennard

1. On a hill far a - way Stood an old rug-ged cross; The em - blem of
2. Oh, that old rug-ged cross, So de - spised by the world, Has a won-drous at -
3. To the old rug-ged cross I will ev - er be true, It's shame and re -

suf - fering and shame. And I love that old cross Where the dear - est and best,
trac - tion for me; For the dear Lamb of God, Left His glo - ry a - bove,
proach glad- ly bear; Then He'll call me some day To my home far a- way,

For a world of lost sin - ners was slain.
To bear it to dark Cal - va - ry. So I'll cher - ish the old rug - ged
Where His glo - ry for - ev - er I'll share.

cross, Till my tro - phies at last I lay down; I will cling to the

old rug - ged cross, And ex - change it some day for a crown.

The Old Rugged Cross

1913

For God so loved the world that He gave His only begotten Son, that whoever believes in Him should not perish but have everlasting life. John 3:16

George Beverly Shea recalls seeing George Bennard, author of this hymn, many times at Winona Lake Bible Conference in Indiana. "Though a preacher—a good one—he would sometimes sing," wrote Mr. Shea. "His voice was not trained or out of the ordinary, but he had great feeling and expression and could really put over any hymn. I remember how moved I was the first time I heard him sing his own 'The Old Rugged Cross . . . .' What a distinguished looking man—slight of build, short, with glasses, the most memorable thing about him was his long, white hair."

George Bennard was born in Youngstown, Ohio, shortly after the end of the Civil War. His father, a coal miner, moved the family to Iowa, and there George came to Christ through the ministry of the Salvation Army. He felt impressed to train for the ministry, but his plans were disrupted when his father's death left him responsible for his mother and sisters. He was sixteen years old. Instead of theological school, he worked by day and devoted his spare time to books.

Eventually George's obligations lessened, and he was able to move to Chicago, marry, and begin in ministry with the Salvation Army. Later he was ordained by the Methodist Episcopal church and became a traveling evangelist.

On one occasion, after a difficult season of ministry, George realized he needed to better understand the power of the Cross of Christ. He later said, "I was praying for a full understanding of the Cross . . . I read and studied and prayed . . . The Christ of the Cross became more than a symbol . . . It was like seeing John 3:16 leave the printed page, take form, and act out the meaning of redemption. While watching this scene with my mind's eye, the theme of the song came to me."

It took several months for the words to formulate in his mind. As he preached through the Midwest, George would carry the words with him, working on them, polishing them, and sometimes singing them in his meetings. It always struck a chord with his audiences.

At last, his hymn finished, George went to the home of his friends, Rev. and Mrs. L. O. Boswick, and sang it for them. After the last note, he looked at them and asked, "Will it do?"

The Boswicks were so moved that they helped pay the fees to have it printed, and it soon began appearing in hymnbooks across America.

The Love of God

F. M. Lehman   F. M. Lehman

1. The love of God is great-er far, Than tongue or pen can ev-er tell,
2. When years of time shall pass a-way And earth-ly thrones and king-doms fall,
3. Could we with ink the o-cean fill And were the skies of parch-ment made,

It goes be-yond the high-est star And reach-es to the low-est hell;
When men, who here re-fuse to pray, On rocks and hills and moun-tains call;
Were ev-'ry stalk on earth a quill And ev-'ry man a scribe by trade.

The guilt-y pair, bowed down with care, God gave His Son to win;
God's love so sure shall still en-dure, All mea-sure-less and strong;
To write the love of God a-bove Would drain the o-cean dry;

His err-ing child He rec-on-ciled And par-doned from his sin.
Re-deem-ing grace to A-dam's race The saints' and an-gels' song.
Nor could the scroll con-tain the whole Tho stretched from sky to sky.

The Love of God
1917

Praise the LORD! Oh, give thanks to the LORD, for He is good! For His mercy endures forever. Psalm 106:1

*T*his hymn was written in a citrus packing house in Pasadena, California, by a German-born Christian named Frederick M. Lehman. At age four, Frederick and his family had immigrated to America, settling down in Iowa. Converted to Christ at age eleven while walking through a crabapple orchard, Frederick eventually entered the ministry and pastored churches in the Midwest. But his greatest love was gospel music, and he compiled five songbooks and published hundreds of songs.

In 1917, his finances had gone sour, and he found himself working in a packing factory in Pasadena, moving thirty tons of lemons and oranges a day. One morning as he arrived at work, a song was forming in his mind. He had been thinking about the limitlessness of God's love, and during breaks he sat on an empty lemon crate and jotted down words with a stubby pencil.

Arriving home that evening, he went to the old upright piano and began putting notes to his words. He finally had a melody and two stanzas, but almost all gospel songs of that era had at least three stanzas. At length, he thought of some lines he had recently heard in a sermon:

> *Could we with ink the ocean fill and were the skies of parchment made,*
> *Were every stalk on earth a quill, and every man a scribe by trade,*
> *To write the love of God above would drain the ocean dry,*
> *Nor could the scroll contain the whole though stretched from sky to sky.*

That verse perfectly formed the third stanza, but who had written it? As Frederick heard the story, it was composed on the wall of an insane asylum by an unknown inmate. Perhaps someone did find it there, but we now know the words originally came from the pen of an eleventh-century Jewish poet in Germany named Meir Ben Isaac Nehorai.

Frederick lived the rest of his life in California, writing a number of hymns before his death in 1948. One of his most popular gospel songs, now outdated and forgotten, was based on the wonder of a new-fangled invention that was sweeping over America. It was called "The Royal Telephone."

> *Central's never "busy," always on the line;*
> *You may hear from heaven almost any time . . . .*
> *Telephone to glory, O what joy divine!*
> *I can feel the current moving on the line . . . .*

Wonderful Grace of Jesus

Haldor Lillenas

Haldor Lillenas

1. Won-der-ful grace of Je - sus, Great-er than all my sin.
2. Won-der-ful grace of Je - sus, Reach-ing to all the lost.
3. Won-der-ful grace of Je - sus, Reach-ing the most de - filed.

How shall my tongue de - scribe it? Where shall its praise be - gin?
By it I have been par - doned, Saved to the ut - ter - most.
By its trans - form - ing pow - er Mak - ing Him God's dear child.

Tak - ing a - way my bur - den, Set - ting my spir - it free.
Chains have been torn a - sun - der, Giv - ing me lib - er - ty.
Pur - chas - ing peace and heav - en For all e - ter - ni - ty.

For the won - der - ful grace of Je - sus reach - es me.
For the won - der - ful grace of Je - sus reach - es me.
And the won - der - ful grace of Je - sus reach - es me.

Wonderful Grace of Jesus

1918

Through Him we have received grace . . . Romans 1:5a

Worship leaders around the world owe a debt of gratitude to Lillenas Publishing Company, which was started by the author of this hymn, Haldor Lillenas. He was born in the fjord district of Norway in 1885, and, as a child, immigrated to the United States with his family. From his youth, Haldor had a musical bent, a talent that served him well when he entered the ministry in 1910 in the newly established Church of the Nazarene.

Between his sermons and visits, Haldor took musical studies by correspondence and soon began writing gospel songs. In 1919, he published his first book, and three years later he organized his own publishing house in Indianapolis, Indiana, where he was serving as pastor of the First Church of the Nazarene. For the next decade, Haldor preached, traveled, wrote hymns, and published songbooks.

In 1930, the Nazarene Publishing House in Kansas City, Missouri, became interested in expanding its fledgling efforts in the field of music. They agreed to purchase Lillenas Publishing Company provided that Haldor himself would move to Kansas City and manage it. He remained in that role until he retired in 1950, then served in an advisory capacity until his death in Aspen, Colorado, in 1959. Today Lillenas Publishing Company is one of the largest church music publishers in the world, owning more than 20,000 song copyrights.

"Wonderful Grace of Jesus" is the best known of the 4,000 hymns Haldor himself wrote. He later gave this account of how it came to be composed:

In 1917, Mrs. Lillenas and I built our first little home in the town of Olivet, Illinois. Upon its completion, we had scarcely any money left to furnish the little home. Having no piano at the time, and needing an instrument of some kind, I managed to find, at one of the neighbor's home, a little wheezy organ which I purchased for $5.00. With the aid of this instrument, a number of my songs were written which are now popular, including "Wonderful Grace of Jesus." It was sung by the great chorus, in 1918, at the Northfield, Massachusetts Bible Conference, being introduced for the first time by Homer Hammontree.

Not yet having started his own publishing house, he sold his soon-to-be-famous hymn for $5.00—just enough to pay for the organ on which it was composed.

I'd Rather Have Jesus

Rhea F. Miller

George Beverly Shea

1. I'd rath-er have Je-sus than sil-ver or gold; I'd rath-er be
2. I'd rath-er have Je-sus than men's ap - plause; I'd rath-er be
3. He's fair-er than lil-ies of rar-est bloom; He's sweet-er than

His than have rich-es un-told; I'd rath-er have Je-sus than
faith-ful to His dear cause; I'd rath-er have Je-sus than
hon-ey from out the comb; He's all that my hun-ger-ing

hous-es or lands. I'd rath-er be led by His nail-pierced hand.
world-wide fame. I'd rath-er be true to His ho-ly name.
spi - rit needs. I'd rath-er have Je-sus and let Him lead.

Than to be the king of a vast do-main Or be held in sin's dread sway.

I'd rath-er have Je-sus than an-y-thing This world af-fords to-day.

I'd Rather Have Jesus

1922

For what profit is it to a man if he gains the whole world and loses his own soul?
Matthew 16:26a

George Beverly Shea, "America's beloved gospel singer," has traveled with the Billy Graham evangelistic team since 1946. He was born in 1909 in Winchester, Ontario, where his dad served as pastor of the Wesleyan Methodist Church. Bev's mother, the church organist, had a piano that came from England; and, seated in front of its keys, she became a sort of "human alarm clock" for the family. Every weekday morning, striking an E-flat chord, she would sing Eliza Hewitt's old song:

> *Singing I go along life's road, | Praising the Lord, praising the Lord,*
> *Singing I go along life's road, | For Jesus has lifted my load.*

On Sundays, she chose a different selection, Isaac Watts' hymn:

> *Lord, in the morning Thou shalt hear | My voice ascending high;*
> *To Thee will I direct my prayer, | To Thee lift up mine eye.*

When Bev was 21, he began working for the Mutual Insurance Company of New York, assisting medical examiners in obtaining information relating to the applicant's health history. Among those who came into the office was Fred Allen, host of a coast-to-coast radio talent show. Learning that Bev liked to sing, Mr. Allen arranged an audition, and a few weeks later Bev found himself singing "Go Down Moses" to a nationwide audience on the National Broadcasting Company. Though he lost the contest to a yodeler, he received fifteen dollars and a taste of widespread fame.

One Sunday shortly afterward, Bev sat down at his mother's organ to practice for the morning church service. His eyes fell on a clipping she had left for him there, a poem written in 1922 by Mrs. Rhea F. Miller. As Bev read the words, they spoke to him about his own aims and ambitions in life. An appropriate melody came easily, practically composing itself.

When Bev's mother came in from the kitchen, he played and sang it for her. Wrapping both arms around him, she placed a wet cheek against his. In church that morning, Bev sang "I'd Rather Have Jesus" publicly for the first time. It later became a sort of "signature song" expressing his own decisions in life.

> *I'd rather have Jesus than men's applause, | I rather be faithful to His dear cause;*
> *I'd rather have Jesus than worldwide fame, | I'd rather be true to His holy name . . .*

Turn Your Eyes Upon Jesus

Helen H. Lemmel

Helen H. Lemmel

1. O soul, are you wea-ry and trou - bled? No light in the
2. Thro' death in - to life ev - er - last - ing He passed, and we
3. His word shall not fail you He prom - ised; Be - lieve Him, and

dark-ness you see? There's light for a look at the Sav - ior, And
fol - low Him there; O - ver us sin no more hath do - min - ion For
all will be well; Then go to a world that is dy - ing, His

life more a - bun - dant and free!
more than con - qu'rors we are! Turn your eyes up - on Je - sus,
per - fect sal - va - tion to tell!

Look full in His won - der - ful face, And the things of

earth Will grow strange-ly dim In the light of His glo - ry and grace.

Turn Your Eyes Upon Jesus
1922

. . . let us run with endurance the race set before us, looking unto Jesus, the author and finisher of our faith . . . Hebrews 12:1–2

Helen Howarth Lemmel was born in England in 1863, into the home of a Wesleyan minister who immigrated to America when Helen was a child. She loved music, and her parents provided the best vocal teachers they could find. Eventually Helen returned to Europe to study vocal music in Germany. In time, she married a wealthy European, but he left her when she became blind, and Helen struggled with multiple heartaches during midlife.

At age 55, Helen heard a statement that deeply impressed her: "So then, turn your eyes upon Him, look full into His face and you will find that the things of earth will acquire a strange new dimness."

"I stood still," Helen later said, "and singing in my soul and spirit was the chorus, with not one conscious moment of putting word to word to make rhyme, or note to note to make melody. The verses were written the same week, after the usual manner of composition, but nonetheless dictated by the Holy Spirit."

⌒⊃

Pastor Doug Goins of Palo Alto, California, and his parents, Paul and Kathryn Goins, both 82, of Sun City, Arizona, knew Helen in Seattle. "She was advanced in years and almost destitute, but she was an amazing person," said Doug. "She made a great impression on me as a junior high child because of her joy and enthusiasm. Though she was living on government assistance in a sparse bedroom, whenever we'd ask how she was doing, she would reply, 'I'm doing well in the things that count.'"

One day, the Goins invited her to supper. "We had never entertained a blind person before," recalled Kathryn, "and it was interesting. Despite her infirmities, she was full of life. I remember how amused we were when, following supper, she said, 'Now if you will lead me to the bathroom, I'll sit on the throne and reign.'"

"But she was always composing hymns," said Kathryn. "She had no way of writing them down, so she would call my husband at all hours and he'd rush down and record them before she forgot the words."

Helen had a small plastic keyboard by her bed. There she would play, sing, and cry. "One day God is going to bless me with a great heavenly keyboard," she'd say. "I can hardly wait!"

Helen Lemmel, who wrote nearly 500 hymns during her lifetime, died in Seattle in 1961, thirteen days before her 98th birthday.

Great Is Thy Faithfulness

Thomas O. Chisholm

William M. Runyan

Great Is Thy Faithfulness

1923

Your mercy, O LORD, is in the heavens; your faithfulness reaches to the clouds.
Psalm 36:5

T he author of this hymn, Thomas Obediah Chisholm, was born in a log cabin in Kentucky. At age 16, he began teaching school, despite the paucity of his own education. He came to Christ at age 27 under the ministry of evangelist H. C. Morrison. But Chisholm's health was unstable, and he alternated between bouts of illness and gainful employment in which he did everything from journalism to insurance to evangelistic work. Through all the ups and downs, he discovered new blessings from God every morning. The third chapter of Lamentations 3 became precious to him: *His compassions fail not. They are new every morning; Great is Your faithfulness* (Lamentations 3:22–23).

Thomas later admitted there was no dramatic story behind the writing of "Great is Thy Faithfulness." While serving the Lord in Vineland, New Jersey, Thomas sent several poems to his friend, musician William Runyan, who was so moved by this one that he prayed earnestly for special guidance in composing the music. Runyan was in Baldwin, Kansas, at the time, and the hymn was published in 1923 in Runyan's private song pamphlets.

"It went rather slowly for several years," Thomas recalled. Then Dr. Will Houghton of the Moody Bible Institute of Chicago discovered it, and would say in chapel, "Well, I think we shall have to sing 'Great is Thy Faithfulness." It became an unofficial theme song for the Institute; and when Houghton died, it was sung at his funeral.

Still, it remained relatively unknown until popularized around the world by George Beverly Shea and the choirs at the Billy Graham Crusades.

Thomas spent his retirement years in a Methodist Home for the Aged in Ocean Park, New Jersey, where he was frequently seen walking by the ocean and along town streets. Tom Rich, a resident of Ocean Park, recalls his pleasant demeanor as he dropped by the diner, sat on park benches, and fellowshipped with friends at Ocean Park's summer Bible conferences.

Thomas died in Ocean Park in 1960. During his lifetime he wrote 1,200 poems and hymns. In addition to "Great is Thy Faithfulness," he is the author of the well-known "O To Be Like Thee," and the hymn, "Living for Jesus."

Living for Jesus, a life that is true,
Striving to please Him in all that I do;
Yielding allegiance, glad hearted and free,
This is the pathway of blessing for me.

Little Is Much When God Is in It

Kittie Louise Suffield

Kittie Louise Suffield

1. In the har - vest field now rip-ened, There's a work for all to do;
2. Does the place you're called to la - bor Seem so small and lit - tle known?
3. When the con - flict here is end - ed And our race on earth is run;

Hark, the voice of God is call - ing, To the har - vest call - ing you.
It is great if God is in it And He'll not for - get His own.
He will say if we are faith - ful, Wel - come home, My child well done.

Lit - tle is much when God is in it, La - bor not for wealth or fame;

There's a crown and you can win it, If you go in Je - sus' name.

Little Is Much When God Is in It

c. 1924

A little one shall become a thousand, and a small one a strong nation. I the LORD, will hasten it in its time. Isaiah 60:22

O ne snow-blanketed night, Canadian Fred Suffield awoke to an urgent pounding on his door. A half-frozen man reported that a train had stalled in the blizzard, and the passengers were in danger of freezing to death. Lighting a lantern, Fred followed the man to the site and led the travelers back to his house. Later one of the passengers, Kittie, wrote a thank you note. Fred replied, and Kittie wrote back. Their correspondence led to courtship and to marriage.

Some time later, Fred and Kittie attended a church in Ottawa pastored by Rev. A. J. Shea, and there they gave their lives to the Lord. As the couple grew in Christ, they entered the ministry of evangelism. One summer they invited Shea's teenage son, George Beverly, to spend a month with them in Westport, Ontario, holding evangelistic meetings. One night, accompanied by Kittie on the piano, Bev attempted to sing, but his voice cracked on the high notes, and he sat down mortified, vowing never to sing again.

Kittie wouldn't hear of it, suggesting he sing in a lower key. He did, and he kept on singing, and singing, and singing.

Many years passed, and in June of 2000, Billy Graham came to Nashville, Tennessee, for a four-night mission. My wife and I were privileged to attend a reception for the Graham team just before the meetings began, and George Beverly Shea, 92 at the time, rose to sing. His rich baritone voice broke into a song that had been written 73 years before by Fred and Kittie: "Little Is Much When God Is in It."

I thought it a strange choice of hymn. We were on the verge of the greatest evangelistic effort in Nashville's history, headlined by the most famous evangelist in the world. And Bev Shea's song was about the littleness of our efforts. But later I realized how perfectly the song fit. Compared to this great mission to untold multitudes, our own individual ministries seemed small and insignificant. But God uses little things in great ways. A tiny acorn may produce a forest. A spark may ignite a revival. A small church might produce the next far-famed evangelist.

Don't be discouraged if your place seems small. You're doing more good than you know.

Precious Lord, Take My Hand

Thomas A. Dorsey

George N. Allen

1. Pre - cious Lord, take my hand, Lead me on, help me
2. When my way grows drear, Pre - cious Lord, lin - ger

stand; I am tired, I am weak, I am worn;
near; When my life is al - most gone,

Thru the storm, thru the night, Lead me on to the
Hear my cry, hear my call, Hold my hand lest I

light, Take my hand, pre - cious Lord, lead me home.
fall; Take my hand, pre - cious Lord, lead me home.

Precious Lord, Take My Hand

1932

Be strong and of good courage, do not fear nor be afraid of them; for the LORD *your God, He is the One who goes with you. He will not leave you nor forsake you.*
Deuteronomy 31:6

Some people think this great old gospel song was written by the famous big bandleader Tommy Dorsey. It wasn't; the author was named Thomas Andrew Dorsey, and he was the son of a Black revivalist preacher.

Thomas was born in a small town in Georgia in 1899. When he was about eleven, the Dorseys moved to Atlanta where Thomas was quickly enamoured with the blues and began playing piano at a vaudeville theater. Later the family moved to Chicago where he attended classes at the College of Composition and Arranging. Soon he was on stage under the name "Georgia Tom," playing barrelhouse piano in one of Al Capone's Chicago speakeasies and leading jazz bands.

Thomas was converted at the National Baptist Convention in Chicago in 1921, and began writing gospel songs and trying to get them published. It was discouraging at first. He later said, "I borrowed five dollars and sent out 500 copies of my song, 'If You See My Savior,' to churches throughout the country . . . It was three years before I got a single order. I felt like going back to the blues."

He didn't, and gradually his reputation grew and his work became known.

In August, 1932, while leading music in St. Louis, he was handed a telegram bearing the words, "Your wife just died." He rushed to a phone to call home, but all he could hear over the line was "Nettie is dead! Nettie is dead!" A friend drove him through the night, and he arrived home to learn that his baby boy had also died.

"I began to feel that God had done me an injustice," Thomas later said. "I didn't want to serve Him anymore or write any more gospel songs." But the next Saturday, while alone in a friend's music room, he had a "strange feeling" inside—a sudden calm and a quiet stillness. "As my fingers began to manipulate over the keys, words began to fall in place on the melody like drops of water falling from the crevice of the rock:

> *Precious Lord, take my hand*
> *Lead me on, let me stand*
> *I am tired, I am weak, I am worn . . ."*

Today Thomas A. Dorsey is remembered as the "Father of Gospel Music" and the author of hundreds of gospel songs including his equally famous, "Peace in the Valley."

He Lives

Alfred H. Ackley

Alfred H. Ackley

1. I serve a ris - en Sav - ior. He's in the world to - day.
2. In all the world a - round me I see His lov - ing care;
3. Re - joice, re - joice, O Chris - tian. lift up your voice and sing.

I know that He is liv - ing; what - ev - er men may say.
And tho' my heart grows wea - ry I nev - er will de - spair.
E - ter - nal hal - le - lu - jahs to Je - sus Christ the King.

I see His hand of mer - cy. I hear His voice of cheer,
I know that He is lead - ing thro' all the storm - y blast.
The hope of all who seek Him, the help of all who find.

And just the time I need Him. He's al - ways near.
The day of His ap - pear - ing will come at last.
None oth - er is so lov - ing, So good and kind.

He Lives

1933

He is not here; for He is risen, as He said. Matthew 28:6a

Why should I worship a dead Jew?" That question—and a dreadful sermon—inspired this hymn.

Alfred Henry Ackley was born in Pennsylvania in 1887.* He showed great promise as a child, and his musician-father personally tutored him before sending him to New York City to study music. From there, it was on to the Royal Academy of Music in London. Alfred then returned to the States to attend Westminster Seminary in Maryland, and he was ordained into the Presbyterian ministry in 1914. After pastoring a church in his home state of Pennsylvania, Alfred was called to a congregation in California.

It was there in 1932, that Alfred met a Jewish man to whom he began witnessing. But the man resisted the Christian faith, saying, "Why should I worship a dead Jew?"

That statement played on Alfred's mind as he prepared his Easter Sunday message. Rising early to prepare for the day, Alfred flipped on the radio as he shaved and was astonished to hear a famous liberal preacher in New York say: "Good morning—it's Easter! You know, folks, it really doesn't make any difference to me if Christ be risen or not. As far as I am concerned, His body could be as dust in some Palestinian tomb. The main thing is, His truth goes marching on!"

Alfred wanted to fling the radio across the room. "It's a lie!" he exclaimed. His wife rushed into the bathroom, asking, "Why are you shouting so early in the morning?"

"Didn't you hear what that good-for-nothing preacher said?" Alfred replied.

That morning, Ackley preached with great vigor on the reality of Christ's Resurrection, and he did the same at the evening service. But later that night, he was still exercised over his friend's question and the morning's radio sermon. "Listen here, Alfred Ackley," his wife said at last. "It's time you did that which you can do best. Why don't you write a song about it and then maybe you'll feel better?"

Alfred went to his study, opened the Bible, and re-read the Resurrection account from Mark's Gospel. A thrill went through him, and he began writing the words to "He Lives." A few minutes later, he was at the piano putting it to music, not dreaming it would become one of the church's most triumphant Easter hymns.

---

*Alfred's older brother, Bentley, was also a renowned gospel songwriter who traveled with the Billy Sunday/Homer Rodeheaver evangelistic team as pianist. Bentley later became a composer and editor with the Rodeheaver Publishing Company, writing over 3,000 hymns and gospel songs.

Beyond the Sunset

Virgil P. Brock

Blanche Kerr Brock

1. Be-yond the sun-set, O bliss-ful morn-ing, When with our Sav-ior, heav'n is be-gun. Earth's toil-ing end-ed, O glo-rious dawn-ing. Be-yond the sun-set, when day is done.

2. Be-yond the sun-set, no clouds will gath-er, No storms will threat-en, no fears an-noy. O day of glad-ness, O day un-end-ing, Be-yond the sun-set, e-ter-nal joy.

3. Be-yond the sun-set a hand will guide me, To God the Fa-ther, whom I a-dore. His glo-rious pres-ence, His words of wel-come, Will be my por-tion on that fair shore.

4. Be-yond the sun-set, O glad re-un-ion, With our dear loved ones who've gone be-fore. In that fair home-land, we'll know no part-ing, Be-yond the sun-set for-ev-er-more.

Beyond the Sunset

1936

And God will wipe away every tear from their eyes; there shall be no more death, nor sorrow, nor crying. There shall be no more pain, for the former things have passed away. Revelation 21:4

Homer Rodeheaver's name will live as long as gospel music is sung. He began his career as song director for the Billy Sunday campaigns, then went on to establish a publishing company that produced hundreds of the era's most popular gospel songs. Both Billy Sunday and Homer Rodeheaver settled down in beautiful Winona Lake, Indiana, home of a renowned Bible conference center and seminary. The Rodeheavers built an expansive home on Rainbow Point which became a center of fellowship for Christians traveling through the area.

During the summer of 1936, the Rodeheaver School of Music was in session at Winona Lake Bible Conference, and "Rody" invited all the faculty members to Rainbow Point for the evening. Among them were the well-known Christian musicians, Virgil Brock and his wife, Blanche Kerr Brock.

On this particular evening, the sunset was fabulous. As the faculty members talked about the splendor of the setting sun against the lake, one of them—a blind man named Horace Burr, Virgil's cousin—exclaimed, "My, that sure is a wonderful sunset. Thanks so much for picturing it for me. I would have missed a lot if you folks hadn't been here to describe it."

When someone commented on Horace's "seeing," he replied, "I *can* see. I see through other people's eyes, and I think I often see more; I see beyond the sunset."

By and by the conversation shifted to the subject of heaven. Someone asked if we can really visualize what lies beyond death's door. Recalling Horace's words, Virgil replied, "Horace Burr has never seen the glory of an earthly sunset, yet was blessed as we tried to describe it to him. In the same way we, as Christians, have never seen what is beyond, but God in His love and promise has told us in the Bible of the glory that is awaiting us beyond the sunset."

Back in their own lodgings later that evening, Virgil and Blanche re-lived the evening. Sitting down together at an old piano, they began putting together words and music. "To us it seemed as if a bright light of truth had streamed into our hearts and lives and had become a song," Virgil later said.

The song was completed that evening and dedicated to Horace and Grace Burr.

Search Me, O God

J. Edwin Orr

Maori Melody

1. Search me, O God, and know my heart to - day;
2. I praise Thee, Lord, for cleans - ing me from sin;
3. Lord, take my life, and make it whol - ly Thine;
4. O Ho - ly Ghost, re - vi - val comes from Thee;

Try me, O Sav - ior, know my thoughts, I pray.
Ful - fill Thy Word, and make me pure with - in.
Fill my poor heart with Thy great love di - vine.
Send a re - vi - val, start the work in me.

See if there be some wick - ed way in me;
Fill me with fire where once I burned with shame;
Take all my will, my pas - sion, self and pride;
Thy Word de - clares Thou wilt sup - ply our need;

Cleanse me from ev - ery sin and set me free.
Grant my de - sire to mag - ni - fy Thy name.
I now sur - ren - der, Lord in me a - bide.
For bless - ings now, O Lord, I hum - bly plead.

Arranged by Mark Hill

Search Me, O God
1936

Search me, O God, and know my heart; Try me, and know my anxieties; And see if there is any wicked way in me, and lead me in the way everlasting. Psalm 139:23–24

When I was a student at Columbia International University in South Carolina, a small, peppery, gray-haired Irishman came to lecture. He was brisk and plain-spoken, and his subject was revival. J. Edwin Orr had studied the history of revivals like no one else; as it happened, I had just read one of his many books on the subject.

When I requested an appointment, he agreed to see me in the lobby of the men's dormitory. Perhaps it was his shyness, but he seemed uncomfortable chatting with me. Instead of looking in my direction and engaging in conversation, he gazed straight ahead and answered my questions with short replies. After several fruitless exchanges, I decided to ask him one last thing.

"Dr. Orr, besides praying for revival, what can I do to help bring it about?" Without a moment's pause, he glanced in my direction gave me an answer I've never forgotten: "You can let it begin with you."

That was exactly the point of this hymn, which he had written years before, in 1936, during an intense springtime revival convention in the town of Ngaruawahia, on the North Island of New Zealand. There had been an attitude of unusual expectancy about the meetings, and prayer meetings proliferated across the city. Many students were coming to Christ, and the area began overflowing with the testimonies of those being saved and renewed in Christ.

One day Dr. Orr heard four Aborigine girls sing a beautiful song entitled, "The Song of Farewell," the first words being, "Now is the hour when we must say good-bye." Unable to get the lovely Polynesian tune out of his mind, Dr. Orr began singing it to himself using words from Psalm 139. These words he jotted down on the back of an envelope while standing in the post office at Ngaruawahia, and they were first published in his book, *All You Need.*

⸻

While this is a wonderful hymn to sing, it is a "dangerous" prayer to offer. We all have sins within us of which we're unaware, for the heart is deceitful above all things. But as we submit ourselves to the searchlight of God's Spirit, we can discover the habits that need to be confessed and the attitudes that need to be changed. As God cleanses us, the result will be . . . revival, one that begins with us.

It Is No Secret

It Is No Secret

<u>1949</u>

For whoever calls on the name of the Lord shall be saved. Romans 10:13

T hough the 1949 Los Angeles Crusade was to launch Billy Graham to world-wide fame, the meetings appeared to get off to a slow start. Arriving in Los Angeles before the crusade, Mr. Graham gave a news conference, then eagerly waited for the next day to see how the crusade would be publicized. Not a single newspaper carried the story.

But among the supporters Graham *did* have was the influential Presbyterian Bible teacher Henrietta Mears, who invited Billy to her home in Beverly Hills to speak to a group of Hollywood personalities. Present that day was a hard-drinking star of cowboy westerns named Stuart Hamblen who also hosted one of the most popular afternoon radio shows on the West Coast. He was infamous for his gambling and brawling.

The two men took a liking to each other, and Billy longed to win Stuart to Christ. But as the three-week campaign neared its end, there was no sign that the big cowboy was under conviction.

Sensing that momentum for the meetings was building, the local crusade organizers wanted to extend them; but Billy was hesitant, having never done that before. He put out a "fleece," and asked God for a sign. The next morning at 4:30, he was awakened in his room at the Langham Hotel by a phone call. It was Stuart Hamblen, and he was in tears. Billy woke his wife and friends, who gathered in another room to pray while Stuart and his wife, Suzy, drove to the hotel. That night, Stuart gave his heart to the Lord Jesus.

It was the sign Billy needed to extend the meetings.

Meanwhile, Stuart excitedly told the story of his conversion on his radio show, and the local newspapers picked up the story. Soon all of Los Angeles was buzzing about the Billy Graham meetings. The resulting publicity launched a half-century of mass evangelism virtually unparalleled in Christian history.

Shortly afterward, Stuart Hamblen reportedly met movie star John Wayne on a street in Los Angeles. "What's this I hear about you, Stuart?" asked the actor.

"Well, Duke, it's no secret what God can do."

"Sounds like a song," said John. Stuart went home, sat down at his piano and wrote "It Is No Secret." He went on to write 225 other songs before his death in 1989.

His Name Is Wonderful

Audrey Mieir   Audrey Mieir

His name is Won - der - ful, His name is Won - der - ful, His name is Won - der - ful,

Je - sus, my Lord; He is the Might - y King, Mas - ter of ev - 'ry - thing;

His name is Won - der - ful, Je - sus, my Lord. He's the Great Shep - herd, The Rock of all

ag - es, Al - might - y God is He. Bow down be - fore Him, Love and a -

dore Him, His name is Won - der - ful, Je - sus my Lord.

His Name Is Wonderful

<u>1959</u>

Therefore God also has highly exalted Him and given Him the name which is above every name. Philippians 2:9

This song was born in a small church. In an era when bigger is better and success is usually measured by statistics, it's important to remember that small churches can still do great things.

Audrey Mae Mieir born on May 12, 1916, and attended L.I.F.E. Bible College. After marrying Charles B. Mieir in 1936, she was ordained to the Gospel ministry in the International Church of the Foursquare Gospel.

Audrey was a gifted pianist and an inspiring worship leader, song director, and choral clinician. In the 1950s, she was working in her brother-in-law's church, Bethel Union Church in Duarte, California, a suburb of Los Angeles. Christmas fell on Sunday that year, and the church was decorated with pine boughs. The choir loft was now a manger scene, and the young people had worked hard on the performance.

"As the morning service began," Audrey later said, "I was almost overwhelmed with the fragrance, the sounds, and most of all, with the gentle moving of the Spirit in that church. The pastor stood to his feet, opened the Bible, and said, 'His name shall be called Wonderful.' I tell you the truth, that's all it took. I wrote the words and music in the flyleaf of my Bible. In the Sunday evening service, I taught the chorus to a group of young people, and it was sung for the first time."

But Audrey had only written the first part of the song, and though it was well-received, it needed more. A friend told her, "Audrey, it's a good song but there just isn't enough of it. Maybe you could write a bridge for it." Audrey went to lunch that day with her friend's advice ringing in her ears. She ordered a hamburger, opened her Bible, and found a list of names given to Jesus in the Scripture. She jotted some of them down on her napkin. After returning to her office, Audrey went to the piano and began writing: "He's the great Shepherd, the Rock of all ages, Almighty God is He . . . ."

Though it was inspired on Christmas day by a traditional Christmas text, "His Name Is Wonderful" has never been pegged as a Christmas hymn. It's been a favorite of Christians around the world throughout the year.

The All Sufficient King

Robert J. Morgan

Jerry Carraway

1. We come, O God, in-to your courts, We en-ter through your gate.
2. We step in-to Your Ho-ly Place To walk and live in light.
3. That an-cient tent, O Lord, is You! Our safe a-bid-ing place.

We scan the al-tar where the Lamb Dis-plays Your love so great.
To feed on You and of-fer prayer Like in-cense in Your sight.
A shel-ter in the wil-der-ness Is your sus-tain-ing grace.

We bring our hands and heart and head Where sin-ful dust does cling
O Great High Priest, we sing to You En-throned be-hind the veil.
How might-y does Your Word re-veal The All Suf-fi-cient King

Be-fore the lav-er of your Grace That makes us pure and clean.
Be-tween the an-gels is our Lord Who al-ways does things well.
To You to-day our praise we bring To you our an-thems ring.

The All Sufficient King

2002

Not with the blood of goats and calves, but with His own blood He entered the Most Holy Place once for all, having obtained eternal redemption. Hebrews 9:12

I had long aspired to preach a series of sermons on God's Tent—the Tabernacle. This is the Old Testament's premier "type" of Christ, and fifty chapters in the Bible are devoted to it; but for a long time, I was intimidated by the immensity of the subject. Finally the general outlines of this wonderful topic broke through. I realized that the high white linen curtains surrounding the Tabernacle represent the holiness of God, which separates us from His presence; but there is one entrance, a wide gate, on the Eastern side near the encamped tribe of Judah. That gate represents **Christ our Savior,** our access into God's presence.

Entering, we come to the altar, which represents **Christ our Sacrifice.** Moving east to west, we pass the bronze laver or basin, where the priests wash their hands and feet. This represents **Christ our Sanctifier,** who daily cleanses and purifies us. Proceeding on, we come to the Tabernacle itself. In the first room is the golden candlestick, the table of showbread, and the altar of incense, signifying **Christ our Sufficiency**—the Light of the World, the Bread of Life, and the One who ever lives to intercede for us.

Passing reverently behind the veil into the Most Holy Place, we discover **Christ our Sovereign,** for that room contains the ark of the covenant, the earthly footstool of God's heavenly throne (1 Chronicles 28:2).

One night in the spring of 2002, while attending a conference at the University of Edinburgh, I was unable to sleep. Clicking on the desk lamp in my small room, I visualized myself entering the Tabernacle complex and walking across the courtyard into the Most Holy Place. I was overwhelmed with the awesome privilege of coming boldly right to the throne of the Almighty. The words of this hymn came quickly and easily.

⌒⊃

You, too, can be a hymnist. As you study the Bible, take time to compose your thoughts and devotions into verse form. If you aren't a musician, find a familiar old melody and create new stanzas for it. If no one sings your hymn but you, it will still bless your own soul and please the heart of God. But you might share a copy with your worship leader at church. The world's best hymns, after all, have yet to be written.

Alphabetical by Title

304

Author/Songwriter

First Line of Hymn

A mighty fortress is our God, 14
Abide with me, 118
Alas! and did my Savior bleed, 32
All creatures of our God and King, 10
All glory, laud, and honor, 6
All hail the power of Jesus' name!, 76
All the way my Savior leads me, 194
All to Jesus I surrender, 238
Almighty Father, strong to save, 136
Am I a soldier of the cross, 42
Amazing grace! How sweet the sound!, 78
And can it be that I should gain, 44
Angels from the realms of glory, 90
Another year is dawning, 186

Be not dismayed whate'er betide, 258
Be thou my Vision, 4
Behold the glories of the Lamb, 30
Behold the Savior of mankind, 28
Beyond the sunset, O blissful morning, 292
Blessed assurance, Jesus is mine!, 182

Christ the Lord is ris'n today, Alleluia!, 50
Come Thou fount of every blessing, 64
Crown Him with many crowns, 124

Day by day and with each passing moment, 154
Do not wait until some deed of greatness, 272
Does Jesus care when my heart is pained, 252

Eternal Father, strong to save, 136

Face to face with Christ, my Savior, 244
Fairest Lord Jesus; Ruler of all nature, 24
Father, whate'er of earthly bliss, 66
For the beauty of the earth, 148

God be with you 'til we meet again, 204
God is the refuge of His saints, 40
God moves in a mysterious way, 72
Good King Wenceslas looked out, 126

Great is Thy faithfulness, O God my Father, 284
Guide me, O Thou great Jehovah, 60

Hallelujah! Hallelujah! Hallelujah!, 54
Hark! the herald angels sing, 48
Have Thine own way, Lord!, 262
He leadeth me, O blessed thought!, 144
His name is Wonderful, 298
Holy, Holy, Holy, Lord God Almighty!, 98
How firm a foundation, 82

I am so glad that our Father in heaven, 176
I come to the garden alone, 270
I gave My life for thee, 140
I hear the Savior say, 156
I heard the voice of Jesus say, 116
I must tell Jesus, 232
I need Thee ev'ry hour, 178
I serve a risen Savior, 290
I sing the mighty power of God, 34
I will sing of my Redeemer, 192
I'd rather have Jesus than silver or gold, 280
In heav'nly love abiding, 122
In the cross of Christ I glory, 96
In the harvest field now ripened, 286
It came upon the midnight clear, 120
It is no secret what God can do, 296

Jesus calls the children dear, 236
Jesus loves me! this I know, 138
Jesus shall reign wherev'r the sun, 36
Jesus! what a friend for sinners, 268
Jesus, I am resting, resting, 198
Jesus, I my cross have taken, 94
Jesus, Lover of my soul, 52
Jesus, the very thought of Thee, 8
Joyful, joyful, we adore Thee, 264
Just as I am, without one plea, 112

Lead, kindly Light, 106
Like a river glorious, 200
Lord, speak to me, that I may speak, 180

307

308